Managing Sustainability

Managing Sustainability is a comprehensive guide to governing, leading, and managing a successful sustainability-focused business.

Being a socially and environmentally responsible business is a worthy goal for many people; however, turning the goal into reality is a daunting process. This book takes a clear and practical approach to the "nuts-and-bolts" of achieving this goal, and covers steps to be taken by directors and executives to create and implement appropriate strategies, policies, and management systems. It recognizes that corporate social responsibility (CSR) is like any other important management initiative and requires proactive leadership from the top of the organization. Key topics include:

- Understanding how CSR is changing the traditional fiduciary duties of directors and officers
- Developing and implementing internal governance instruments to provide a foundation for decision-making around CSR
- Integrating CSR into the duties and responsibilities of the chief executive officer and other members of the C-suite team, as well as into their compensation arrangements
- Conducting continuous audits and assessments of the sustainability governance and management framework using certification and rating systems to evaluate and improve CSR performance and effectiveness

Current and aspiring leaders wishing to build a sustainability-centered business will appreciate the straightforward and actionable guidance offered by this book.

Alan S. Gutterman is the Founding Director of the Sustainable Entrepreneurship Project (www.seproject.org), a best-selling author of legal and business publications and a widely recognized business counselor.

Managing Sustainability

Alan S. Gutterman

Routledge
Taylor & Francis Group

NEW YORK AND LONDON

First published 2021
by Routledge
52 Vanderbilt Avenue, New York, NY 10017

and by Routledge
2 Park Square, Milton Park, Abingdon, Oxon OX14 4RN

Routledge is an imprint of the Taylor & Francis Group, an informa business

British Library Cataloguing-in-Publication Data
A catalogue record for this book is available from the British Library

Library of Congress Cataloging-in-Publication Data
Names: Gutterman, Alan S., 1955– author.
Title: Managing sustainability / Alan S. Gutterman.
Description: New York: Routledge, 2020. |
Includes bibliographical references and index. |
Identifiers: LCCN 2020028810 (print) | LCCN 2020028811 (ebook) |
ISBN 9780367518554 (hardback) | ISBN 9780367518547 (paperback) |
ISBN 9781003055440 (ebook)
Subjects: LCSH: Social responsibility of business. |
Industrial management—Environmental aspects. |
Strategic planning—Environmental aspects.
Classification: LCC HD60 .G88 2020 (print) | LCC HD60 (ebook) |
DDC 658.4/083—dc23
LC record available at https://lccn.loc.gov/2020028810
LC ebook record available at https://lccn.loc.gov/2020028811

ISBN: 978-0-367-51855-4 (hbk)
ISBN: 978-0-367-51854-7 (pbk)
ISBN: 978-1-003-05544-0 (ebk)

Typeset in Times New Roman
by codeMantra

Contents

Preface

Corporate sustainability and corporate social responsibility (CSR) are like any other important management initiatives and require proactive leadership from the top of the organization. In fact, it is clear that the "tone at the top" is an important factor in the success or failure of any sustainability initiative and that the directors, executive officers and senior managers of the organization are uniquely positioned to act as internal champions of sustainability and proactively communicate with everyone in the organization on a daily basis about the impact of new environmental and social products, services and activities (e.g., philanthropic projects) and sustainability-related systems and processes. Sustainability requires a paradigm shift by organizations, pushing them to look beyond economic performance to consider the impact of their activities on the environment and society in which they operate and on stakeholders other than the owners of the organization; however, the pursuit of sustainability relies on many of the same basic governance and management processes used everywhere in the business world (e.g., planning, acquiring and deploying resources, building products and systems and monitoring execution of day-to-day operations). At the same time, the emergence of corporate sustainability has fueled interest in new skill sets including sustainable leadership and ethical management.

Being a socially and environmentally responsible business is a worthy goal for many people; however, turning the goal into reality is a daunting process. Successfully governing, leading and managing a sustainability-focused business begins with understanding the fundamental principles and activities associated with corporate governance, leadership and management that are outlined in the opening chapter of this volume. Thereafter we turn to a comprehensive menu of the subjects, issues and activities associated with sustainability governance and management to present and discuss the relevant research and suggestions for integrating sustainability into the practice of management. The table of contents for this volume serves as a valuable checklist for the steps that need to be taken:

* Understanding how sustainability is changing the traditional fiduciary duties of directors and officers including the ascendance of the stakeholder-focused model

- Ensuring that the board of directors integrates environmental and social responsibility into the governance structure and the traditional roles and responsibilities of directors
- Designing and implementing an effective framework for board oversight of sustainability and CSR and development and implementation of organizational strategies that integrate meaningful sustainability commitments and targets
- Designing effective internal organizational structures and systems for managing sustainability initiatives and programs and supporting sustainability and CSR commitments and expectations such as preparation and distribution of sustainability reports and stakeholder engagement
- Integrating sustainability into the duties and responsibilities of the chief executive officer and other members of the C-suite team, as well as into their compensation arrangements, and developing job responsibilities and performance metrics for a new breed of sustainability executives
- Understanding the leadership styles, behaviors and actions that have been identified as being the most effective for leading sustainability-focused initiatives
- Implementing formal management systems relating to sustainability-related issues such as the environment, social responsibility and supply chain security and processes for collecting and analyzing information to assess the performance and effectiveness of sustainability-related initiatives
- Identifying and counseling directors, officers, managers and employees on ethical issues that will arise as they discharge their responsibilities with respect to sustainability and work to enhance and maintain the reputation of the organization
- Developing and implementing internal governance instruments—codes, policies and procedures—to guide organizational members on their sustainability-related duties and responsibilities and provide a foundation for decision-making
- Understanding the organizational changes that may be necessary in order to embed sustainability into the company's organizational culture and the important role that the practice of sustainable human resources management plays in that process
- Understanding the relationship between technology management and sustainability and the importance of sustainable product design and use, sustainable manufacturing and sustainable information technology management
- Understanding the role of sustainability reporting and communications and developing the processes required for disseminating information to stakeholders relating to the company's sustainability initiatives

- Conducting continuous audits and assessments of the sustainability governance and management framework through the use of certification and rating systems in order to evaluate and improve sustainability performance and effectiveness

The author hopes and anticipates that sustainability management will eventually converge into what is considered mainstream management principles and that every manager will apply the tools discussed in this book in the normal course of their activities. Although the coverage in this volume is extensive, it does not cover everything. For example, managers will need to be attentive to the actions of their value chain partners and invest time and resources in engaging with specific stakeholders including investors, workers, customers and members of the community in which the company operates. Consideration must be given to the role of businesses in respecting human rights, and sustainability performance is also becoming an important factor in capital raising activities as interest in impact investing accelerates. To learn more about each of these topics, as well as the subjects covered in this volume, visit the author's Sustainable Entrepreneurship Project website (www.seproject.org). Reference should also be made to the author's volume on *Sustainability and Corporate Governance*, which is being published by Routledge contemporaneously with this volume.

Alan S. Gutterman
Oakland, California
September 2020

1   Governance, Leadership and Management

Consideration and debate regarding sustainability in the 21st century has involved integrating long-standing concerns about economic growth and social equity with concern for the carrying capacity of natural systems.[1] Interest in corporate sustainability surged after the United Nations World Economic and Development Commission popularized the term "sustainable development" in its famous 1987 "Brundtland Report" and researchers began to adapt the concept to companies by declaring that they could pursue sustainability by meeting their present needs without compromising the ability of future generations to meet their own needs.[2] During the 1990s and early 2000s, academics and practitioners began to argue that corporate sustainability required simultaneous attention to, and satisfaction of, environmental, social and economic standards.[3] For example, Dyllick and Hockerts suggested that when the fundamental principles of sustainable development are translated to the firm level, it leads to defining corporate sustainability as "meeting the needs of a firm's direct and indirect stakeholders (such as shareholders, employees, clients, pressure groups, communities, etc.), without compromising its ability to meet the needs of future stakeholders as well".[4] A few years later, Laughland and Bansal described "business sustainability" as follows:

> Business sustainability is often defined as managing the triple bottom line – a process by which firms manage their financial, social, and environmental risks, obligations and opportunities. We extend this definition to capture more than just accounting for environmental and social impacts. Sustainable businesses are resilient, and they create economic value, healthy ecosystems and strong communities. These businesses survive external shocks because they are intimately connected to healthy economic, social and environmental systems.[5]

The steadily growing attention to corporate sustainability has been accompanied by a rise in the popularity of corporate social responsibility (CSR). Like sustainability generally, researchers and commentators have suggested a variety of definitions for CSR. One of the simplest descriptions of CSR is actions taken by a company to further some social good which is outside of the company's immediate interests yet required by law. Many of the definitions are strikingly similar to those suggested for corporate sustainability, such as Davis' description of CSR as being "the firm's considerations of, and response to, issues beyond the . . . economic, technical, and legal requirements of the firm to accomplish social benefits along with the traditional economic gains which the firm seeks".[6] Some have focused on CSR as a strategic tool that increases the competitiveness of the company and strengthens the company's reputation, each of which ultimately contributes to improved company performance. As noted above, definitions of corporate sustainability tend to incorporate the dimensions of the "triple-bottom-line" and conceptualize corporate sustainability as the long-term maintenance of responsibility from economic, environmental and social perspectives.

The consensus is that both CSR and corporate sustainability are based on attempting to operate businesses in a more humane, ethical and transparent way[7]; however, there is an important distinction: CSR is generally seen as being a voluntary action in and of itself or as part of the company's CSR strategy, while corporate sustainability is an organizational practice that is integrated into the entire business and business strategy of the company. This is important to understand because integrating sustainability into organizational practices is a time-consuming process that is heavily influenced by the organization's history, people, interests and action. The specific organizational practices that are related to sustainability are those that are implemented in order to reduce the adverse environmental and social impacts of the company's business and operations.

Sustainability requires organizations to look beyond traditional economic performance to consider the impact of their activities on the environment and society in which they operate; however, pursuit of sustainability relies on many of the same basic governance and management processes that have been developed in the business world. As such, in order to implement and practice effective sustainability management, directors, executive officers and senior managers must understand several fundamental topics: corporate governance, leadership and management. While considered separately, the topics are closely related and overlapping and, in fact, there is debate about how best to distinguish "leadership" and "management". In addition, one of the most important jobs of the members of the governance group, the board of directors in the case of a corporation, is selecting the management team, providing them with directions and monitoring and evaluating how the skills and actions of the managers (e.g., planning, acquiring and deploying resources, building products and systems and monitoring execution of day-to-day operations) have contributed to achievement of the overall goals and objectives set by the governance group.

Corporate Governance

Corporate governance can be thought of as the way in which corporations are directed, administered and controlled, and the actual activities of the directors and senior executives, the persons responsible for the governance and management of the corporation, have been referred to as steering, guiding and piloting the corporation through the challenges that arise as it pursues its goals and objectives. Jamali et al. explained that the "control" aspect of corporate governance encompassed the notions of compliance, accountability and transparency, and how managers exert their functions through compliance with the existing laws and regulations and codes of conduct.[8] At the board level, the focus is on leadership and strategy and directors are expected to deliberate, establish, monitor and adjust the corporation's strategy; determine and communicate the rules by which the strategy is to be implemented; and select, monitor and evaluate the members of the senior executive team who will be responsible for the day-to-day activities associated with the strategy. In addition, directors are expected to define roles and responsibilities; orient management toward a long-term vision of corporate performance; set proper resource allocation plans; contribute know-how, expertise and external information; perform various watchdog functions; and lead the firm's executives, managers and employees in the desired direction.[9]

Corporate governance has been a matter of intense focus and debate for public companies over the last few years, and a wide array of new statutes and regulations have been adopted that impact fiduciary obligations of directors and officers to shareholders; the composition and responsibilities of the audit and other committees of the board of directors; and the duties of professional advisors to public companies, notably accountants and lawyers. While this has created additional expense and risk for public companies, it has also raised the bar for privately held companies that are now expected to meet higher standards with respect to internal controls and ensure the appropriate compliance and risk management programs have been implemented and followed. Corporate governance does demand investment of significant resources, including the time and attention of senior management; however, the effort can pay substantial dividends in terms of employee morale and creating a position impression and reputation in the investment community and among the consumers of the company's products and services.

Setting the strategy for the corporation obviously requires consensus on the goals and objectives of the corporation's activities and the parties who are to be the primary beneficiaries of the performance of the corporation. Traditionally, directors were seen as the agents of the persons and parties that provided the capital necessary for the corporation to operate—the shareholders—and corporate governance was depicted as the framework for allocating power between the directors and the shareholders and holding the directors accountable for the stewardship of the capital provided by investors. In that framework, based on "shareholder primacy" famously championed by Friedman and others,[10] the principal participants were the shareholders, management and board of directors; however, the scope of corporate governance began to change during the 1990s as new and different goals for corporate activities were suggested. Sir Adrian Cadbury, Chair of the UK Commission on Corporate Governance, famously offered the following description of corporate governance and the governance framework in the Commission's 1992 Report on the Financial Aspects of Corporate Governance:

> Corporate governance is concerned with holding the balance between economic and social goals and between individual and communal goals. The governance framework is there to encourage the efficient use of resources and equally to require accountability for the stewardship of those resources. The aim is to align as nearly as possible the interests of individuals, corporations and society.

Cadbury's formulation of corporate governance brought an array of other participants, referred to as "stakeholders" (i.e., employees, suppliers, partners, customers, creditors, auditors, government agencies, the press and the general community), into the conversation and other influential bodies soon followed suit. For example, the principles of corporate governance of the Organisation for Economic Cooperation and Development clearly state that the corporate governance framework should recognize the rights of stakeholders (i.e., employees, customers, partners and the local community) as established by law and encourage active co-operation between corporations and stakeholders in creating wealth, jobs and the sustainability of financially sound enterprises. The focus on interested parties beyond shareholders is the hallmark of a broader view of corporate governance that emphasizes the responsibilities of business organizations to all of the different stakeholders that provide it with the necessary resources for its survival, competitiveness and success.[11] In this conception, managers remain primarily accountable to the stockholders who have placed their wealth in the hands of those managers; however, managers, particularly the members of the board of directors, are also responsible to groups of stakeholders who have made equally significant contributions to the corporation and these stakeholder responsibilities impose additional constraints on managerial action and the primacy of shareholder rights.[12]

The ascendency of the stakeholder perspective to challenge traditional shareholder primacy has led many to observe that corporate sustainability and governance have actually converged and the challenges for companies have gone beyond deciding whether they have duties to be socially responsible to developing new business and corporate governance models for long-term sustainability.[13] The drive toward, and pace of, convergence of corporate sustainability and governance has turned on a variety of key factors including improvements in information technology and a surge of globalization that has resulted in greater interconnection between stakeholders and companies, recognition of the role that sustainability and CSR and taking a values-based approach to governance and decision-making can have on improving motivation and productivity among employees, the desire of companies to protect their reputation and build trust in an era of corporate scandals, the need to take steps to ensure that the benefits of globalization are shared more broadly and the ascendency of new types of corporate leaders dedicated to advancing sustainability and CSR competencies in their organizations and linking sustainability issues with mainstream business issues. Also important has been the recognition of investors that CSR can and does have a positive impact on the financial and overall performance of their portfolio companies and the growing attention that directors have paid to environmental and social responsibility while developing their governance frameworks.[14] In addition, governments have become more involved with regulating activities in areas such as the environment, labor relations and reporting, which means that companies have had to expand the scope of their compliance operations.[15]

Leadership

Governance is the means by which companies can be effectively led and the key players in the governance structure—the directors and executive officers—must accept and embrace their leadership responsibilities. In the management context, leadership has been consistently identified as playing a critical role in the success or failure of organizations, and some surveys have pegged up to 45% of an organization's performance on the quality and effectiveness of its leadership team.[16] However, while leadership has been rigorously studied and discussed for centuries, a consensus regarding how the term "leadership" can and should be defined has been elusive. In this regard, Stogdill observed that "there are almost as many definitions of leadership as there are persons who have attempted to define the concept" and Fiedler wrote that "[t]here are almost as many definitions of leadership as there are leadership theories—and there are almost as many theories of leadership as there are psychologists working in the field".[17] The researchers involved in the influential Global Leadership and Organizational Effectiveness project defined leadership as "... the ability of an individual to influence, motivate, and enable others to contribute toward the effectiveness and success of the organizations of which they are members".[18]

While leaders can be distinguished from managers, leaders nonetheless are responsible for a number of the same functions typically categorized as "managerial" such as setting goals and designing strategic plans to achieve those goals, communicating directives to other members of the organization, overseeing execution of the organizational strategy and setting guidelines for motivating organizational members and assessing their performance. Based on the research and observations on the subject, all leaders, regardless of their position, are engaged in the following core roles and activities[19]:

- Selecting and defining goals and objectives for the organization; designing strategic plans to achieve those goals and objectives; and identifying, promoting and managing changes required to achieve future goals and objectives
- Communicating ideas about their vision for the organization and providing directions to other members of the organization regarding actions to be taken to realize the vision
- Designing and implementing an organizational structure that promotes efficient flow of information and collaboration among members of the organization to develop new products and services and solutions for problems and issues raised by customers
- Overseeing execution of the organizational strategy and establishing procedures for assessing the performance of organizational members
- Implementing human resources management practices that support their vision and provide members of the organization with access to training necessary to maintain and improve the skills required for them to positively participate in the execution of the vision
- Engaging in proactive pursuit and collection of information from internal and external sources and implementation of procedures for efficient analysis and dissemination of relevant information among members of the organization
- Engaging in behaviors that support organizational members and enhance their feelings of personal worth and importance
- Engaging in behaviors that facilitate interaction among organizational members; encourage members to develop close and mutually satisfying relationships; create high quality teams; and train members of the organization on team building techniques
- Engaging in behaviors that motivate organizational members to achieve excellent performance and fulfill the goals set for the organization using a range of techniques such as formal authority, role modeling, delegation of authority, setting specific and challenging goals, and adroit and intelligent use of rewards and punishments
- Engaging in behaviors that support achievement of the organizational performance goals, including activities such as coordinating, planning and scheduling and providing organizational members with the requisite tools, materials and technical knowledge necessary for them to do their jobs

- Engaging in behaviors consistent with service as a steward of the assets, resources, mission, reputation and legacy of the organization including selection and development of potential future leaders and representing the organization with integrity in the communities in which it operates

While there is arguably consensus about the core leadership roles and activities, execution depends heavily on "leadership style": how the leader interacts with his or her followers and his or her "manner and approach of providing direction, motivating people and achieving objectives".[20] Although there are a number of different models of leadership style, three fundamental dimensions are often represented: the leader's approach to influencing the behavior of his or her followers; the manner in which decisions regarding the direction of the group are made, with a specific emphasis on the level of participation offered to followers; and the balance struck between goal attainment and maintaining harmony within the group (sometimes referred to as group "maintenance").[21] For example, two alternative approaches to influencing the behavior of followers are the transactional leadership, which views the leader-follower relationship as a process of exchange, and transformational leadership, which is particularly relevant to sustainability and relies on the leader's ability to communicate a clear and acceptable vision and related goals that engender intense emotion among followers that motivates them to buy into and pursue the leader's vision. Contrasting styles for decision-making are found when distinguishing authoritarian (autocratic) and participative (democratic) leaders. Finally, the balance between goals and maintenance is emphasized in those models, such as Blake and Mouton's Grid Theory, that analyze the degree to which leaders exhibit task and/or relationship orientation in their interactions with followers.

Management

Given that "management" has been so widely studied and practiced for literally thousands of years, it is not surprising to find a wide array of possible definitions of the term. A number of definitions of "management" have focused on the specific tasks and activities that all managers, regardless of whether they are overseeing a business, a family or a social group, engage in, such as planning, organizing, directing, coordinating and controlling. One of the simplest, and often quoted, definitions of management was offered by Mary Parker Follett, who described it as "the art of getting things done through people".[22] The notion of "management through people" can also be found in the work of Weihrich and Koontz, who defined management as "the process of designing and maintaining an environment in which individuals, working together in groups, accomplish efficiently selected aims".[23] As time has passed, management has come to be recognized as one of the core factors of production along with machines, materials, money, technology and people. It is well known that productivity has become a leading indicator of organizational performance, and Drucker has argued that "[t]he greatest opportunity for increasing productivity is surely to be found in knowledge, work itself, and especially in management".[24] While the skills and styles of individual managers will always be relevant, more attention and reliance is being placed on the "management systems" used by organizations to manage their structures, processes, activities and resources in order that their products or services meet the organization's objectives.[25]

In order to understand whether someone is being an effective manager, it is necessary to have some idea of the expectations regarding the person's roles and activities within the organization. A number of different approaches have been taken in creating models of managerial functions or activities. Fayol famously argued that there were five principle managerial functions—planning, organizing, commanding, coordinating and controlling—and others have accepted these categories and added a handful of others such as staffing and rewarding. Mintzberg criticized Fayol's "five functions" as being an inaccurate reflection of the complex and chaotic nature of the manager's tasks and suggested an alternative model of the ten core "roles", or organized sets of behaviors, identified with a managerial position, which he divided up into three groups: interpersonal roles, informational roles and decisional roles. Others have pointed out that it is useful to distinguish between "functional" and "general" managers, each of whom has their own unique duties, responsibilities and skill requirements. The position or level of the manager in the organizational hierarchy is also likely to be relevant to his or her roles and activities: "first-line" managers focus primarily on supervision of operational employees, "middle managers" focus primarily on supervising the first-line managers and/or staff departments and "top-level" or "senior" managers focus on setting the strategic direction for the entire organization.[26]

Researchers and commentators have attempted to identify the skills, motivations and behaviors that managers and administrators must have in order to effectively carry out their duties and responsibilities. There is no single answer since the particular skills that a specific manager may need will vary depending on whether he or she is engaged in "general" or "functional" management and where the manager fits into the overall organizational hierarchy, and other situational factors certainly play an important part in determining what might be "effective management" in a specific context. Mintzberg's efforts to identify some of the distinguishing characteristics of managerial work, which ultimately led to the creation of his model of "managerial roles", were accompanied by his assessment that effective managers must recognize and master a number of important "managerial skills", including development and nurturing of peer relationships (i.e., liaison contacts), negotiation and conflict resolution skills, the ability to motivate and inspire subordinates, establishment and maintenance of information networks, the ability to communicate effectively when disseminating information and the ability to make decisions in conditions of extreme ambiguity and allocate resources, and he argued that the entire process of identifying the various managerial roles and related skills, while not guaranteeing that a manager will be effectiveness and successful, provided a framework for setting priorities and establishing a managerial training regimen.[27] Mintzberg's work provided support for managerial skills posited by others: the need to deal with an unrelenting pace of activities and decisions, the need to cope with complexity, the need to manage the scarce resources of time and attention, preferences for verbal media and the need to create and nurture communication relationships with superiors, outsiders and subordinates.

As with other topics that have been intensely reviewed in the management literature, there is a wide array of definitions of the term "management style". A fairly simple approach is to view management style simply as the way that an organization is managed.[28] Not surprisingly, there is no single management style that applies in all instances, and the style that might be used in any particular situation, and its effectiveness, will be influenced by a number of factors including the type of organization, business purpose and activities of the organization, size of the organization, operating environment, corporate culture, societal culture, information technology and communication and, finally, the personal style and behavior of the owner or chief executive.[29] Moreover, management styles will change as firms transition to new business models based on changing trends in the marketplace, such as greater emphasis on quality and customer service and satisfaction.[30]

Notes

1 T. Dyllick and K. Hockerts, "Beyond the Business Case for Corporate Sustainability", *Business Strategy and the Environment*, 11 (March 2002), 130.
2 I. Montiel, "Corporate Social Responsibility and Corporate Sustainability: Separate Pasts, Common Features", *Organization and Environment*, 21(3) (September 2008), 245, 254 (citing UN World Commission on Environment and Development, *Our Common Future* (Oxford: Oxford University Press, 1987), 43).
3 See P. Bansal, "Evolving Sustainably: A Longitudinal Study of Corporate Sustainable Development", *Strategic Management Journal*, 26(3) (2005), 197; and T. Gladwin and J. Kennelly, "Shifting Paradigms for Sustainable Development: Implications for Management Theory and Research", *Academy of Management Review*, 20(4) (1995), 874.
4 T. Dyllick and K. Hockerts, "Beyond the Business Case for Corporate Sustainability", *Business Strategy and the Environment*, 11 (March 2002), 130, 131.

5 P. Laughland and T. Bansal, "The Top Ten Reasons Why Businesses Aren't More Sustainable", *Ivey Business Journal* (January/February 2011), http:// iveybusinessjournal.com/publication/the-top-ten-reasons-why-businesses-arent-more-sustainable/ (accessed April 23, 2020).

6 K. Davis, "The Case For and Against Business Assumption of Social Responsibilities", *American Management Journal*, 16 (1973), 312.

7 M. Marrewijk, "Concepts and Definitions of CSR and Corporate Sustainability: Between Agency and Communion", *Journal of Business Ethics*, 44(2) (May 2003), 95.

8 D. Jamali, A. Safieddine and M. Rabbath, "Corporate Governance and Corporate Social Responsibility Synergies and Interrelationship", *Corporate Governance*, 16(5) (2008), 443–444 (citing K. MacMillan, K. Money, S. Downing and C. Hillenbrad, "Giving Your Organization SPIRIT: An Overview and Call to Action for Directors on Issues of Corporate Governance, Corporate Reputation and Corporate Responsibility", *Journal of General Management*, 30 (2004), 15; and A. Cadbury, "The Corporate Governance Agenda", *Journal of Corporate Governance, Practice-Based Papers*, 8 (2000), 7).

9 K. MacMillan, K. Money, S. Downing and C. Hillenbrad, "Giving Your Organization SPIRIT: An Overview and Call to Action for Directors on Issues of Corporate Governance, Corporate Reputation and Corporate Responsibility", *Journal of General Management*, 30 (2004), 15; A. Cadbury, "The Corporate Governance Agenda", *Journal of Corporate Governance, Practice-Based Papers*, 8 (2000), 7; and J. Page, *Corporate Governance and Value Creation* (University of Sherbrooke, Research Foundation of CFA Institute, 2005).

10 Milton Friedman, the Nobel Prize winning economist, declared that the exclusive goal of corporate activities was to maximize value for the owners of the corporation (i.e., the shareholders) and companies did make a positive social contribution by running a profitable business, employing people, paying taxes and distributing some part of their net profits to shareholders. Another argument often made for the shareholder primacy approach to corporate governance was that requiring management to invest time and effort in devising ways to create additional social benefits beyond the honest pursuit of profits within the boundaries of the law would dilute management's focus, undermine economic performance, and thereby ultimately undermine social welfare. C. Williams, "Corporate Social Responsibility and Corporate Governance", in J. Gordon and G. Ringe (Eds.), *Oxford Handbook of Corporate Law and Governance* (Oxford: Oxford University Press, 2016), 34, Retrieved from http://digitalcommons.osgoode.yorku.ca/scholarly_works/1784 (accessed April 23, 2020).

11 K. MacMillan, K. Money, S. Downing and C. Hillenbrad, "Giving Your Organization SPIRIT: An Overview and Call to Action for Directors on Issues of Corporate Governance, Corporate Reputation and Corporate Responsibility", *Journal of General Management*, 30 (2004), 15.

12 J. Page, *Corporate Governance and Value Creation* (University of Sherbrooke, Research Foundation of CFA Institute, 2005); and N. Kendall, "Good Corporate Governance", *Accountants' Digest*, 40 (1999).

13 M. Rahim, *Legal Regulation of Corporate Social Responsibility: A Meta-Regulation Approach of Law for Raising CSR in a Weak Economy* (Berlin: Springer, 2013), 13, 44 (citing M. Blowfield and J. Frynas, "Setting New Agendas: Critical Perspectives on Corporate Social Responsibility in the Developing World", *International Affairs*, 81(3) (2005), 499, 504).

14 Investors and other stakeholders have increasingly turned their attention to assessing and grading companies and their directors and senior management teams against emerging standards that cut across three dimensions

now commonly referred to as "ESG": environmental, social and governance. With respect to the environment, the focus is on how a company performs as a "steward of nature" through its policies and practices with respect to impacting climate change, sustainability, carbon footprint, water usage, pollutants and conservation. The social dimension focuses on how the company manages its stakeholder relationships and includes criteria relating to non-discrimination, working conditions, gender equality, diversity and inclusivity, fair pay, health and safety and community engagement. Governance in this framework is concerned about the actions of the company's leaders with respect to adhering to corporate governance principles, shareholders' rights, boardroom diversity, participation by other stakeholders, alignment of executive compensation with performance objectives, audits and internal controls and business ethics. The criteria are continuously expanding to include company's lands, manufacturing facilities, offices and transportation modalities as well as human rights due diligence. Adapted from J. Chen, "Environmental, Social, and Governance (ESG) Criteria", https://www.investopedia.com/terms/e/environmental-social-and-governance-esg-criteria.asp (accessed April 23, 2020); and S. Seiden, "Recruiting ESG Directors" (Harvard Law School Forum on Corporate Governance and Financial Regulation, October 27, 2019), https://corpgov.law.harvard.edu/2019/10/27/recruiting-esg-directors/ (accessed April 23, 2020).

15 C. Strandberg, *The Convergence of Corporate Governance and Corporate Social Responsibility: Thought-Leaders Study* (Ottawa: Canadian Co-operative Association, March 2005), 8–9. Traditional compliance activities have also been impacted by the convergence of corporate sustainability and governance as companies have begun to move "beyond the law" to develop processes to understand and comply with a growing range of self-regulatory regimes focused on various aspects of businesses' environmental and social responsibilities.

16 B. Bass, *Bass & Stogdill's Handbook of Leadership: Theory, Research, and Managerial Applications* (3rd ed.) (New York: Free Press, 1990); D. Day and R. Lord, "Executive Leadership and Organizational Performance: Suggestions for a New Theory and Methodology", *Journal of Management*, 14(3) (1988), 453–464.

17 R. Stodgill, *Handbook of Leadership* (New York: Free Press, 1974), 259; F. Fiedler, *Leadership* (Morristown, NJ: General Learning, 1971), 1.

18 R. House, P. Hanges, M. Javidan, P. Dorfman and V. Gupta (Eds.). *Culture, Leadership, and Organizations: The GLOBE Study of 62 Societies* (Thousand Oaks, CA: Sage, 2004), 15.

19 A. Gutterman, *Practicing Leadership* (New York: Business Expert Press, 2018). See also D. Dudley, *This Is Day One: A Practical Guide to Leadership That Matters* (New York: Hachette Books, 2018).

20 C. Fertman and J. van Liden, "Character Education: An Essential Ingredient for Youth Leadership Development", *NASSP Bulletin*, 83(609) (October 1999), 9–15. See also R. Ashkenas and B. Manville, *Harvard Business Review Leader's Handbook* (Cambridge, MA: Harvard Business Press, 2018).

21 R.W. Scholl, Changing *Leadership Style* (2000).

22 M. Follett, "Dynamic Administration" in H. Metcalf and L. Urwick (Eds.), *Dynamic Administration: The Collected Papers of Mary Parker Follett* (New York: Harper & Row, 1942).

23 H. Weihrich and H. Koontz, *Management: A Global Perspective* (10th ed.) (New York: McGraw-Hill, 1993).

24 P. Drucker, *Management, Tasks, Responsibilities, Practices* (New York: Harper & Row, 1973), 69.

25 See Chapter 8 (Management Systems) in this volume for further discussion of designing and implementing quality and management systems based on ISO 9001 (quality), ISO 14001 (environment) and ISO 26000 (social responsibility). See also A. Gutterman, *Practicing Management* (New York: Business Expert Press, 2018).

26 Managers interested in overviews of managerial roles, activities, skills and styles should review L. Belker, M. McCormick and G. Topchik, *The First Time Manager* (6th ed.) (New York: AMACOM, 2012); S. Lebowitz, "10 Books Every First-Time Manager Should Read" (January 29, 2016), https://www. inc.com/business-insider/books-new-managers-should-read.html (accessed April 23, 2020); K. Blanchard and S. Johnson, *The New One Minute Manager* (New York: William Morrow, 2015); *The Essential Manager's Handbook: The Ultimate Visual Guide to Successful Management* (London: DK Publishing, 2016); and *The Harvard Business Review Manager's Handbook: The 17 Skills Leaders Need to Stand Out* (Cambridge, MA: Harvard Business Review Press, 2017).

27 H. Mintzberg, "The Manager's Job: Folklore and Fact", *Harvard Business Review*, 53(4) (July–August 1975), 49–61. Information regarding Mintzberg's own studies of managerial work was collected in H. Mintzberg, *The Nature of Managerial Work* (New York: Harper & Row, 1973).

28 T. Quang and N. Vuong, "Management Styles and Organisational Effectiveness in Vietnam", *Research and Practice in Human Resource Management*, 10(2) (2002), 36–55.

29 Id.

30 S. Dolan and S. Garcia, "Managing by Values: Cultural Redesign for Strategic Organizational Change at the Dawn of the Twenty-First Century", *Journal of Management Development*, 21(2) (2002), 101–117.

2   Sustainability in the Boardroom

Corporate social responsibility (CSR) and corporate sustainability initiatives are most effective when CSR principles have been integrated into the company's governance and management processes and organizational culture. CSR governance begins at the top of the organization with the board of directors, which has been charged by emerging corporate governance guidelines and stakeholder expectations with responsibility for oversight of the environmental and social impacts of the company's operations. The directors and members of the senior executive team must proactively respond to the serious challenges confronting business, and society in general, from neglect of important environmental and social issues. Governance policies and procedures must explicitly address the concerns of all of the company's stakeholders, not just shareholders but also employees, the environment, customers, supply chain partners, community members and business partners. Ideas regarding organizational design need to be re-visited in order to coordinate CSR activities. Finally, continuous efforts need to be made in order to establish and maintain an organizational culture in which all of the members share the same views and values regarding the importance of balancing economic, environmental and social responsibility in order to achieve the level of collaboration necessary to pursue sustainability initiatives.

Directors' Adoption of Sustainability Oversight Responsibilities

Governance processes relating to CSR cannot be effective unless and until the directors are brought on board and while there is evidence that directors are acknowledging and adopting sustainability oversight responsibilities the uptake remains far from universal. In 2017, researchers on corporate sustainability from the MIT Sloan Management Review and The Boston Consulting Group (BCG) reported that while 86% of companies agreed that boards should play a strong role in their company's sustainability efforts, only 48% said their CEOs are engaged, and even fewer (30%) agreed that their sustainability efforts had strong board-level oversight.[1] The researchers cautioned that a company's top executives and board members needed to be mindful of the interests and expectations of investors and noted that corporate leaders must recognize that an increasing number of shareholders are (literally) invested in whether a company's environmental, social and governance (ESG) activities connect with its financial success.[2] Noting that improving board engagement on sustainability issues faced several hurdles (e.g., the unclear financial impact of developing sustainable business practices, competing priorities, a lack of sustainability expertise among board members and short-termism), the researchers recommended that steps to be taken to improve directors' expertise with respect to sustainability through training, new appointments to the board and accessing external expertise through external/independent advisory boards.

Support for CSR programs by the board of directors is an important element of the requisite "tone at the top" for increasing the chances of success for CSR. Board members must understand that CSR programs are consistent with their traditional role and duty to effectively manage the legal, financial and reputational risks to the company that arise from the environmental and social impacts of the company's activities. Board members must insist that CSR be integrated into the company's strategic decision-making and performance management and assessment systems, a priority which includes allocating sufficient resources to ensure that personnel are able to efficiently engage with the company's stakeholders. In addition, board members must push for creating and maintaining systems that provide them with information they need to understand and evaluate the company's CSR programs.

Directors' Roles and Responsibilities

The focus on sustainability has extended the traditional roles and responsibilities of directors and created new ones.[3] Many agree that CSR principles are typically embedded into governance practices such as disclosure and reporting, risk management oversight, board composition and diversity and compensation. Disclosure and reporting on social, environmental and ethical issues has become commonplace among larger companies and has expanded to include specific details on policy implementation and stakeholder engagement. In addition, the main standards developed for non-financial reporting, such as the Global Reporting Initiative, have incorporated several disclosure items relating to the internal governance framework including the independence and expertise of directors; board-level processes for overseeing the identification and management of economic, environmental and social risks and opportunities, and the linkage between executive compensation and achievement of financial and non-financial goals.

The growing emphasis on CSR means that boards need to be able to draw on the skills, knowledge and experiences of a more diverse group of members, a requirement that is consistent with calls for better gender and ethnicity diversity in the boardroom. Boards also need to develop new compensation and rewards systems that take CSR into account and prioritize metrics and success indicators that are broadly defined from a longer-term perspective.[4] In addition, as boardroom focus on sustainability has increased, it is expected that directors become more involved in integration of strategy and sustainability; paying attention to stakeholder perspectives and engagement; overseeing the production of, and approving, sustainability reports; and ensuring that management is appropriately accountable for sustainability performance, and compensated properly in light of that performance.[5]

Framework for Board Oversight of Sustainability

CSR and corporate sustainability are broad and challenging topics and the directors must carefully consider how the board's duties and responsibilities will be discharged and allocated among board members. The structure and processes a board creates to oversee CSR and corporate sustainability will vary based on a number of factors, such as the size and complexity of the company's operations (including its supply chain and whether operations are international), its industry, the magnitude of the company's CSR risks and opportunities, the degree to which CSR issues are central to the company's strategy, and the level of director expertise regarding relevant CSR issues.[6] One well-known corporate governance advisor has counseled that directors should begin the process of developing an oversight framework for CSR and corporate sustainability by asking and answering the following questions[7]:

- How should concerns regarding CSR and corporate sustainability be integrated into the board's discussions on strategy and risk oversight?
- To what extent should CSR and corporate sustainability topics be included as standalone agenda items for board meetings?
- What information should be provided to directors (e.g., data on how the company's efforts compare to those of its peer companies, leading industry standards, and the CSR-related priorities of key shareholders and proxy advisory firms)?
- Which metrics should the board and members of the executive team focus on in considering progress against CSR and corporate sustainability goals (e.g., goals involving reduction of water usage and emissions, reducing on-the-job injuries and employee turnover, or improving workforce diversity and employee retention)?
- What process should be used for drafting and reviewing public disclosures about the company's CSR and corporate sustainability efforts?

The entire board also needs to consider whether it has the full team and resources necessary to effectively and credibly carry out its oversight responsibilities. For example, consideration needs to be given to the following issues and questions[8]:

- Does the board have a sufficient number of members to staff the requisite standing and special committees and to meet expectations of investors and other stakeholders with respect to diversity and ability to effectively engage with stakeholders?
- Does the board include directors who have knowledge of, and experience with, the company's businesses?
- Are all of the directors able to devote sufficient time to preparing for and attending board and committee meetings?
- Does the board have processes in place to ensure that directors receive all of the data, presented in a clear and objective manner, which is critical for them to be able to make sound decisions on strategy, compensation and capital allocation?
- Does the board have procedures in place to ensure that directors receive continuous training and education on the rapidly expanding list of topics that will appear on the board's agenda?

The answers to each of the questions above are pivotal in formalizing the board's approach to sustainability governance. Each situation is different; however, reference should be made to the following best practices adapted from suggestions included in a UN Global Compact publication[9]:

- Create a standing board committee devoted to sustainability-related issues with a portfolio that includes reviewing and monitoring the sustainable development, environmental, health and safety and community development policies and activities of the company on behalf of the board
- Integrate periodic review of the company's environmental, sustainability and safety policies and reports into the board's formal duties and responsibilities along with ensuring effective communication with stakeholders through transparent disclosures
- Include adherence to sustainability standards and values in the company's Corporate Code of Conduct, which should be reviewed and endorsed annually by the board, and include sustainability in applicable policies and procedures and in the company's corporate performance scorecard
- Include sustainability initiatives in the company's long-term strategy and provide for regular and continuous monitoring of the performance of such initiatives
- Include sustainability in the formal job descriptions of the CEO and other members of the executive team, executive compensation

policies and executive performance objectives and provide that the lead sustainability executive has a direct reporting relationship to the board

- Require that directors become generally knowledgeable of the company's stakeholder interests and sustainability impacts and risks and formalize procedures for ensuring that the legitimate interests of stakeholders are considered in board decisions and that the overall quality of stakeholders' relations is monitored
- Provide that the board's governance and nominating committee implement board diversity policies and measures and maintain oversight responsibility of diversity policy implementation (e.g., sustainability should be included as a skill within the director skills matrix and sustainability topics and opportunities should be included in director continuing education)
- Ensure that sustainability information is proactively provided to institutional and socially responsible investors and other stakeholders and that information is provided to all stakeholders on how to contact the board directly with questions, concerns and ideas regarding the company's sustainability initiatives and performance
- Provide that a specific board committee (e.g., the audit committee) will monitor compliance with the Code of Conduct by ensuring all directors become thoroughly familiar with the Code and acknowledge their support and understanding of the Code
- Ensure that all members of the board receive quarterly updates of the company's ethics and compliance program and sustainability-related initiatives
- Develop, implement and enforce polices relating to fair operating practices (i.e., ethical conduct, anti-bribery and anti-corruption), environmental and sustainability, CSR, human rights, occupational health and safety, governmental relations and lobbying, and philanthropy and donations

In addition, the records of the deliberations of the board should make it clear that members of the board understand and accept their responsibility for setting the "tone at the top" in adhering to and enforcing the company's sustainability policies, values and commitments. Among other things, time at board meetings should be set aside for educating directors on their traditional fiduciary duties as established by statute and case law, as well as their emerging sustainability-related responsibilities as set forth in voluntary standards that go "beyond the law". Directors should also be reminded that their oversight duties with respect to compliance and risk management have been expanded to include sustainability and issues succumbed therein such as human rights.

While the entire board should consider the questions posed above, and CSR and corporate sustainability need to have an important place on the agenda for full board meetings, larger companies typically follow the advice described above and rely on one or more committees when it comes to allocating specific tasks and tapping into specialized resources and expertise.[10] One approach that is growing in popularity is the creation of public policy/CSR, social and cultural responsibility and/or environmental responsibility, health, safety and technology committees composed of a sub-group of the entire board that is charged with focusing more time and effort on sustainability generally and important topics within sustainability. In addition, other committees may be asked to provide support relating to specific CSR and corporate sustainability topics that are closely related to their regular activities, although it is important to avoid too much dilution of effort by making sure that the actions and activities of all committees are coordinated and the results reported upward to the entire board during the portion of the board meetings allocated to the consideration of CSR and corporate sustainability. Examples include[11]:

- *Nominating Committee*: In discharging its responsibilities with respect to identifying and recruiting new directors who can broaden the range of experience and expertise available to the full board and its committees, the nominating committee should pay specific attention to identifying candidates with experience in evaluating and overseeing CSR and corporate sustainability initiatives, such as CEOs of other companies that have achieved positive recognition for their sustainability efforts. The nominating committee can also contribute to the socially responsible profile of the company by ensuring that the board is diverse and represents all the company's key constituencies and that members have skills and experience necessary to engage effectively with stakeholders regarding CSR, corporate sustainability and identify and manage risks. The committee should integrate sustainability criteria into its processes for identifying director candidates and evaluating director performance.
- *Governance Committee*: While some companies allocate responsibility for director training and education to the nominating committee of the board, the governance committee is generally responsible for those activities and should ensure that CSR, corporate sustainability and the specific issues and topics included therein are given a place on board's education agenda.[12] For example, the governance committee should ensure that all directors are adequately versed in the sustainability-related topics of most interest to investors such as climate change and identifying and mitigating the risks associated with climate change. Education and training should also cover emerging trends in the sustainability area. The governance committee will also often be tasked with reviewing corporate policies on sustainability.
- *Audit Committee*: Many commentators focus on how CSR and corporate sustainability initiatives help companies manage and

reduce risks. As such the audit committee of the board, which is generally the committee responsible for risk assessment and management, should include CSR and corporate sustainability on its agenda and work with the company's external and internal auditors to ensure that the sustainability topics are covered in audit activities and internal controls and that financial reporting procedures take into account emerging requirements for sustainability-related reporting. The audit committee should also understand the risks and opportunities relating to reporting the sustainability performance of the company, ensure the quality and timeframe of sustainability and other corporate disclosures, monitor research and development on sustainability and ensure compliance with new regulations and non-binding standards on sustainability along with other committees formed to focus specifically on compliance activities.[13]

- *Compensation and Organizational Development Committee*: The compensation and organizational development committee should carefully review the compensation and incentive programs, and accompanying evaluation procedures, established for the company's senior executives to ensure that they are consistent with the company's CSR and corporate sustainability initiatives and performance targets. Executive compensation has often been criticized as being tied too closely to short-term performance and weighting financial performance too heavily will dissuade executives from investing in sustainability initiatives that may be more difficult to objectively assess for value (e.g., improving energy efficiency, reducing greenhouse gas emissions, meeting health and safety targets or improving leadership diversity).[14] The compensation committee should be proactively engaged in dialogue with the company's investors regarding sustainability and executive compensation.[15] The committee should also oversee the company's human resources development programs to ensure that they include CSR and corporate sustainability topics.

- *Disclosure and Reporting Committee*: One of the fundamental principles of CSR and corporate sustainability is more transparency by companies with respect to their operational activities and their actual and potential impact on stakeholders beyond investors. As such, it is important for the board to recognize the importance of disclosure and reporting by establishing a separate committee on the topic and ensuring that sufficient resources are assigned to understanding and complying with mandatory reporting requirements and creating effective sustainability reports that comply with the emerging guidelines such as those developed by the Global Reporting Initiative. In particular, the committee needs to ensure appropriate funding and support for the more comprehensive internal reporting processes required for CSR and corporate sustainability analysis and reporting.

- **Risk Management and Compliance Committee**: The risk management and compliance committee, which often is separated into two committees, should expand its traditional role and responsibilities to include oversight of management of risks relating to sustainability issues and compliance with sustainability-related laws and regulations. When engaging in compliance oversight the committee should be prepared to coordinate with other board committees such as the audit committee, which brings its expertise in assessing compliances with specified standards, and committees focused on specific regulated issues such as the environment and health and safety.

Boards may supplement formal "hard governance" mechanisms for sustainability (i.e., board committees) with external advisory panels that comprise experts either on sustainability in general or on specific topics relevant to the company's industry or otherwise of particular interest to the company such as health, nutrition or renewal energy.[16] When these panels have a direct line to the entire board, they can enhance the efforts of directors to understand sustainability issues and help the board with the collection and assessment of stakeholder opinions regarding the company's sustainability strategy and performance. Another type of external advisory panel is a "stakeholder advisory group", which includes representatives of one or more stakeholder groups who are available for consultation on specific topics or a variety of sustainability issues. External panels generally meet as a full group two to four times a year and panel members should be available between meetings for ad-hoc consultations with the board and/or senior management.[17]

Board Composition

Along with finding the appropriate structure for oversight of sustainability, boards must address the composition of the director team to ensure that it both demonstrates certain key values associated with social responsibility and includes members with the appropriate sustainability mindset and skills required to execute on sustainability commitments. Important issues and characteristics for board composition relative to sustainability are independence (i.e., separating the chief executive and chairperson positions and recruiting external directors), diversity (i.e., gender diversity, which has led to imposition of quotas to remedy under-representation of women on corporate boards, and including representatives of key foreign markets as companies globalize their operations), stakeholder representation (i.e., a director elected to the board specifically to represent the interests and perspectives of non-investor stakeholders, a concept that admittedly has yet to be widely adopted apart from a handful of jurisdictions with "dual board" corporate governance structures), cultures, age and viewpoints, each of which has a clear relationship to sustainability.[18]

KPMG noted that another important issue with respect to board composition is making sure that the directors have the relevant experience and expertise to identify and understand CSR risks and opportunities and to intelligently and effectively oversee management's handling of these issues. Companies have begun recruiting directors with specific expertise and experience on topics that will likely be most important to the company from a strategic perspective, such as "climate change", and realize that having a board with strong CSR expertise sends a signal to investors and other stakeholders that CSR issues are a priority in the boardroom. The entire board, through its nominating and governance committee, should add relevant CSR expertise to the criteria used to identify and select future candidates; however, a CSR skill set should be just one of several tools that a candidate brings to the board. For example, while a director may have extensive experience in working on a particular social issue, he or she needed to be familiar and comfortable with the financial analysis tools that will be used to develop a business case for a particular CSR initiative and the associated performance metrics. In addition, steps should be taken to educate all members of the board on CSR issues, especially those directors who lack background in the area.[19]

Sustainability Governance Policies and Processes

Companies often designate a corporate secretary or another person to oversee administrative matters relating to governance processes. Someone in this position would normally be expected to maintain relevant governance processes and structures through regular reviews and updates to the board manual and other governance documents; keep current on evolving practices in corporate governance and advise the board and the board's governance committee; serve as chief expert and advisor on all corporate governance matters for directors and employees; serve as executive liaison to the governance committee; and administer the corporate code of conduct and other board policies.[20] With respect to sustainability, a Global Compact publication recommended that the aforementioned traditional duties be supplemented to include monitoring the external environment to remain fully informed of corporate sustainability governance trends, emerging issues and best practices, especially those of relevance to the sector or key issues; informing the governance committee on trends and changes in best practice corporate sustainability governance and regulator expectations; determining and implementing amendments to governing documents, processes and structures to incorporate sustainability oversight roles for the board; ensuring that executives and key employees understand the emerging trends in corporate sustainability governance; and, along with members of the executive team, ensuring that the board regularly reviews, updates and monitors compliance with corporate sustainability policies.

Sustainability Education and Training for Board Members

In addition to seeking out board members with specific experience and skills relevant to sustainability, companies must ensure that all of their directors are continuously educated on sustainability in general as well as the subtopics of sustainability that are the foundation of the company's goals and commitments. Director education and training in sustainability is important for several reasons. First, directors who are unable to recognize and respond to sustainability issues are derelict in their duties with respect to risk management since those issues pose a substantial risk to the company's reputation, brand and license-to-operate. Second, directors need to understand sustainability in order to properly select and oversee senior leadership to ensure that a "culture of sustainability" is created and maintained from the very top of the organization. Finally, directors are responsible for the long-term strategy and direction of the company and in discharging those duties and making leadership decisions they need to understand how strategic management of sustainability and innovation can improve business performance.[21] Sustainability training is often assigned to the board's nominating and governance committee which will be responsible for determining the curriculum and identifying internal faculty members and external training providers such as universities with expertise in various sustainability issues.

A Global Compact publication recommended that all board members should have generic sustainability skills and knowledge such as basic awareness of sustainability and how it affects the organization; basic understanding of what is corporate sustainability; ability to identify at a high level the most material sustainability impacts of and on the organization, its value chain, industry and operating context; knowledge of key stakeholders and their priorities and issues; understanding of how poor sustainability performance can create reputational and other risks; ability to articulate how sustainability relates to the purpose and strategy of the organization; understanding of sustainability trends generally and as they affect the industry and their impact on the company; and knowledge of the company's business case for sustainability, including how sustainability can contribute to long-term value creation such as the ability to attract and retain talent and stimulate innovation.[22]

Competencies and Remuneration of the Executive Team

Selecting the CEO and other members of the executive team, and setting the right performance criteria and incentives with respect to pursuit and achievement of the company's sustainability commitments and targets, is a unique and important responsibility of the board of directors. Surveys, such as one completed by Boyden in 2017 among adults in the United Kingdom, repeatedly confirm that the public strongly believes that the

CEO must play an active role in the CSR activities of his or her company and act as a spokesperson for those activities.[23] Participation and engagement by employees throughout the organization is essential for effective CSR implementation and the CEO is the only person in a position to communicate and demonstrate the values associated with CSR in a way that will integrate CSR into the corporate culture and the way that employees work on a day-to-day basis. At the very beginning, during the recruitment process, directors must include in their selection criteria that candidates have the ability to demonstrate solid understanding of the complex sustainability issues that affect the business environment; commit to operate in accordance with the highest social, environmental and ethical standards; and provide a track record of producing excellent financial results with due consideration for the interests and concerns of different stakeholders.[24] While all of this is certainly applicable to the selection of the CEO, the same level of rigor should be applied to filling all the spots on the executive team.

Once candidates for CEO and the other spots on the executive team have been selected, incentives must be put in place in their compensation arrangements that reward long-term performance and that are aligned with the sustainability priorities and targets established by the board. Not only does this impact the decisions that the executive team make but it also sends a strong message to employees and external stakeholders about how sustainability is valued and taken seriously at the top of the organization. It is no secret that incentive elements of executive compensation arrangements have long been tied to financial performance and increasing shareholder value as demonstrated by improvements in share prices. Certainly financial success is important to the long-term viability of the business and provides the CEO and other senior executives with access to the capital necessary to remain competitive and pursue and commercialize innovative products, services and technologies; however, there is growing interest among stakeholders, including many institutional investors still very interested in financial returns, to create links between executive compensation and sustainability measures (i.e., metrics based on environmental, social and governance targets).

Investor and Stakeholder Engagement

Publicly acknowledging the value and importance of multiple stakeholders and proactively supporting stakeholder engagement is an important element of the board's responsibilities for shaping the company's framework for accountability, control, and risk management and directors should take steps to embed stakeholder engagement in the company's overall governance framework.[25] Researchers on corporate sustainability from the MIT Sloan Management Review and BCG, noting that while 90% of executives believed that stakeholder collaboration was essential to sustainability success, only 47% said their companies collaborated with stakeholders strategically.[26] The researchers noted that companies that were walking the talk on sustainability were much more likely than other companies to be involved in more collaborations with a more diverse group of collaborators and identify more reasons to collaborate in order to achieve their sustainability goals. In addition, companies that did the best job with respect to strategic collaborations enjoyed the benefits of top management support and a solid process infrastructure for partnering that included ensuring that each stakeholder relationship was launched with clearly defined roles, reporting frameworks, clear governance structures and thoughtful and complete due diligence on prospective partners. Among the key steps that directors should take with regard to stakeholder engagement and collaboration are the following[27]:

- Define stakeholder engagement, transparency, integrity and ethical relationships with stakeholders as core values of the company
- Identify, discuss and prioritize key risks associated with changing societal expectations about the roles of business in general and the company in particular
- Determine the board's financial and non-financial information needs for decision-making, management oversight, and monitoring key stakeholder relationships associated with generating value and wealth
- Discuss and approve key performance indicators for social, environmental and financial performance with input from investors and other internal and external stakeholders
- Approve a policy for external reporting to all stakeholders of financial and non-financial results from the company's activities and the governance processes that the board and senior management have created to ensure that sustainability is integrated into long-term strategic planning
- Proactively integrate discussion of stakeholder issues into annual meetings of shareholders rather than reacting to sustainability-focused proposals initiated by activists
- Discuss the risks and impacts of projects and operations and provide transparent disclosure information to shareowners and other key stakeholder groups
- Convene stakeholder forums and invite key stakeholder representatives to address board meetings and participate in permanent stakeholder panels formed to provide continuous input to directors and senior management

Sustainability has become an important issue for the major institutional investors and asset managers and the marketplace is seeing an increase in smaller, more specialized investment funds that are primarily oriented toward providing capital to companies that excel in their ESG practices and which focus on ESG-oriented activities such as climate change and impact investing. The goal of these investors is to encourage their portfolio companies to contribute to the successful pursuit of environmental and social outcomes which continuing to provide investors with a suitable financial return and companies interested in attracting these types of capital providers need to pay special attention to the tools and metrics that they use for their investment decisions including negative/exclusionary screening, best-in-class positive screening, ESG integration, "impact" and business models focusing on high profile sustainability themes (e.g., cleantech, infrastructure, energy-efficient real estate or sustainable forestry).[28]

Notes

1 D. Kiron, G. Unruh, N. Kruschwitz, M. Reeves, H. Rubel and A. M. zum Felde, "Corporate Sustainability at a Crossroads: Progress toward Our Common Future in Uncertain Times", *MIT Sloan Management Review* (May 2017), 15.
2 Id. Investors and other stakeholders assess and grade companies and their directors and senior management teams against emerging standards that cut across three dimensions: "environmental", which focuses on how a company performs as a "steward of nature" through its policies and practices with respect to impacting climate change, sustainability, carbon footprint, water usage, pollutants and conservation; "social", which focuses on how the company manages its stakeholder relationships and includes criteria relating to non-discrimination, working conditions, gender equality, diversity and inclusivity, fair pay, health and safety and community engagement; and "governance", which focuses on the actions of the company's leaders with respect to adhering to corporate governance principles, shareholders' rights, boardroom diversity, participation by other stakeholders, alignment of executive compensation with performance objectives, audits and internal controls and business ethics. The criteria are continuously expanding to include company's lands, manufacturing facilities, offices and transportation modalities as well as human rights due diligence. Adapted from J. Chen, "Environmental, Social, and Governance (ESG) Criteria", https://www.investopedia.com/terms/e/environmental-social-and-governance-esg-criteria.asp (accessed April 23, 2020); and S. Seiden, "Recruiting ESG Directors" (Harvard Law School Forum on Corporate Governance and Financial Regulation, October 27, 2019), https://corpgov.law.harvard.edu/2019/10/27/recruiting-esg-directors/ (accessed April 23, 2020).
3 For further discussion of roles and responsibilities of directors, see A. Gutterman, *Corporate Governance: An Introduction to Theory and Practice* (Oakland, CA: Sustainable Entrepreneurship Project, 2019) Retrieved from www.seproject.org.
4 C. Strandberg, *The Convergence of Corporate Governance and Corporate Social Responsibility: Thought-Leaders Study* (Ottawa: Canadian Co-operative Association, March 2005), 9–10.
5 The Global Compact LEAD, Discussion Paper: Board Adoption and Oversight of Corporate Sustainability.
6 *ESG, Strategy and the Long View: A Framework for Board Oversight* (Netherlands: KPMG LLP, 2017), 18.

7 H. Gregory, "Corporate Social Responsibility, Corporate Sustainability and the Role of the Board", *Practical Law Company* (July 1, 2017), 3.

8 Adapted from M. Lipton, S. Rosenblum, K. Cain, S. Niles, V. Chanani and K. Iannone, "Some Thoughts for Boards of Directors in 2018" (New York: Wachtell, Lipton, Rosen & Katz, November 30, 2017), Retrieved from http://www.wlrk.com/webdocs/wlrknew/WLRKMemos/WLRK/WLRK.25823.17.pdf (accessed April 23, 2019).

9 *The Essential Role of the Corporate Secretary to Enhance Board Sustainability Oversight: A Best Practices Guide* (New York: United Nations Global Compact, September 2016).

10 *A New Agenda for the Board of Directors: Adoption and Oversight of Corporate Sustainability* (New York: Global Compact LEAD, 2012).

11 For further discussion of the activities and operations of many of the committees described below, see A. Gutterman, *Sustainability and Corporate Governance* (New York: Routledge, 2020).

12 Many companies combine the activities of nominating and governance into a single committee called the Nominating and Governance Committee and some even include the term "Responsibility" in the committee name.

13 R. Sainty, "Engaging Boards of Directors at the Interface of Corporate Sustainability and Corporate Governance", *Governance Directions* (March 2016), 85, 87.

14 For further discussion, see G. Lewis, *In-Depth: Linking Compensation to Sustainability* (March 2016), Retrieved from glasslewis.com (accessed April 23, 2020).

15 R. Sainty, "Engaging Boards of Directors at the Interface of Corporate Sustainability and Corporate Governance", *Governance Directions* (March 2016), 85, 87.

16 The Global Compact LEAD, Discussion Paper: Board Adoption and Oversight of Corporate Sustainability.

17 D. Grayson and A. Kakabadse, *Towards a Sustainability Mindset: How Boards Organize Oversight and Governance of Corporate Responsibility* (London: Business in the Community, 2012), 10–11 (also including feedback from a group of experienced members of experts' panels and corporate advisory groups with respect to sustainability on "critical success factors" for ensuring the effectiveness and value-added contribution of such panels for companies).

18 *A New Agenda for the Board of Directors: Adoption and Oversight of Corporate Sustainability* (New York: Global Compact LEAD, 2012), 12. See also S. Seiden, "Recruiting ESG Directors" (Harvard Law School Forum on Corporate Governance and Financial Regulation, October 27, 2019), https://corpgov.law.harvard.edu/2019/10/27/recruiting-esg-directors/ (accessed April 23, 2020 and providing recommendations on recruiting "ESG talent" for director positions including eliminating director age maximums that arbitrarily eliminate otherwise valuable candidates with unique sustainability-related expertise related to long periods of focus on relevant issues and accepting "newbies" (i.e., people who have never served on a public board) with relevant experience drawn from a pool that includes non-CEOs that are either part of the C-suite or report into the C-suite, high-ranking former government or military officials, non-profit CEOs, academic officers and faculty and others with the right combination of expertise and emotional intelligence to thrive and lead (not just get along) in the boardroom).

19 Id. at 18.

20 *The Essential Role of the Corporate Secretary to Enhance Board Sustainability Oversight: A Best Practices Guide* (New York: United Nations Global Compact, September 2016).

21 The Global Compact LEAD, Discussion Paper: Board Adoption and Oversight of Corporate Sustainability.

22 *The Essential Role of the Corporate Secretary to Enhance Board Sustainability Oversight: A Best Practices Guide* (New York: United Nations Global Compact, September 2016).

23 CEOs and the New CSR Priority (Boyden Executive Monitor, September 2017), https://www.boyden.com/media/ceos-and-the-new-csr-priority-2909935/index.html (accessed April 23, 2020).

24 *A New Agenda for the Board of Directors: Adoption and Oversight of Corporate Sustainability* (Global Compact LEAD, 2012), 8.

25 For detailed discussion of stakeholder engagement, see A. Gutterman, *Stakeholders and Stakeholder Engagement: A Guide for Sustainable Entrepreneurs* (Oakland, CA: Sustainable Entrepreneurship Project, 2019) Retrieved from www.seproject.org.

26 D. Kiron, G. Unruh, N. Kruschwitz, M. Reeves, H. Rubel and A. M. zum Felde, "Corporate Sustainability at a Crossroads: Progress toward Our Common Future in Uncertain Times", *MIT Sloan Management Review* (May 2017), 17.

27 Adapted from *Stakeholder Engagement and the Board: Integrating Best Governance Practices* (Washington, DC: International Finance Corporation and Global Corporate Governance Forum, 2009), 16–17.

28 A. Krauss, P. Kruger and J. Meyer, *Sustainable Finance in Switzerland: Where Do We Stand?* (Zurich: Sustainable Finance Institute, September 2016), 15.

3 Organizational Design for Sustainability

While sustainability has become an important issue for many companies, they often struggle with understanding and implementing "sustainable organizational design principles" into their infrastructures and supply chains.[1] Surveys have found that while a large percentage of executives worldwide say that they believe that sustainability is important to the financial success of their companies, less than half of them were actually taking steps to embed sustainability into their core business practices.[2] A study by Accenture found that a majority of the chief executive officers (CEOs) who had embraced the UN's Global Compact principles had adopted policies on and programs for sustainability; however, of that group "comparatively few had made the necessary operational changes in their supply chains and distribution systems or established sustainability goals and controls for their lines-of-business".[3] Companies need to take organizational design for sustainability seriously, particularly since research has shown that building sustainability into business units doubles an organization's chance of profiting from its sustainability activities.[4]

Griffiths and Petrick identified three key elements in the traditional organizational design of larger corporations that likely impede their ability to adapt to the specific requirements of sustainability. The first problem is that larger corporations rely on established task routines that promote the status quo, which means that new theories regarding the company's value to society and the proposed practices associated with those theories are generally seen as threats by entrenched interests that prefer to continue their heavy reliance on routines and "command-and-control" style management systems. Second, the hierarchical "command-and-control" organizational structures generally used by larger corporations impede access, and assignment of value, to input from stakeholders of the corporation, all of whom are important actors in sustainability initiatives. Finally, corporations operating under traditional organizational design principles did not have departments with "specialized environmentally relevant knowledge to recognize, act on, and transfer to other parts of the organization".[5] In the same vein, Sampselle argued that the traditional bureaucratic organizational design still used by many large companies was ill-suited to identifying opportunities to capture value-oriented trends in a value-oriented context and that while many of these companies already had the requisite technology and other core competencies to take on significant sustainability initiatives, they lacked the appropriate organizational design to deploy their resources in a manner that allowed them to interact efficiently with their various stakeholders.[6]

While there is reason to be disheartened about shifting organizational design to promote sustainability-focused strategies, many observers believe that large corporations can indeed "become much more efficient at modifying inputs, throughputs and outputs to reduce their negative impact on the ecology" and learn and embrace the potential competitive advantages associated with these improvements to their operation and product management systems.[7] Griffiths and Petrick effectively advocated for recognition of several attributes for organizational structures that should be used in order to institutionalize sustainable practices including architectural processes that capture and use sustainability information that is integrated into strategic decision-making about innovative solutions necessary for maintaining a sustainable business (e.g., network organizations, virtual organizations and communities of practice), incorporate employees' knowledge into strategic decision-making and rapidly respond to sustainability opportunities and threats.[8] Also important is creating multiple and diverse entry points into the organization in order for companies to capture and use sustainability information for strategic purposes and ensuring that relevant information is not confined to specialist units but is instead diffused throughout the organization for wider use in strategic decisions.[9]

Designing Organizational Structures for Sustainability

The alignment of organizational design and sustainability should begin with the development of a sustainability strategy and accompanying goals and priorities. In order for the sustainability strategy to be effective and successful, it must align with the structure, competencies and culture of the company. Strategies should be based on an overall vision for the company and a set of commitments that serve as the foundation for strategies and tactics and bind all of the business units together to work toward a common purpose. Commitments should be pursued through a combination of corporate policies, sustainability policies and employee initiatives. Companies should embed sustainability into their organizations through cross-functional teams, clear targets and key performance indicators. Experiences of various companies have illustrated that it is important to introduce smaller organizational structures into the mix that facilitate mobilization of local communities to work on issues that will contribute to sustainability in their communities.[10]

When designing the organizational structure for sustainability, several important principles need to be considered[11]:

- While placement within the organizational structure is an issue, and may vary depending on the circumstances, there should generally be some form of formal sustainability function overseen by a single designated senior executive. While sustainability may be new to the company, leadership should be vested in someone who has the requisite credentials and experience working in the area. Science and engineering backgrounds are helpful and common and it is also a significant advantage if the sustainability executive has worked inside the organization since relationships and networking will be important in establishing the initiative and understanding how to integrate sustainability into existing operational habits.
- The sustainability initiative, and the accompanying changes to the organizational structure, must have executive sponsorship and the CEO must be a visible proponent of the sustainability vision for the company. Executive sponsorship accelerates engagement by employees and business units, but even better results can be expected if the CEO is proactive and assume personal leadership of a highly visible sustainability program.
- Structure is driven by the specific sustainability-related commitments that are made by the board of directors and members of the senior executive team following consultation with internal and external stakeholders. Examples of sustainability-related commitment topics include climate change, waste reduction and management, resource consumption, education, human rights, community engagement and procurement (i.e., supply chain management). Commitments should be pursued through a combination of corporate policies, sustainability policies and employee initiatives.
- The board of directors should also signal its support of the sustainability initiative by creating a separate committee dedicated to sustainability and corporate social responsibility or designating one director to provide oversight to sustainability-related initiatives. As is the case with the CEO, board members should do more than just oversee the ideas of others and should actively initiate or drive a sustainability-related initiative.
- As companies grow and the scope of the sustainability initiative expands, consideration should be given to creating other forms of organizational engagement such as executive sustainability advisory councils (i.e., members of the senior leadership team, including an executive sponsor, who reported to the CEO), mid-level employee sustainability councils, "green teams" and external advisory councils with representative from key external stakeholders.

- The sustainability executive should be supported by a cross-functional advisory team with members drawn from corporate communications, operations, legal, sales and marketing, human resources and environment, health and safety (EH&S). Creation of such a team provides the executive with access to divergent views from throughout the company and also facilitates sharing of best practices and regular communications across internal organizational boundaries to make sure that everyone is aware of what is being done on sustainability and that programs are properly coordinated and aligned with the company's strategic vision and stated goals for sustainability.

- The sustainability executive should also be supported by resources exclusively available to the sustainability function. Generally, this includes managers for metrics and reporting, social programs and communications/public affairs/marketing. Internal support for day-to-day operation and reporting allows the sustainability executive to remain focused on strategic considerations and necessary outward communications with board members, the CEO and other executives, external stakeholders and the other forms of organizational engagement mentioned above.

- Staffing levels for sustainability-related activities are driven by a number of factors including the size and stage of development of the company, the importance of sustainability to the mission and overall strategic goals of the company, risk and industry. These factors also influence the focus of sustainability activities, which generally include a mix of environmental issues, philanthropy and community relations, governance/risk/compliance, human rights and employee relations.

- The core responsibilities for implementing the sustainability programs should be vested in departments have close ties to stakeholders and the requisite decision-making powers with respect to issues related to the programs. Common choices include the corporate, legal or public affairs departments.

- The leader of the sustainability initiative should have a direct reporting relationship with both the CEO and the board of directors in order to send a signal to employees and other stakeholders about the important of the initiative and provide the initiative with access to the support and resources available from high-level executives and managers in other departments.

- An organizational structure should be selected that achieves the appropriate level of interaction with employees and creates value to the business. The optimal structure may change over time as the sustainability initiative gains traction and becomes more embedded in day-to-day operations and decisions.

- Clear procedures regarding decision rights should be established, recognizing the integration of sustainability programs and goals often challenge existing decision rights. It is important to identify the types of decisions that will need to be made, the parties that will be involved in making those decisions and the managers who will be entrusted with implementing the decisions.

- Sustainability performance must be integrated into day-to-day management activities and compensation programs and responsibilities, performance reviews and compensation models for all employees must be aligned with the company's sustainability objectives in order to encourage and reward contributions to innovation and creative problem solving.

- In order to achieve the requisite integration and employee buy-in, programs must be created to develop a basis awareness of the company's sustainability strategy, goals and priorities, educate employees about opportunities and support employee efforts.

- The internal structure should be aligned with the external structure that the company relies upon to engage with stakeholders since one of the most important aspects of a sustainability program is external accountability. External stakeholders need to know that their concerns and questions will be addressed and that begins with knowing how best to access the company.

- The sustainability strategy must include both transparent goals with metrics that can be evaluated by both internal and external stakeholders and provision for reporting on the results of the sustainability programs.

Organizational Structures for Sustainability

Companies that are relatively new to sustainability often begin with a fairly simple "stand-alone" structure based on treating the sustainability program as a separate function like finance, operations or marketing.[12] A high level executive, often given the title "chief sustainability officer" (CSO) will oversee the function and reports directly to the CEO from the same level in the organizational hierarchy as other C-level executives. The job of the CSO, which is discussed in more detail in a separate chapter of this publication however, is to begin the difficult process of engaging the business units that are overseen by other C-level executives. The CSO should be given adequate resources to carry out his or her responsibilities including support from various sustainability directors worked primarily inside the sustainability function. The advantages of this type of structure is that it creates a group that is solely focused on and responsible for initiating and implementing sustainability-related activities and serves as a magnet for recruiting the specialized skills necessary for sustainable programs to be successful. However, a stand-alone approach has several critical drawbacks: sustainability is not integrated into the rest of the organization; limited buy-in from employees because they are not accountable to the sustainability function; and funding challenges since the function is typically focused on reducing costs as opposed to business development.

Companies often attempt to address and resolve some of the key shortcomings of the stand-alone structure by designing an "integrated structure" that recognizes and promotes reporting relationships between the sustainability directors, still sitting primarily in the sustainability function, and the business units. Advantages of this approach include enablement of organization-wide integration and the creation of direct ties between the sustainability experts and the business units, thereby allowing the sustainability expertise to be available for supporting sustainability programs in the business units. The enhanced access for the sustainability directors also encourages and improves employee buy-in, although there is still no formal accountability and the actions of employees with respect to sustainability are largely determined by the priorities of the leaders of their specific business unit. In fact, the main problem with this structure is that responsibility and accountability remain disperse; however, the structure can be helpful for companies with sustainability goals that are primarily focused on reducing costs and efficiency.

Another more advanced and dynamic structure for sustainability is referred to as an "embedded structure" and actually transfers the sustainability directors out of the sustainability function and into each of the business units and functions themselves. The sustainability director reports both to the leader of the business unit or function and back to the CSO—a matrix structure that can cause issues with respect to authority. Advantages of the embedded structure include the ability to select and implement sustainability programs that drive business value and become part of the company's core business and the opportunities to encourage significant buy-in from all employees. However, the embedded structure makes it more difficult for the CSO to coordinate sustainability activities across the organization and efforts may be duplicated. An embedded structure is considered to be the most advanced of the basic structures for sustainability and generally makes sense for mature organizations that have a good basic understanding of sustainability already integrated into their business units and are looking for revenue-generating opportunities.

Regardless of the particular structure adopted by an organization to facilitate its sustainability initiatives, it is essential to have executive sponsorship and visible and proactive support from the CEO and other members of the executive team and the board of directors. The leader of the sustainability initiative should have a direct reporting relationship with both the CEO and the board of directors in order to send a signal to employees and other stakeholders about the important of the initiative and provide the initiative with access to the support and resources available from high-level executives and managers in other departments. Clear procedures regarding decision rights should be established, recognizing the integration of sustainability programs and goals often challenge existing decision rights. Sustainability initiatives will only be successful if employees are engaged and in order to achieve the requisite integration and employee buy-in, programs must be created to develop a basis awareness of the company's sustainability strategy, goals and priorities, educate employees about opportunities and support employee efforts. Sustainability performance must be integrated into day-to-day management activities and compensation programs and responsibilities, performance reviews and compensation models for all employees must be aligned with the company's sustainability objectives in order to encourage and reward contributions to innovation and creative problem solving.

The CSO or other leader of the sustainability initiative must establish relationships with the business and relevant functions in all of the company divisions and organizational units such as health, safety and environment; ethics and compliance; legal; product development; manufacturing; public affairs; marketing and communications; human resources and procurement. As companies grow larger, the CSO will have an entire sustainability leadership team to assist in sustainability oversight and coordination. For example, as mentioned above a company may create directorships for specific sustainability topics such as philanthropy; sustainability strategy and stakeholder engagement; EH&S and business continuity; communications and reporting; social business and special projects.

The efforts of the CSO will often be supported by a "sustainability board" that includes representatives from all relevant functions and divisions and is dedicated to ensuring that sustainability activities are directed, guided and coordinated across the company and that duplication is minimized, results are reported and best practices are quickly shared. The sustainability board should have its own charter that describes the board's responsibilities and composition. For example, the board might be assigned responsibility for approving and/or recommending to the corporate social responsibility (CSR) committee of the board (and ultimately the entire board) an overall sustainability strategy, sustainability targets, sustainability policies, external sustainability positions, sustainability materiality assessment, sustainability communication and reporting approach, sustainability stakeholder engagement plan and major environmental, social and governance index submissions. The sustainability board may also convene sustainability dialogue sessions with external stakeholders on the sustainability topics that are most material to the company's business, develops reports for internal and external use and ensure that information regarding sustainability activities is shared throughout the organization. The role of the board is to be particularly mindful of the cross-divisional/cross-functional implications of sustainability activities and thus it is important for board to include the leaders of all business and functional units. The CSO or other sustainability leader should chair the sustainability board and one or more directors from the board-level CSR committee should have ex-officio participation rights. The board should meet no less frequently than quarterly and should be adequately supported by specialists working with the company's dedicated sustainability group or unit.

One of the notable features about a sustainability-focused organizational structure is the emphasis on aligning the internal structure of the company with an external structure that is designed to promote direct, intense and continuous engagement with stakeholders. This begins with making sure that the core responsibilities for implementing the sustainability programs are vested in departments have close ties to stakeholders and the requisite decision-making powers with respect to issues related to the programs. Assessment of the organizational structure should reveal clear paths for stakeholders to express their concerns and pose questions to the company and provision should be made for both transparent goals for stakeholder relationships and metrics that can be used by both internal and external stakeholders to evaluate how well the structure is performing. Evaluation and reporting should be done on a regular basis, generally quarterly or bi-annually, and should be accompanied by informal face-to-face discussions among the managers of the sustainability initiatives and the employees reporting to them and members of the stakeholder constituencies they are serving. Performance measurement and reporting should be taken seriously and the results should be used to identify and implement the structural changes that will be needed as the sustainability initiative gains traction and becomes more embedded in day-to-day operations and decisions.[13]

Complete and Partial Organizing for Corporate Social Responsibility

Rasche et al. set out to examine how sustainability and CSR is organized and why certain organizational forms are used frequently to coordinate CSR activities, while other forms are less widespread.[14] In particular, they were interested in how and why companies might choose among popular CSR initiatives such as cross-sector partnerships, internal codes of conduct or signing on to multi-stakeholder or industry-wide standards when deciding how best to pursue a CSR-related goal such as combatting human rights abuses. They argued that companies (through their boards of directors and senior executives) and other CSR "organizers" (e.g., non-governmental organizations, governments and standard-setters) generally choose between two distinct types of "organizing" when it comes to CSR. The first type is a "complete" organization, which is feasible when the organizers have access to all of the elements needed to achieve organized orders (i.e., membership, hierarchy, rules, monitoring and sanctioning). The second type is a "partial" organization, which is used in instances when the organizers do not have access to all of the organization elements. Illustrations of partial organizations include cross-sector partnerships between companies and NGOs and CSR standards evolving from multi-stakeholder consultations.[15]

Rasche et al. observed that "CSR has varied enormously by context, particularly the context of place, or national business systems" and that "the most important characteristic to note in CSR is its susceptibility to change".[16] In the context of considering how CSR initiatives are organized, the most interesting change has been a shift from CSR principally being a more "corporate-centered" to a more "corporate-oriented" concept.[17] Specifically, in the early 1960s, when CSR was first emerging, it was generally thought of a matter of corporate discretion, wholly apart from law or public policy, meaning that companies decided on their own on how to implement CSR initiatives and the CSR was typically conducted through "complete" organization (i.e., centered inside the formal boundaries of the company). Recently, however, the responsibility for defining the concept of CSR has broadened beyond the company itself to include numerous actors in the environment in which the company operates: government, civil society, professionals and other businesses. As such, the spotlight has shifted to how the actions and practices of the company impact its supply chain, workers, use of resources and the consumption and disposal of its products and services, and the aforementioned actors have organized their interests in the practices of companies through "partial" organization (e.g., membership rules for partnerships, standards setting, and methodologies for monitoring and imposing sanctions of company misbehaviors).

While CSR has become more "corporate-oriented", companies continue to deploy the strategies and methods of complete organization to CSR, not surprising since companies remain ultimately responsible for their actions relating to CSR. For example, more and more companies are explicitly integrating CSR principles and goals into their missions and strategies, and investment in internal CSR capacity (i.e., personnel and technologies) has increased.[18] However, organizational practices must now take into account the interests and concerns of external actors who bring with their own ideas and expectations regarding norms and standards and the role of companies in pursuing their business objectives in a way that incorporates community benefit alongside traditional economic goals. All this means that companies must become more adept at understanding and balancing both "complete" and "partial" organizational techniques when developing and implementing their CSR initiatives.

While many organizations have organized their CSR activities internally using all or most of the elements of complete organization, the details are often based on external standards, including an increasing volume of laws and regulations and popular global standards for CSR reporting. It is also commonplace for organizations to engage in CSR outside and among formal organizations that are partial organizations (e.g., multi-stakeholder standards-setting groups) in those instances where the organizers do not have access to all of the organizational elements.[19] Companies have also recognized that they are no longer the sole actor with respect to CSR and must rely on partial organization to gain access to complementary resources that have been developed by and/or with others, such as knowledge and legitimacy (e.g., publicly adopting the Global Reporting Initiative (GRI) standards and participating in GRI working groups on sustainability and reporting).[20] Rasche et al. noted that partial organizations are less formal and thus easier to promote to potential actors who would otherwise be reluctant to collaborate, such as organizations that regularly compete with one another in the marketplace.[21] Partial organizations also provide organizers with more flexibility to identify common ground that can be used for the foundation of a CSR initiative. This often allows organizers to create change more quickly than attempt to convince organizations to radically change their internal formal organizations. For example, the introduction of a type of partial organization, the "standards" developed under the umbrella of the International Integrated Reporting Framework (integratedreporting.org), has been a catalyst in moving companies away from traditional "sustainability reporting" into "integrated reporting".

Notes

1 D. Sampselle, *Sustainable Organization Design Principles*, OTMT 608.13. Sampselle explained that while "sustainable organization design" was often used to refer to organization designs that preserve financial sustainability, his meaning of the term was organizational design principles for "triple bottom line businesses" (i.e., businesses simultaneously pursuing profits, socially responsible treatment of the people in their organizations and environmental responsibility in the way in which they conduct their businesses). Id.
2 Id. (citing P. Mirvis, B. Googins and S. Kinnicutt, "Vision, Mission, Values: Guideposts to Sustainability", *Organizational Dynamics*, 39 (2010), 316).
3 Id.
4 D. Kiron, G. Unruh, N. Kruschwitz, M. Reeves, H. Rubel and A.M. zum Felde, "Corporate Sustainability at a Crossroads: Progress toward Our Common Future in Uncertain Times", *MIT Sloan Management Review* (May 2017), 11.
5 A. Griffiths and J. Petrick, "Corporate Architectures for Sustainability", *International Journal of Operations and Production Management*, 21(12) (2001), 1573–1574 (see original text for additional citations to research on each of the identified impediments).
6 D. Sampselle, *Sustainable Organization Design Principles*, OTMT 608.13, 8.
7 A. Griffiths and J. Petrick, "Corporate Architectures for Sustainability", *International Journal of Operations and Production Management*, 21(12) (2001),

1573, 1576 (see, e.g., P. Shrivastava, "The Role of Corporations in Achieving Ecological Sustainability", *Academy of Management Review*, 20(4) (1995), 936; and E. Weizsacker, A. Lovins and L. Lovins, *Factor Four: Doubling Wealth, Halving Resource Use* (London: Earthscan Publications, 1998)).

8 A. Griffiths and J. Petrick, "Corporate Architectures for Sustainability", *International Journal of Operations and Production Management*, 21(12) (2001), 1573, 1581–1583.

9 Id. at 1581.

10 D. Sampselle, *Sustainable Organization Design Principles*, OTMT 608.13, 8.

11 H. Farr, *Organizational Structure for Sustainability* (July 14, 2011), http:// abettercity.org/docs/events/BCBS%20Hayley%20Farr_28%20July%202011. pdf (accessed April 23, 2020);, *Structuring and Staffing Corporate Responsibility: A Guidebook* (Northampton, MA: Corporate Responsibility Officers Association, 2010); A. Longsworth, H. Doran and J. Webber, "The Sustainability Executive: Profile and Progress" (PWC, September 2012); and National Association for Environmental Management, EHS & Sustainability Staffing and Structure: Benchmark Report (November 2012).

12 The discussion in this paragraph is adapted from H. Farr, *Organizational Structure for Sustainability* (July 14, 2011), http://abettercity.org/docs/events/ BCBS%20Hayley%20Farr_28%20July%202011.pdf (accessed April 23, 2020).

13 A number of interesting and useful studies of sustainability structures and staffing are available including *Structuring and Staffing Corporate Responsibility: A Guidebook* (Northampton, MA: Corporate Responsibility Officers Association, 2010); A. Longworth, H. Doran and J. Webber, "The Sustainability Executive: Profile and Progress" (PWC, September 2012); D. Baumann-Pauly, C. Wickert, L. Spence and A. Scherer, *Organizing Corporate Social Responsibility in Small and Large Firms: Size Matters* (University of Zurich: Chair of Foundations of Business Administration and Theories of the Firm Working Paper Series No. 204, December 2011); and National Association for Environmental Management, EHS & Sustainability Staffing and Structure: Benchmark Report (November 2012). For further discussion, see A. Gutterman, *Sustainability and Corporate Governance* (New York: Routledge, 2020).

14 A. Rasche, F. de Bakker and J. Moon, "Complete and Partial Organizing in Corporate Social Responsibility", *Journal of Business Ethics*, 115 (July 2013), 651.

15 The arguments made by Rasche et al. were grounded in the work of Ahrne and Brunsson, who believed that an organization could be understood as a type of decided social order in which one or more of the following five elements existed: membership, hierarchy, rules, monitoring and sanctions. See G. Ahrne and N. Brunsson, "Organization Outside Organizations: The Significance of Partial Organization", *Organization*, 18(1) (2011), 83.

16 A. Rasche, F. de Bakker and J. Moon, "Complete and Partial Organizing in Corporate Social Responsibility", *Journal of Business Ethics*, 115 (July 2013), 651, 653 (citing D. Matten and J. Moon, "'Implicit' and 'explicit' CSR: A Conceptual Framework for a Comparative Understanding of Corporate Social Responsibility", *Academy of Management Review*, 33(2) (2008), 404; and J.-P. Gond and J. Moon, "Corporate Social Responsibility in Retrospect and Prospect" in J.-P. Gond and J. Moon (Eds.), *Corporate Social Responsibility: A Reader* (London: Routledge, 2011), 1).

17 J. Moon, *Corporate Social Responsibility: A Very Short Introduction* (Oxford: Oxford University Press, 2014).

18 A. Rasche, F. de Bakker and J. Moon, "Complete and Partial Organizing in Corporate Social Responsibility", *Journal of Business Ethics*, 115 (July 2013), 651, 654 (citing J. Moon, "The Institutionalisation of Business Social Responsibility: Evidence from Australia and the UK", *The Anahuac Journal (Mexico)*, 5(1) (2004), 40; K. Bondy, J. Moon and D. Matten, "An Institution of Corporate Social Responsibility (CSR) in Multi-National Corporations (MNCs): Form and Implications", *Journal of Business Ethics*, 111(2) (2012), 281; and R. Strand, *In Praise of Corporate Social Responsibility Bureaucracy* (Copenhagen: Copenhagen Business School PhD Series (26.2012))).

19 Id. at 656.

20 For further discussion of the role of CSR in gaining legitimacy for organizations, see also T. Emtairah and O. Mont, "Gaining Legitimacy in Contemporary World: Environmental and Social Activities of Organisations", *International Journal of Sustainable Society*, 1(2) (2008), 134.

21 A. Rasche, F. de Bakker and J. Moon, "Complete and Partial Organizing in Corporate Social Responsibility", *Journal of Business Ethics*, 115 (July 2013), 651, 659–660.

4 Strategic Planning for Sustainability

Corporate sustainability and social responsibility initiatives had been subject to criticism from both sides of the ideological spectrum.[1] On the left advocates from civil society have often questioned the fundamental motivations of corporations' actions under the umbrella of corporate social responsibility (CSR), arguing that in most cases corporate support for environmental and social programs was nothing more than a public relations campaign designed primarily, if not solely, to boost brand reputations as another means for achieving the primary corporate objective of maximizing profits. At the other end of the spectrum CSR has been denounced as inappropriate and unnecessary in a capitalist society where the responsibility of business is to create financial returns for its shareholders and the larger economy and environmental and social issues should be left to the government and civil society. Both sides have also complained about the lack of metrics to evaluate the efficacy of CSR programs, a situation that is all the more problematic given that businesses are generally driven and managed through precise tools designed to track and analyze the performance of every investment decision.[2]

In spite of the criticisms, sustainability and CSR have become mainstays of business activities: the percentage of large global companies professing to practice some form of sustainability and CSR has been steadily increasing, sustainability reporting has become the norm and businesses of all sizes are subject to sustainability and CSR drivers including the philanthropic motivations of their employees and the expectations of other stakeholders such as customers and investors. As such, sustainability management now includes finding a way to forge a coherent strategy that is can accommodate the broad range of sustainability and CSR activities including corporate funding of community activities, grants for nonprofits/NGOs, environmental sustainability programs to reduce energy and resource use, "cause" marketing and comprehensive system-level efforts to remake a business's entire value chain.[3]

Rangan et al. argued that while they believed that every company needed a sustainability and CSR strategy, few of the many companies that had already adopted sustainability were practicing it with a formal strategy. They found that the common situation was a portfolio of disparate sustainability and CSR programs and initiatives, some of which supported core strategy and others of which appeared adjacent and discretionary.[4] The diversity of sustainability and CSR activities cited above is one issue; however, developing a strategic orientation is complicated by the fact that each company has its own unique set of drivers and motivations for sustainability and CSR and ideas and responsibilities for those initiatives come from all parts and levels of the organization. Moreover, while it makes sense to identify a specific business logic and rationale for each sustainability initiative, the reality is that companies often take on causes and projects that have little or no connection to their core competencies or business strategy. As such, Rangan et al. cautioned that while they were arguing for a sustainability strategy, it was not something that could or should be completely absorbed into the company's core business strategy.[5]

Companies proactively engaged in sustainability and CSR are in many ways no different than any other business: their business model needs to generate sufficient profits for the company to survive and grow (i.e., to achieve the sustainability necessary for it to be around long enough to achieve its social and/or environmental goals as well as generate income for its investors, managers and employees). As such, sustainable companies still need to understand and apply traditional business planning techniques; however, they also need to integrate their sustainability and CSR projects and initiatives into their strategic goals and business and operating plans. Hohnen and Potts noted that there is no "one-size-fits-all" framework or method for pursuing a sustainability strategy and that each company must consider its own unique characteristics and circumstances when implementing, expanding or modifying its sustainability programs and policies.[6] Among other things, these characteristics and circumstances include the company's overall mission and purpose, organizational culture, external environment and risk profile, operating conditions and existing relationships with stakeholders.

Strategic planning for sustainability is far from easy or precise, if only because it requires that simultaneous consideration be given not only to economic performance and development, but also to environmental protection and the social wellbeing of employees and other persons and groups outside of the organization. Companies and their managers are struggling to find and deploy the tools and practices that are necessary for balancing and reconciling the "triple bottom line" of profits, planet and people. Clearly a company cannot contribute to sustainable development on a long-term basis unless it remains "in business" and this often means taking actions thought necessary for financial survival at the expense of other actions that would be environmentally or socially preferable. Even when businesses clearly understand that respecting the environment and society are necessary it may take time for them to make the necessary changes in their operational activities and it is not always possible for companies to avoid actions that might cause short-term environmental or social harm. In those situations, however, companies need to take responsibility for their actions and remediate the damage, such as by committing to build new skills and find meaningful employment for workers laid off as part of a downsizing of operations in a specific community. Another challenge is that the empirical data that manages are used to having for their financial analysis is not as readily available for environmental and societal issues and the information that does exist is continuously changing, often technically ambiguous and subject to competing interpretations that not only make internal decision making more difficult but also muddle the regulatory environment in which businesses must operate.

The path for developing and pursuing a sustainability strategy will be different for each company and will depend on its unique characteristics and circumstances; however, it is generally recognized that an effective strategy must be based on accepting the need for organizational change, a commitment to continuous improvement and strong board-level vision and oversight. Maon et al. suggested that sustainability strategy development and implementation could be considered as an organizational change process (i.e., moving from a present to a future state), or as a new way of organizing and working, with the ultimate aim being to align the organization with the dynamic demands of the business and social environment through the identification and management of stakeholder expectations.[7] Companies can consult international instruments that provide guidance and ideas for designing and implementing an effective and comprehensive CSR initiative and which have been vetted and endorsed by governments and civil society alike. Among the sources for companies to choose from are the Organisation for Economic Co-operation and Development Guidelines for Multinational Enterprises; the International Labour Organization Tripartite Declaration of Principles concerning Multinational Enterprises and Social Policy and Core Labour Standards; the UN Global Compact Principles; the Global Reporting Initiative Sustainability Reporting Guidelines; the International Organization for Standardization standards; the AccountAbility AA1000 Series; and the Social Accountability International SA8000 standard.[8]

In addition, there is a growing body of empirical research that has helped to build consensus on the elements of an effective framework for developing sustainability strategies including assessing current sustainability norms, standards and practices by benchmarking against competitors and universal standards; engaging key stakeholders to raise awareness of sustainability, solicit positive participation in the sustainability strategy process and mobilize commitment for significant organizational change; defining the specific sustainability and CSR commitments and goals and articulating a clear business case for each of them; developing an integrated strategic plan to achieve the selected sustainability goals and embed sustainability into organizational strategy;

implementing the plan and the initiatives linked with sustainability and CSR; establishing internal and external communications regarding sustainability and CSR commitments and performance; evaluating, verifying and reporting on sustainability progress; and institutionalizing the sustainability strategies and policies by embedding sustainability into corporate culture and values and aligning organizational systems to support sustainability commitments.[9]

For example, the UN Global Compact, which has been described as the largest policy initiative for businesses that are committed to aligning their operations and strategies with universally accepted principles of sustainability and CSR, has issued guidance on implementation and integration of sustainability that notes that in many ways implementing sustainability is like any other management task and called for defining sustainability goals, taking into account the issues and ideas that should have been identified during stakeholder engagement; implementing programs with a view toward achieving the goals in a timely manner; checking to make sure that the goals are being achieved through some sort of assessment or auditing process; and dealing with problems and non-conformance to goals through quality management techniques (i.e., "Plan-Do-Check-Act").[10] Hohnen and Potts suggested an implementation framework for sustainability strategy based on the suggestions of the UN Global Compact—they referred to it as "Plan-Do-Check-Improve"—but which placed more emphasis on measuring and evaluating performance, identifying opportunities for improvement and engaging with stakeholders on implementing changes and improvements.[11]

The UN Global Compact also referred to an alternative systems-based approach to continuous sustainability improvement that focused more on ensuring that sustainability was integrated into organizational strategy and included four repeating stages[12]:

- Assessment: Mapping, benchmarking and gap analysis; internal CSR surveys; non-financial risk assessment; stakeholder engagement; due diligence and international standards
- Strategy: Policy development; environment and climate change; community investment; supplier code of content; human resources and measurement and monitoring system
- Implementation: Senior management buy-in; staff involvement; staff training and capacity building; roll out policies; action plans; alignment with international standards; measurement and monitoring and supply chain integration
- Communications: Internal; external; targeted; reporting and disclosure; case studies and leadership

While first published in the early 1990s, guidance from the International Institute for Sustainable Development in collaboration with Deloitte &

Touche and the World Business Council for Sustainable Development remains relevant today and suggests the following steps for the process of creating a sustainability strategy and managing an enterprise based on sustainable development principles[13]:

- Perform a stakeholder analysis to identify all the parties that are directly or indirectly affected by the enterprise's operations and set out the issues, concerns and information needs of the stakeholders with respect to the organization's sustainable development activities.
- Assess the current position to determine the degree to which the company's activities line up with sustainable development principles, a process that requires evaluating the company's overall strategy, the performance of specific operations, and the effect of particular activities. This process should compare the company's current performance with the expectations of the stakeholders, review management philosophies and systems, analyze the scope of public disclosures on sustainability topics, and evaluate the ability of current information systems to produce the required data should be evaluated.
- Set sustainable development policies and objectives including articulating the basic values that the enterprise expects its employees to follow with respect to sustainable development, incorporating sustainable development objectives as an additional dimension of business strategy, setting targets for operating performance and establishing an effective external monitoring system that gathers information on new and proposed legislation; industry practices and standards, competitors' strategies, community and special interest group policies and activities. trade union concerns and technical developments (e.g., new process technologies).
- Establish a social responsibility committee of the board of directors with responsibility for setting corporate policies on sustainable development and monitoring their implementation and for dealing with issues such as health and safety, personnel policies, environmental protection, and codes of business conduct.
- Decide on a strategy taking into account the performance of other comparable organizations and with a focus on narrowing the gap between the current state of the corporation's performance and its objectives for the future. The strategy should be supported by a plan that describes how and when management expects to achieve the stated goals and the various milestones that must be reached along the way. Once the strategy and the general plan have been approved, detailed plans should be prepared indicating how the new strategy will affect operations, management systems, information systems and reporting. Plans should be reviewed and approved by senior management following consultation with employees throughout the organization.

- Design and execute an implementation plan for the management system changes that are needed in order to achieve sustainable development objectives, a process that normally includes changing the corporate culture and employee attitudes, defining responsibilities and accountability, and establishing organizational structures, information reporting systems and operational practices.

- Develop a supportive corporate culture to ensure that the organization and its people give their backing to the sustainable development policies. In most cases, managers will need to be retrained to change attitudes that have traditionally emphasized wealth management for the owners of the enterprise. An effort should also be made to develop a culture that emphasizes employee participation, continuous learning and improvement.

- Develop appropriate measures and standards of performance taking into account the company's sustainable development objectives and standards that have been established by government and other public agencies.

- Develop meaningful reports for internal management and stakeholders, outlining the enterprise's sustainable development objectives and comparing performance against them. Directors and senior executives use internal reports to measure performance, make decisions and monitor the implementation of their policies and strategies. Shareholders, creditors, employees and customers, as well as the public at large, use external corporate reports to evaluate the performance of a corporation, and to hold the directors and senior executives accountable for achieving financial, social and environmental objectives.

- Enhance internal monitoring processes to help directors and senior managers ensure that the sustainable development policies are being implemented. Monitoring can take many forms, such as reviewing reports submitted by middle managers, touring operating sites and observing employees performing their duties, holding regular meetings with subordinates to review reports and to seek input on how the procedures and reporting systems might be improved, and implementing an environmental auditing program.

While each of the frameworks suggested above are organized and described as an orderly continuum of steps, the reality is that developing and implementing a sustainability initiative requires that a number of activities be carried out at once. One of the first things that should be done is to getting a good idea about what the company stands for and how it operates, a process which includes document review, interviews and observation. Concerns of internal stakeholders, such as employees, need to be identified and analyzed. At the same time, it is essential to determine who the company's most important external stakeholders are and collect information on how those stakeholders have interacted with the company and what their expectations might be with respect to the company's CSR programs. Community concerns are particularly noteworthy even though the company's relationships with other stakeholders, such as investors, customers, lenders and supply chain partners, have a more direct impact on economic performance. Companies need to reach out to members of their communities through publications, open houses and workshops to develop and implement ideas about how the company can be a better community member. Finally, the interests and concerns of society-in-general and regulators should be monitored on a continuous basis and companies should establish and maintain contacts with NGOs, advocates for civil society, legislators and representatives of regulatory agencies with influence over topics that are relevant to the company.

Becoming a sustainable business, or improving a company's current performance with respect to acting in an environmentally and socially responsible manner, requires the same sort of strategic approach as any other major corporate initiative. However, while strategic planning for sustainability has become a recognized discipline, companies and their directors and senior executives must acknowledge and seek to overcome various specific challenges the fluidity of the concepts of sustainability and CSR, ongoing debate about the allocation of responsibilities for sustainable development between governments and business, understanding and adopting new performance measures that go beyond financial results to include environmental and social dimensions, reconciling the difficult tradeoffs that often must be resolved when implementing sustainable business practices, effectively communicating with stakeholders to explain the long-term approach that is necessary for implementing sustainability and CSR and the need to adopt new processes for decision making in the boardroom and implement internal controls that track sustainability and facilitate sustainability reporting.

Companies can overcome these challenges if they understand and follow certain best practices when determining and implementing their sustainability strategies and making investments in sustainability-related projects. First of all, companies need to align their sustainability investment activities with an overriding business mission and vision and focus those activities on projects that are both a natural fit for the company and which are perceived by the intended beneficiaries as valuable to them. In addition, companies need to set aside adequate resources to support sustainability initiatives on a long-term basis. This means integrating sustainability into the regular strategic planning and budgetary processes, rather than treating the topic as a discretionary matter that is addressed in an *ad hoc* fashion, and maintaining sufficient funding to ensure meaningful impact. Provision should also be made for hiring and supporting a professional, dedicated management function for the sustainability initiatives, and resources planning should be flexible enough to involve employees beyond volunteerism including allowing them to participate in sustainability initiatives as part of their regular day-to-day roles. Finally, strategies, goals and performance should also be continuously and clearly communicated throughout the company so that everyone knows the direction that has been selected and the steps that have been planned.[14]

Notes

1 K. Rangan, L. Chase and S. Karim, *Why Every Company Needs a CSR Strategy and How to Build It* (Cambridge, MA: Harvard Business School Working Paper 12-088, April 5, 2012), 1.

2 On the ideological debate over CSR, see A. Karnani, "Doing Well by Doing Good: The Grand Illusion", *California Management Review,* 53(2) (Winter 2011), 69; and D. Windsor, "Corporate Social Responsibility: Cases For and against" in M. Epstein and K. Hanson (Eds.), *The Accountable Corporation: Corporate Social Responsibility* (Volume 3) (Westport, CT: Praeger Publishers, 2006), 41–43.

3 K. Rangan, L. Chase and S. Karim, *Why Every Company Needs a CSR Strategy and How to Build It* (Cambridge, MA: Harvard Business School Working Paper 12-088, April 5, 2012), 3.

4 See also B. Googins and S. Rochlin, "Corporate Citizenship Top to Bottom: Vision, Strategy, and Execution" in M. Epstein and K. Hanson (Eds.), *The Accountable Corporation: Corporate Social Responsibility* (Volume 3) (Westport, CT: Praeger Publishers, 2006), 116–117.

5 K. Rangan, L. Chase and S. Karim, *Why Every Company Needs a CSR Strategy and How to Build It* (Cambridge, MA: Harvard Business School Working Paper 12-088, April 5, 2012), 4.

6 P. Hohnen (Author) and J. Potts (Editor), *Corporate Social Responsibility: An Implementation Guide for Business* (Winnipeg: International Institute for Sustainable Development, 2007), 18.

7 F. Maon, V. Swaen and A. Lindgreen, Mainstreaming the Corporate Responsibility Agenda: A Change Model Grounded in Theory and Practice (IAG-Louvain School of Management Working Paper, 2008), 8 (citing P. Dawson, *Understanding Organisational Change: Contemporary Experience of People at Work* (London: Sage, 2003); and J. George and G. Jones, *Understanding and Managing Organizational Behavior* (Reading, MA: Addison-Wesley, 1996)).

8 P. Hohnen (Author) and J. Potts (Editor), *Corporate Social Responsibility: An Implementation Guide for Business* (Winnipeg: International Institute for Sustainable Development, 2007), vii. Companies can also refer to guidelines prepared by local and regional governments which presumably were prepared with reference to specific local conditions and societal values and generally benefit from participation by representatives of business, government and labor. Id.

9 For a survey of the literature regarding frameworks about sustainability implementation, see F. Maon, V. Swaen and A. Lindgreen, Mainstreaming the Corporate Responsibility Agenda: A Change Model Grounded in Theory and Practice (IAG- Louvain School of Management Working Paper, 2008), 39, 56–58 (see also Figure 1: Proposed Integrative Framework at 62 of publication).. Frameworks discussed included H. Khoo and K. Tan, "Using the Australian Business Excellence Framework to Achieve Sustainable Business Excellence", *Corporate Social Responsibility and Environmental Management,*

9(4) (2002), 196–197; M. Werre, "Implementing Corporate Responsibility— The Chiquita Case", *Journal of Business Ethics*, 44(2–3) (2003), 247; V. Panapanaan, L. Linnanen, M. Karvonen and V. Phan, "Roadmapping Corporate Social Responsibility in Finnish Companies", *Journal of Business Ethics*, 44(2) (2003), 133; and J. Cramer, "Experiences with Structuring Corporate Social Responsibility in Dutch Industry", *Journal of Cleaner Production*, 13(6) (2005), 583.

10 UN Global Compact, *Training of Trainers Course Guidance Manual* (New York: UN Global Compact), 36.

11 P. Hohnen (Author) and J. Potts (Editor), *Corporate Social Responsibility: An Implementation Guide for Business* (Winnipeg: International Institute for Sustainable Development, 2007), 19.

12 UN Global Compact, *Training of Trainers Course Guidance Manual* (New York: UN Global Compact), 39–40.

13 *Business Strategy for Sustainable Development: Leadership and Accountability for the '90s* (Winnipeg: International Institute for Sustainable Development, jointly with Deloitte and Touche; Business Council for Sustainable Development, 1992).

14 Adapted from "Best Practice in Corporate Social Investment", https://next-generation.co.za/best-practice-in-corporate-social-investment-csi/ (accessed May 6, 2020).

5 The CEO and Sustainability

The main member of the executive team, and the person with the most responsibility for, and control over, the organizational design of the company, is the chief executive officer, or "CEO". While the CEO "reports" to the board of directors and the board of directors is vested with more legal authority than any officer of the company, including the CEO, it is the CEO to whom the directors turn for leadership in setting strategy and putting the company's assets and other resources to work in order to achieve the stated goals and objectives of the company. The CEO is almost always a member of the board of directors and, until recently, the common practice among larger corporations was for the CEO to also serve as the chairperson of the board of directors. While it is now the general rule that public companies, as well as many larger privately-held companies, will fill a majority of the seats on the board of directors with outsiders (i.e., non-employees and persons who do not represent a large shareholder block), it is nonetheless still true that the CEO exerts significant influence over the board even in those circumstances.

CEO Duties, Responsibilities and Roles

Regardless of the stage of evolution of a company, CEO has a broad, if not overwhelming, set of duties and responsibilities. Some of these duties are formal and prescribed by corporate law and the governing documents of the company or other applicable regulations (e.g., accounting and financial reporting requirements imposed by securities and capital markets regulators); however, most of the expectations imposed on the CEO are often vague and are left to the CEO to define and execute. A CEO is confronted with challenges in a number of different areas and from various stakeholders and he or she must be able to balance and prioritize the demands on his or her time and intellectual resources.

The CEO is, in many ways, the face of his or her company, and the image that he or she presents can have a significant impact on the reputation of the company in the investment community and the general marketplace. The CEO can place his or her imprint on the way a company operates and performs in a number of different ways:

- While the CEO will generally have a team of specialists to assist him or her with respect to organizational strategy and design issues, the CEO is ultimately responsible for establishing and implementing the strategy and setting the major business goals and objectives of the company (including the related decisions about how scarce inputs, such as capital and human resources, will be deployed) and vetting and approving the organizational structure of the company—how responsibilities are allocated within the company, which positions have authority over others, and the policies and procedures for motivating employees and coordinating the activities of different business/functional units.
- The CEO is expected to take the lead in identifying, selecting and managing the other members of the executive team and also should take an active role in filling other key positions within the company and making sure that the company has in place a formal system for making sure that the best talent is tapped to manage the business and that qualified managerial prospects are carefully trained and promoted.
- The CEO is expected to consciously determine the optimal culture for the company and take steps to establish and reinforce the appropriate values and norms associated with that culture. Culture is influenced by the people that the CEO selects for key management positions and the way in which the company expects problems to be solved and decisions to be made.
- Subject to the final approval of the board of directors, the CEO is responsible for setting the rewards to be offered to managers of the company, including the CEO, as incentives for them to pursue and achieve the business goals and objectives of the company. Obviously the potential for conflict-of-interest is high when it comes to deciding the amounts that are to be allocated to managers as opposed to other stakeholders including the shareholders, employees and even customers, and the exercise of discretion with respect to compensation by the CEO will heavily scrutinized by investors and other stakeholders.
- The CEO should take the lead in company efforts to build networks with its key business partners and establish strategic alliances. No company, regardless of its size and volume of resources, can take on every activity necessary for it to be successful and an important element of any company's business strategy is identifying key vendors, distributors, manufacturing partners and other service providers that can become reliable elements within the company's value creation chain.
- It is essential for the CEO to be prepared to oversee the company's activities with respect to globalizing the marketing and sales of the

company's products and services and tapping into resources in foreign markets to improve operational efficiency and the capacity of the company to be continuously innovative.

The Crucial Role of the CEO in Sustainability and CSR Activities

Surveys, such as one completed by Boyden in 2017 among adults in the United Kingdom, have repeatedly confirmed that the public strongly believes that the CEO must play an active role in the sustainability and corporate social responsibility (CSR) activities of his or her company and act as a spokesperson for those activities.[1] Participation and engagement by employees throughout the organization is essential for effective human capital management and CSR implementation, and the CEO is the only person in a position to communicate and demonstrate the values associated with CSR in a way that will integrate CSR into the corporate culture and the way that employees work on a day-to-day basis. It should be noted that CSR has become a significant driver of employee engagement, particularly among Millennials who are more willing to accept lower wages in exchange for working with a company committed to sustainability, and that the CEOs efforts to engage employees in this area will improve the company's ability to attract and retain talented workers. CEOs must also develop the soft skills necessary to communicate and engage with multiple stakeholders, each of which has different values and attitudes about how society should function and the role that the firm should play. CEOs must be able to engage in civil dialogue, approach the problems and challenges that are raised by stakeholders with an open mind and a focus on identifying and implementing innovative solutions and developing tools that will help measure and demonstrate the effectiveness and value of the company's CSR initiatives.

Selecting the CEO and other members of the executive team, and setting the right performance criteria and incentives with respect to pursuit and achievement of the company's sustainability commitments and targets, is a unique and important responsibility of the board of directors. At the very beginning, during the recruitment process, Global Compact LEAD calls on directors to include in their selection criteria that candidates have the ability to demonstrate solid understanding of the complex sustainability issues that affect the business environment; commit to operate in accordance with the highest social, environmental and ethical standards; and provide a track record of producing excellent financial results with due consideration for the interests and concerns of different stakeholders.[2]

Once candidates for CEO and the other spots on the executive team have been selected, incentives must be put in place in their compensation arrangements that reward long-term performance and that are aligned with the sustainability priorities and targets established by the board. When setting "sustainability objectives" for which performance will be measured and compensation determined, emphasis should be on the specific issues and priorities that are material to the company such as the chosen targets for carbon emissions, health and safety incidents, gender diversity or sales of certain categories of sustainable products.[3] Performance measurement with respect to sustainability indicators can be challenging given the lack of necessary data and the need for some level of discretion to be used when objective information is not easily available. When discretion is used, it is important for it to be verifiable and based on an independent process. Sustainability incentives must also be meaningful in the broader context of the executive's entire compensation package.[4]

The CEO and other members of the executive team need to have right capabilities to drive exemplary environmental, social and governance performance.[5] Each member of the executive team should have the ability to think strategically about the issues, communicate clearly and persuasively, and possess sound business knowledge and judgment. As for entire team, it should have the following interdisciplinary and cross-functional competencies:

- The ability to develop trusting relationships with a variety of company constituents before an issue becomes a problem.
- A solid grounding in a wide range of environmental processes, procedures, and technologies; social issues; and governance requirements at the local, state, regional, federal, and international levels.
- A knowledge of financial operations that extends beyond budgeting to an understanding of how finance intersects with sustainability and the ability to make a business case for a new direction.
- Familiarity with technological and process advances and an understanding of the trends in sustainability and their influences on the company and the industry segment.

Specific questions for each member of the executive team regarding awareness of sustainability risks and opportunities in their functional area might include the following:

- Does the chief financial officer incorporate sustainability factors into financial analyses?
- Does the chief marketing officer understand the difference between greenwashing and demonstrable corporate commitment to environmental goals—and that greenwashing not only alienates consumers but also signals to investors that integrity may be a problem in other areas of the company's operations?
- Is the chief human resources officer able to sincerely incorporate the company's sustainability performance into the company's employer

brand, or would employees and potential employees respond skeptically?

- Does the executive team as a whole see environment, society and governance, so-called "ESG", as an issue of long-term competitiveness?

CEO's Guide to being an Effective Sustainability Leader

Since studies are clear that the attitudes, actions and skills of the CEO are essential to the success of sustainability and CSR initiatives and ensuring they are perceived positively among the various stakeholder groups of the company, the CEO must be prepared for his or her role and understand and cultivate the appropriate mindset. For sustainable entrepreneurs, enthusiastic passion for environmentally or socially responsible business activities comes naturally, and he or she will willingly jump into the fray and engage with stakeholders from the very beginning of the venture. However, in order for all this work to be effective, and sustainable and credible, the CEO needs to understand certain "best practices" that have been identified by consultants, scholars and CEOs themselves.

Ethics and Social Responsibility

Ethics and social responsibility need to be important priorities for the CEO. He or she must have and express personal values that support ethical and socially responsible behavior by the company and its employees and must ensure that those values are integrated into the company's culture and communications with external stakeholders. An effective sustainability-focused CEO understands that while output, quality and profitability are all necessary for the long-term success of the company, companies have environmental and social responsibilities beyond making a profit and being ethical and socially responsible is the most important thing a company can do and is essential to the company's long-term profitability, competitiveness and sustainability.

It is the job of the CEO to lead the directors and other members of the executive team in identifying and articulating the specific social responsibility that the company will seek to address and continuously make the case that ethics, social responsibility and profitability can be compatible. In carrying out that role, he or she should ensure that corporate planning and goal setting sessions include discussions of ethics and social responsibility and that decisions regarding operational tactics never include bending or breaking the rules or cutting corners in order to achieve a profit. During those sessions, the CEO should constantly communicate that while operational excellence continues to be an important driver of how a company is perceived, engagement, purpose, integrity and ethical and socially responsible commercialization of products and services have become just as important, if not more important, in the eyes of the public and the way they assess a company's reputation. Ethical and socially responsible behavior should be tracked and measured and factored into assessments of the overall effectiveness of the company.

Public Relations

While a worthy cause is important for creating a sustainable business, sustainability of the company itself depends on developing and maintaining a loyal customer base that will buy the company's products and services and recommend them to others so that the company can survive and fulfill its stated mission. Surveys show that customers will pay a modest premium for sustainable products and services from brands that are trusted and known as being environmentally friendly and for their social value. The public statements and actions of the CEO are important factors in how the company is perceived by its key internal and external stakeholders. As such, the CEO needs to understand and practice the tools of public relations in all of his or her interactions with those stakeholders. For example, an energetic, confident and charismatic CEO generally has an advantage in raising capital from investors and commercial lenders and closing business relationships with strategic partners. On the other hand, poor business and ethical decisions by a CEO will create a crisis that causes investors to flee and destroys morale within the company.

The CEO must develop trust among the company's stakeholders such that they are confident that the CEO is telling the public the truth about what is happening with the company with honesty and good intentions. The CEO must also demonstrate that he or she is committed to taking concrete sustainability actions right now, not just when there is more money and resources are available or a crisis arises that the company needs to address from a defensive posture. The CEO must be perceived as open to listening to stakeholders, engaging in inclusive dialog with them and keeping them informed about decisions that impact the company's sustainability-related initiatives. Finally, the CEO must send a message that he or she is particularly tuned in to managing now only for the present moment but also for tomorrow and the future generations of employees and leaders of the company.[6]

Innovative Ways to Practice CSR

CEOs should look for new and innovative ways to conduct CSR, strategies and methods that are more in line with what businesses do best on a day-to-day basis. For example, rather than replicating the same menu of CSR initiatives that other companies are doing, the CEO should look for ways that their companies can specialize in areas that are consistent with their competitive advantages in the marketplace. Not every company can be like Ben & Jerry's and have a social mission at the core of their brand, but most businesses have a core competency they can deploy, such as the way that UPS has provided logistics support to help deliver emergency supplies. Aggressive collaboration with other companies, and with government policymakers, is another way that companies can have a great environmental and social impact. CEOs building and operating companies in the technology sectors, which require fewer employees than traditional businesses, can nonetheless make a valuable contribution to society by participating in effort to retrain displaced workers so they can be competitive in the new job market. Retraining programs can also help the CEO fill positions at his or her company, since many technology companies are still struggling to find qualified applicants for all of the activities they need in order to be successful. The bottom line is that CEOs should continuously think about how their companies can leverage their core competencies in innovative ways to have a positive impact on society and mitigate and reduce the potential negative effects of their business activities.

Engagement

Gone are the days that the CEO can simply hunker down and spend all of his or her time on internal issues and activities such as product development, manufacturing and human resources issues. It is clear that that a substantial slice of its earnings and opportunities are dependent on the relationships of the company, and its CEO in particular, with external stakeholders. Research confirms that while operational excellence, including returns to investors, remains an important driver of a firm's reputation among the general public, other factors have emerged as drivers of brand goodwill, and thus potential overall value, including engagement, purpose, integrity and the environmental and social impact of the company's products and services.

As such, stakeholder engagement has become a top priority for CEOs and he and she must understand how to do engagement efficiently and successfully. In the past, a CEO would delegate CSR to another person or group and the primary focus was often on philanthropy or modest collaborations with outside groups interested in environmental and social issues and problems. Now the CSR efforts of the company must be integrated into each of its core commercial activities, as well as its overall strategy and operational planning. Even the CEOs of the companies that have enjoyed the most financial success in recent years, such as Tim Cook of Apple, have only a limited amount of time to enjoy increases in revenues and earnings and the development of new products since they must now deal with intense and continuous criticism of the environmental and social impact of their operations and calls for operational changes thought by others to be necessary to achieve diversity and address income inequality.

A good general rule regarding engagement is to authentically communicate often with all of the company's key stakeholders and do so in a way that stakeholders can trust that their concerns and ideas are being heard and considered seriously. The CEO needs to understand that the company's agenda for CSR cannot be dictated by the company and must be mutually agreed upon by the company and each of its stakeholders since CSR has only limited value if it is not perceived by stakeholders as being responsive to their needs and expectations. That said, the CEO must prioritize his or her CSR activities, and the associated engagement, around the issues that are most important for the long-term success and sustainability of the company. For some companies, this may mean getting involved in developing new solutions for environmental problems, which means that the CEO will need to become engaged in industry-wide discussions and work with customers on ideas for new products and employees on how to help them develop the skills necessary to work with new technologies. Many companies have focused on diversity and ensuring that everyone has better opportunities for employment with the company and advancement to higher levels of the organization. The CEO should advocate and demand respect, diversity and inclusion in the workforce and support each employee's capability and desire to be an honest, knowledgeable ambassador to customers, friends, shareholders and public officials. Whatever the issue might be, the CEO needs to be clear about the purposes and goals of the company with respect to CSR, set the proper "tone at the top" and be able to explain to everyone involved with the company, inside and outside, why pursuit and attainment of those goals will be in the best interests of all of the stakeholders. This is particular true for employees since motivated and engaged employees will be more productive and loyal and help the company deliver better results for customers and shareholders.

Stakeholder engagement is not always pleasant and the CEO will often find that the demands and expectations of stakeholders are beyond what the company can reasonably promise or deliver. In those situations, the CEO must remain calm, patience and good-humored and focus on listening to the legitimate concerns of stakeholders and provide stakeholders with reliable information and reasoned analysis with respect to the decisions that are made, always being mindful of the impact of such decisions on all of the stakeholders.

Investor Relations

While discussions of CSR engagement are typically focused on how companies can develop and maintain relationships with stakeholders beyond shareholders, investors still remain first among equals in the stakeholder universe and CEOs need to be particularly careful in how they engage with investors on CSR initiatives. For a long time, caution was needed because many investors were skeptical of their portfolio companies deviating too much from a focus on financial performance, which meant that the CEO need to spend time helping investors understand how the company practice of environmental and social responsibility would ultimately enhance the long-term value of the company and their ownership stake therein. However, the pendulum has swung dramatically among institutional investors that now expect CEOs to develop and lead appropriate CSR initiatives and establish CSR reporting mechanisms. CEOs are not expected to be experts on a particular environmental or social issue, but they do need to have a plan and be able to demonstrate to investors that they have invested adequate resources for the company to fulfill its public commitments on environmental and social topics. Another important role of the CEO in the eyes of investors is oversight of the company's organizational culture and human capital. The CEO should be able to explain to investors how much time and effort he or she spends in talking with employees from all levels of the organization and disseminating a strong message regarding the company's commitments to environmental and social goals. Investors also want evidence that the CEO is creating and maintaining a diverse group of senior managers and other key decision makers and is implementing compensation and performance measurement systems that give due weight to contributions to CSR. Finally, CEO should be prepared to share with large investors the results of the company's own assessment of its CSR initiatives and processes and the steps that the CEO is taking to make necessary improvements in the way in which the company conducts its business.

Personal Values and Risks

While most of what a CEO does with respect to CSR occurs in the public domain, there are very personal issues and risks that the CEO also needs to consider. First of all, there is no such thing as privacy for the CEO when a crisis occurs with respect to whether or not his or her company has failed to fulfill expectations with respect to ethics and social responsibility. The CEO's official actions will be scrutinized and more likely than not someone will pry into personal matters such as whether the CEO's lifestyle is inconsistent with concerns about income inequality. While hopefully any such allegations will have no merit, the spotlight can be stressful for the CEO and his or her family. If there are issues, the CEO's credibility is almost immediately undermined in a way that makes it difficult for him or her to continue and there are surveys that provide support for the proposition that materialistic CEO practices leader to lower CSR and sustainability performance scores. Second, high profile CEOs may be expected to take positions in social and political controversies, even getting involved is not directly related to a specific CSR initiative or goal of the company. Many CEOs, while comfortable with certain social issues, prefer not to become regular participants in the market-place of opinions; however, it has been argued that CEOs are in a unique position to frame the dialogue on certain issues and that CEOs that take a position on a controversial issue can actually bring more new business to the company. Finally, while CEOs that champion CSR initiatives are generally praised for such work when things are going well, research shows that if a CEO has invested in CSR and the firm performs poorly, he or she is much more likely to be dismissed.

Sustainability for the Startup CEO

While sustainability and CSR have been topics of discussion for larger businesses for a long time, relatively little attention was paid to sustainability among small businesses and startups. While prospective sustainable entrepreneurs rightly have concerns about the costs associated with many sustainability practices and CSR-related projects, they are also eager to create and build sustainable businesses based on purpose, innovation, shared value and respect for people and planet.

One of the first things to consider, and arguably the most important decision for the founders of a new company to make, is just who among the initial drivers of the company will assume the position of CEO. In many cases the choice is obvious, but what may seem to make sense in the early days of the company may not be what is necessary as the business model evolves and more and more stakeholder engagement, particularly with investors, becomes necessary. One thing that cannot be overemphasized is that good sustainability-related skills are in addition to, not in lieu of, top-notch leadership and management competencies. It is not sufficient to be passionate about the "cause" if the CEO is not able to grasp basic principles of strategy, finance, sales, marketing and technology.

Another thing to consider is how the sustainability-related energy and skills of the members of the founding team who are not the CEO can be leveraged while not muddying up the messaging from the CEO. The CEO needs to continuously communicate with the other members of the founding team, as well as senior managers brought in to assist with launching the venture, to understand their views on the mission of the enterprise and ensure that everyone is speaking in the same voice when interviewing prospective employees, talking to investors, engaging with strategic partners and going about their business in the communities in which the company is operating. Sometimes new companies will appoint one of the founders to serve as "chief sustainability officer". This is fine; however, the position should be designed to support execution of the CEO's vision and decisions regarding sustainability and CSR rather than a way to separate those issues from the CEO's portfolio.

Whoever is selected as the CEO needs to carefully consider how his or her background will be presented to the company's various stakeholders during the engagement process. Stakeholders will seek out authenticity and practical experience when assessing the skills and trustworthiness of the CEO and the story line needs to be settled well in advance of what will quickly become a tumultuous schedule of meetings and other communications with stakeholders. The "best" scenario is a CEO who can describe how he or she came upon a particular environmental and/or social problem or opportunity and provide his or her experiences in identifying and developing solutions that can credibly form a foundation for a viable business. The CEO also needs to be able to demonstrate how his or her prior professional experiences and network align with the actions that will need to be taken in order for the company to fulfill its mission.

Operationalizing sustainability and CSR is crucial for the startup CEO. Actions speak louder than words and one of the actions that the CEO can take from the very beginning of the company's journey is establishing and maintaining CSR practices and policies that are compatible with the company's size and resources. Many sustainable entrepreneurs argue that they simply have too much to do during the early days of their firm—finishing the first product, hiring new employees, talking with investors to raise seed capital and trying to engage with strategic partners—to worry about implementing formal policies and procedures. They often say that there is no point since it is impossible to know how quickly the company will grow and whatever is agreed upon in the first few months will be obsolete by the end of the first year. While it is true that things are changing quickly during the launch stage, it can be the best time to begin laying the foundation for ethics and social responsibility throughout every aspect of the organization and its activities.

At a minimum, the CEO should establish, in consultation with board members, other members of the senior management team and a representative group of employees from throughout the organization, a mission statement that explicitly incorporates ethical and socially responsible behavior and a concise code of ethics or conduct that can be used by everyone as guiding principles for their decisions and as an agenda for training and orienting new employees about the organizational culture. From the very beginning, the CEO should prioritize employee morale and work to achieve and maintain fluent communication between employees and management so that employees always feel comfortable about sharing their ideas and opinions and there is a cooperative atmosphere that benefits group success. To do this, the CEO must continuously engage with employees throughout the company on fundamental matters such as "mission" and "vision" so that employees understand how to act and how to explain the company's purpose for being to outsiders.

Environmental and social responsibility should also be explicitly woven into strategic planning and performance metrics and the CEO should make sure that the company's sustainability initiatives are tracked formally and reported on regularly to all of the company's stakeholders, even if the company is not yet ready to adopt one of the sophisticated reporting frameworks that have emerged and are now being regularly used by larger businesses. Performance relating to environmental and social responsibility should be formally incorporated into compensation arrangements for the CEO and other senior executives from the very beginning since research shows that CEOs who are compensated based only on economic factors are less motivated to push CSR initiatives. Finally, a compliance program to satisfy specific formal legal requirements should be established, not only for its own sake but as a good first step in implementing one or more of the voluntary certification standards that may be applicable to the business (e.g., ISO 9001 for quality management; ISO 14001 for environmental management; OHSAS 18001 for occupational health and safety and ISO 26000 for social responsibility). While, as mentioned above, small businesses and startups operate under resource constraints that make it impractical for them to implement comprehensive sustainability initiatives on the scope of those that have been adopted by larger companies, they nonetheless can begin by referring to the same authoritative international instruments such as the Organisation for Economic Co-operation and Development Guidelines for Multinational Enterprises and the UN Global Compact Principles, each of which are intended to be applicable to organizations of all sizes.[7]

Notes

1 CEOs and the New CSR Priority (Boyden Executive Monitor, September 2017), https://www.boyden.com/media/ceos-and-the-new-csr-priority-2909935/index. html (accessed April 25, 2020).
2 *A New Agenda for the Board of Directors: Adoption and Oversight of Corporate Sustainability* (Global Compact LEAD, 2012), 8.
3 Id. There is also the option of providing, as is the case in certain extractive industries and the pharmaceutical industry, of using "negative criteria" that is embedded in bonus rules that provide that no bonuses will be paid when incidents of a certain magnitude have occurred. Id. at 8–9.
4 Id. at 9.
5 *Boards and Sustainability: Three Best Practices* (Chicago, IL: Heidrick & Struggles, 2017), 4.
6 For further discussion of "public relations" principles, see the materials available from the Arthur W. Page Society (page.org), a leading global professional association for senior public relations and corporate communications executives and educators.
7 See also International Organization for Standardization, ISO 26000, *Guidance on Social Responsibility: Discovering ISO 26000* (2014) and *Handbook for Implementers of ISO 26000, Global Guidance Standard on Social Responsibility by Small and Medium Sized Businesses* (Middlebury, VT: ECOLOGIA, 2011).

6 Sustainability Executives

The country's first chief sustainability officer (CSO), Linda Fisher, was appointed at DuPont in 2004, and since then many large companies have created a position with that title and other positions within their executive teams that focus on sustainability, environmental impact, corporate responsibility or citizenship.[1] In addition to the CSO title, companies have referred to the position in a number of different ways with titles such as chief responsibility officer, corporate social responsibility officer, corporate social and environmental officer, community and environmental responsibility officer and sustainable development officer.[2] In many cases, the CSO role was originally created by companies to respond to crises that had either not been anticipated or had been largely ignored in the course of their day-to-day strategic and risk management planning.[3] The nature of the crisis usually dictated the initial focus of the CSO role. For example, when companies in the retail industry were confronted with legal and human rights issues in their supply chain, they began to develop organizational responses to monitor and remediate labor practices among their suppliers around the world. Similarly, companies with operations that generated a significant environmental footprint naturally gravitated toward sustainability programs that were focused on preservation of natural resources and reduction of harmful emissions.

As time has gone by, companies have gradually shifted from being reactive to proactive and the emerging definition of the CSO role now includes involvement in overall decision-making and responsibility for embedding sustainability throughout the organization. For many years, "sustainability" fell under the functional description of environmental, health and safety, or "EH&S", and the primary role of the EH&S leader was to handle audit and compliance matters and interact mainly with permit writers, safety inspectors and low-level compliance staff at regulatory agencies. However, a range of pressures and sources forced companies to take a new look at how their EH&S and sustainability activities were managed including aggressive governmental enforcement activities in the US and in the European Union, financial and legal considerations, concerns about climate change and energy costs and availability, the need to develop new technologies to address environmental challenges and intensified scrutiny from public interest groups and the media into sustainability practices generally and oversight of environmental and social matters in supply chains specifically. Companies also had to address the emergence of numerous guidelines and reporting standards for sustainability and social responsibility that were changing the expectations of stakeholders regarding corporate performance and communications.[4]

While at first many companies were reacting to changes in their environment as opposed to taking the initiative to transform their businesses to take into account sustainability, many eventually came to understand the crucial role that EH&S performance played in overall company performance and recognized that EH&S could no longer be treated as a cost center, but instead should be regarded as an important strategic asset that could easily become a significant liability if not properly managed. Companies began to appreciate the significant business benefits of taking a different approach to EH&S and sustainability such as enhanced brand, preservation and enhancement of reputation, decreased costs, protection of assets, increased efficiency and competitive advantage.[5] As time has gone by, companies changed their organizational structures to move away from the traditional practice of having the CSO report into the legal or human resources function toward a new alignment in which the CSO reports directly to the CEO and interacts regularly with other members of the senior executive team as a peer.[6] As discussed below, board members have come to expect a direct communications line with the CSO, another sign that the position is now regarded as being an important driver of company growth and performance and an architect of overall company strategy.

Today the best practice is to have sustainability represented in the C-suite as a catalyst for the strong leadership and support for sustainability initiatives that must emanate from the senior executive team in order for those initiatives to capture the imagination and energy of employees and other stakeholders. The CSO should be sure that sustainability is taken into account when business strategy is being discussed and established in the boardroom and in meetings among senior executives, and should take the lead in communicating with operations managers about how budgets and performance metrics for particular programs have been established taking into account sustainability priorities. The CSO should also join the CEO in engaging with stakeholder groups to explain the company's sustainability strategy and obtain feedback and address concerns. Finally, the CSO should be responsible for ensuring that the company adheres to the continuous process of auditing and evaluating its sustainability activities in order to ensure that its sustainability strategies are coherent and effective.[7]

Coordinating a company's sustainability initiatives in a strategic manner is a challenging task given that companies may be engaged in a diverse set of programs that include philanthropy, value chain activities and wholesale business transformation that may be driven and led by a range of actors including community affairs managers, operations managers and members of the executive team. In order for the CSO to be successful and impactful in all these areas, he or she needs to hold the position as his or her full-time responsibility and be given the resources to do his or her job in the form of a dedicated sustainability unit that would be formally and publicly tasked with coordinating and integrating sustainability initiatives across the organization, even if responsibility for implementation of the various initiatives remains dispersed throughout the company. While the CSO cannot attend every planning meeting or event, representatives of the unit can be knowledgeable participants for each program including have decision rights in the design and execution of programs. The knowledge collected from the activities of the unit will allow the CSO to elevate strategic sustainability topics and priorities to the highest levels within the organization quickly and effectively.[8]

CSO Roles and Competencies

The ideal CSO is an ambassador, visionary and strategist charged with driving commitment to sustainability within the company and across the company's external stakeholders.[9] The CSO position has a number of specific roles and related knowledge requirements. For example, with respect to the company's social sustainability activities the CSO is expected to integrate social responsibility with the company's business strategy and operations. At the same time, the CSO might directly manage, facilitate or participate in the environmental compliance and leadership activities of the company, including identifying, assessing, responding and monitoring environmental risks and opportunities in the company. With respect to governance, the CSO would be expected to be involved in advising the board on its duties relating to oversight of sustainability, business practices and ethics, compliance and risk management, disclosure and transparency, stakeholder communications and monitoring and auditing sustainability initiatives. The CSO's primary internal working relationships would be with the entire board, C-level executive leadership, the board committee(s) assigned responsibilities for sustainability, governance and investor relations and governmental affairs. With regard to external working relationships, the CSO should be communicating regularly with community groups, non-government organizations (NGOs), policy makers and major investors; media, financial and industry analysts; professional CSR organizations; and peer counterparts.[10]

A study conducted by the consulting firm PWC of sustainability executives from 25 global companies recognized as leading on sustainability found that responsibilities and activities among them, and the average percentage of their time spent on each area, broke down as follows: core business and operations, including working on operational improvements, supporting product and service sustainability efforts and engaging suppliers/sourcing (19%); external engagement, including developing partnerships with external groups and reporting externally to stakeholders; internal engagement, including communicating and socializing the case for change, supporting senior executives/C-suite management/ board of directors, engaging employees and the business units in the organization and measuring progress and reporting internally (32%); and developing strategy, including identifying and analyzing sustainability issues, developing sustainability strategy and developing the business case for sustainability (28%).[11]

A guide prepared and distributed by the National Association of Corporate Directors (NACD), which looked at the role of the CSO position from the perspectives of the members of the company's board of directors, listed the following as core duties and responsibilities of the position[12]:

- *Strategy*: Lead development of an overarching sustainability approach directly related to the company's long-term business plans
- *Thought Leadership*: Broaden and raise the company's understanding of what society, customers, employees, investors, and other stakeholders expect
- *Advocacy*: Speak out on behalf of the company's sustainability goals and accomplishments
- *Policies and Programs*: Drive the development and execution of guiding principles and initiatives for the company's sustainability programs
- *Goals and Measurement*: Develop appropriate targets and ways of assessing progress to drive and evaluate the company's performance on sustainability
- *Reporting*: Determine how the company will internally and externally express progress toward accomplishing its sustainability goals and respond to society's increasing demand for greater transparency
- *Stakeholder Engagement*: Build constructive alliances and coalitions with key constituency groups
- *Risk Management*: Identify risks and opportunities based on stakeholder expectations and design proactive mitigation and response strategies
- *Fiscal Oversight*: Through the sustainability strategic and operational planning process, develop an understanding of the fiscal impact of the company's goals and priorities in this area

As for the preferred qualifications for the CSO position, the Corporate Responsibility Officers Association (CROA), which is now called the 3BL Association, has mentioned C-suite executive level experience; a sophisticated understanding of the global sustainability landscape and best practices; being the kind of individual who is sought out for his or her advice and perspective; experience working with and influencing senior company leadership (including the CEO and/or COO), chairperson of the board and board members) on projects that involve the development of new company-wide policies and programs; ability to work successfully with people of diverse functional and cultural backgrounds; demonstrated ability to anticipate trends and issues in business and society; excellent written and oral communications skills; ability to analyze and interpret data; and strong business financial acumen. The required knowledge base and skill set for the CSO position is extremely broad and includes knowledge about economic, social and environmental sustainability, governance, stakeholder engagement and ethics, and skills with respect to strategy development and execution, performance and change management, communications, industry and business acumen and risk management.[13] Critical personality attributes for the CSO include being courageous, ethical, innovative, logical, perceptive, process focused and versatile.[14]

Another view on the necessary competencies for an effective CSO was offered by Heidrick & Struggles, which began with the ability to think strategically, described as the ability to look toward the horizon, identify an opportunity or challenge before it affects the company, and develop and implement a strategy to either take advantage of the opportunity or manage the challenge. Particular attention was given to the creation of business opportunities by the CSO, a marked shift from focusing primarily on prevention, mitigation and compliance. For example, the CSO could proactively seek out technological solutions to environmental problems that simultaneously reduce costs and improve productivity, a true "shared value" proposition. A second key competency for the CSO identified by Heidrick & Struggles was the ability to communicate effectively and translate complex technical concepts and strategies into terms that resonated with the company's top leadership and key constituencies (i.e., employees, investors, lenders, insurers, rating agencies, customers, suppliers, the media and the public). When communicating the CSO needs to be able to adapt his or her tone and approach to a wide range of audiences ranging from the CEO, directors and regulators to each of the employees who would be called upon to change their skills and behaviors in order to execute the sustainability strategy.[15]

Understanding the Role of the C-Suite Sustainability Executive: Directors' View

As noted above, the NACD guide was written from the unique and interesting perspective of directors' oversight of sustainability generally and the CSO in particular. The guide discusses the information and reporting expectations of directors relating to sustainability and recommends that board members require the CSO (or the holder of any other senior sustainability position to provide the following information to them on a regular basis[16]:

- A clear and detailed overview of the sustainability landscape, including a long-term strategic view of sustainability risks and opportunities, and the most material sustainability issues and challenges facing the company and its operations
- Educated perspectives and advice on the business impacts of specific sustainability-related events and activities
- Systematic structure and plan for reporting on sustainability issues on an ongoing basis to a broad list of stakeholders, including customers, investors, employees, board members, the public, and government organizations
- Complete and industry-appropriate sustainability reporting
- Reports on key sustainability planning and implementation issues and effectiveness
- Innovative and creative strategies to embed sustainability into business activities

Implicit in the recommendations included in the NACD guide is the need for regular face-to-face meetings between directors, either the entire board or the members of a committee of the board focusing on sustainability, and the CSO to address questions and issues arising from the information outlined above and on additional topics such as the level of the organization's reporting transparency, particularly in comparison with competitors; the engagement of the CSO in the strategic planning process and the completeness and relevance of strategies for addressing key sustainability issues; the potential risks and opportunities resulting from strategic plans and how the company is prepared to manage risk (i.e., whether the CSO is aware of issues that should be of concern to the company); the quality of the company's sustainability strategy and response plans; whether the objectives of the organization's sustainability function are in alignment with what the stakeholders would expect or desire (i.e., does the sustainability focus match the shareholders' interests); where the company stands from a sustainability perspective in comparison to competitors and to benchmark enterprises; and the areas in the company's business where financial interests conflict with the interests of society and/or the environment.

During the course of meetings and other communications between the CSO and board members, consideration should also be given to identifying ways in which the board can better engage with the sustainability process and provide assistance and support in the implementation of sustainability plans and initiatives. Board members should understand and accept their duties and expectations with regarding to establishing the requisite "tone at the top" relating to sustainability, but they need guidance from the CSO and the CEO about how best to do that. For example, the board should consider whether the CSO has the data that he or she needs to manage sustainability-related risks and solicit the advice of the CSO on how the board should balance business decisions with socioeconomic impact and document those decisions in a manner that allows the CSO to adequately communicate them to stakeholders. The board should also solicit CSO input on the adequacy of the company's sustainability and corporate governance structure and how it might be improved.[17]

Board members should combine their interactions with the CSO with related discussions between them and the CEO relating to the company's sustainability strategies and activities. The goal of these discussions should not only be learning more about with the CEO is doing in his or her position, but also assessing how well the CEO and the CSO are working together. Specific topics for board members to cover with the CEO relating to sustainability recommended in the NACD guide included the effectiveness of the integration of sustainability strategy into business processes, as well as business and investment decision-making; the quality of sustainability culture across the business units and the supporting evidence; the ability of all employees to articulate the company's key sustainability values at all levels and across all geographies; the CEO's views on how sustainability activities can best be integrated into ongoing business activities, clearly and regularly communicated to all stakeholders, including customers, investors, employees, directors, the public and government organizations; and any shift(s) in business models that the company should consider in an effort to make the business more restorative.[18]

Key Factors Supporting and Enabling Success of Sustainability Executives

Having the authority and resources to oversee pursuit and achievement of the company's sustainability goals is certainly a fundamental prerequisite for being a successful CSO, as is the engagement and support of the board of directors and the other members of the executive team. In addition, the holders of the sustainability leadership positions interviewed by PWC for the survey mentioned above provided more insights into the key factors that supported and enabled their success in large business enterprises[19]:

- No matter where the CSO reports, having broad access to and a view across the entire business is critically important. Some of the leaders were indifferent to reporting lines as long as their position was endorsed and sponsored by the board and key executives including the CEO; however, others felt that the position would have the most impact by being seen as a strategic function.

- Wherever the position is located in the organizational hierarchy, internal support from the hosting function is crucial. For example, if the sustainability leader worked out of the company's external affairs group he or she should expect to receive support from the communications and branding teams rather than simply having a desk in the same area as other members of that group without much interaction.
- The most frequently cited "essential tool" for success was a thorough understanding of how the business works, which is crucial for achieving and maintaining credibility internally and for being able to continuously make the business case for sustainability to investors.
- The CSO needs to have access the data that is necessary to support the sustainability strategy, guide the execution of that strategy ensure accountability and measure performance. However, too much data can be distracting and the CSO needs to carefully consider what data is truly necessary for gauging performance and how that data should be presented to different audiences.
- Developing and presenting the business case for sustainability is one of the most important and challenging activities for the CSO and the business case should include a strategic vision and narrative to inspire understanding, commitment, and action and hard data and plans for implementation. In addition, the CSO must have the requisite communication and intercultural skills to effective translate the business case using the language of business and persuade his or her audience to take action on the sustainability agenda and support the sustainability strategy.
- Robust employee engagement is critical for realizing value from the sustainability strategy and the CSO must lead in the development and implementation of initiatives to motivate employees about the company's sustainability agenda and excite them so that they will invest their efforts in the activities necessary for success.
- The CSO must always be looking ahead, scanning the company's external environment and identifying and translating relevant opportunities and threats that can and should be addressed as part of the company's sustainability strategy.
- While the CSO should practice collegiality among the other members of the C-suite, he or she will often find it necessary to take positions that are not popular with other leaders who are still clinging to traditional cultural values and strategic goals that are profit-centric. Effective sustainability leaders are change catalysts seeking to push their companies in new directions and must be prepared to lose their jobs rather than continue to go along with the status quo.
- The CSO should engage with his or her community of colleagues to borrow and share professional best practices, techniques, approaches and information, thus accelerating the pace of change.

The responses of the sustainability leaders in the survey made it clear that leading sustainability requires passion, patience, and a long-term perspective, and that in order to be successful and impactful the CSO needs to be nimble (i.e., able to seize opportunity when it presents itself), passionate about their work and the company's goals, resilient (i.e., able to accept and rebound from failure and pushback), persistent (i.e., willing to repeat the same message ad nauseam), aware and able to anticipate future risks and strategic opportunities and patient (i.e., understanding that change takes time). Among other things, the CSO needs to grapple with the challenges of "continued integration", which requires building and maintaining relationships with senior leadership, fine-tuning operations, using innovation to drive deeper integration into the company's product and service offerings and maintaining the momentum and the spotlight on sustainability.[20] Other challenges for the CSO include how to engage meaningfully with stakeholders, partners and industry peers; how to identify strategic priorities; ensuring that the correct metrics are being tracked and reported; demonstrating and articulating the value of sustainability initiatives; and scaling the sustainability effort.[21]

Rounding Out the Sustainability Team

As discussed elsewhere in this chapter, the preferred approach, assuming there are sufficient resources, is for the CSO position to be supported by a full sustainability leadership team with cross-functional experiences and skills drawn from key areas including corporate communications, operations, human resources, legal and compliance, sales, marketing, philanthropy, community relations and EH&S. As a practical matter, the size of the sustainability leadership team will be determined by factors that are beyond the control of the CSO including the size of the organization, responsibilities assigned to other functional areas and available capital and human resources. Surveys among even the largest organizations find that the CSO generally has to get by with a relatively small number of direct reports and a modest budget, which means that the CSO has to be adept at using their interpersonal skills to develop and maintain cooperative relationships with other parts of the company. In a series of reports on the evolution of the CSO, the Weinreb Group found that CSOs thrived and achieved success when they are able to build and manage multiple teams, and empower sustainability leaders, throughout the organization.[22]

One important sustainability leadership post is the vice president of sustainability, a senior operational role reporting to the CSO and responsible for oversight of the development and implementation of sustainability strategy and managing a team of sustainability specialist experts.[23] Inside the company the vice president of sustainability would work closely with executive leadership, the committee(s) of the board to which sustainability duties and activities have been assigned, business line managers (i.e., supply chain, human resources and environmental affairs), investor relations and governmental affairs and his or her direct reports. Facing outward, he or she would be working with community groups, NGOs and policy makers; media, financial and industry analysts; professional CR organizations and peer counterparts. The required knowledge base and skill set for this position is not quite as broad as for the CSO position; however, he or she must have knowledge of economic, social and environmental sustainability and ethics and have a keen understanding of business conditions in the company's industry and the tools necessary for effective strategy execution and performance and risk management.

As one gets deeper into the staffing of the sustainability function, variations will necessarily be observed given that each organization has its own priorities and resources. As a point of reference regarding the specialist positions that might be created, consideration might be given to five other key sustainability-related positions within the organizational hierarchy mentioned by the CROA[24]:

- *Director of Sustainability Communications*: Responsible for developing and executing a comprehensive, cohesive communications strategy for both internal and external audiences and for the production of the annual sustainability report, and uses the communications strategy to connect and convey broader reputation and social issues to the commercial objectives of the business. Works closely with internal groups like public relations, human resources, government affairs, investor relations, and environmental health and safety as well as with external stakeholders like socially responsible investors, NGOs, customers, etc. The Director of Sustainability Communications plans, develops, and leads the execution of a global sustainability communications plan, aligned with the company's sustainability goals. Candidates should have knowledge about stakeholder engagement and ethics and be skilled in change management, communications and risk management.
- *Director, Philanthropy*: This position is responsible for establishing, leading and managing, a non-profit charitable foundation which awards grants annually to a variety of organizations in communities where the company does business. Duties and responsibilities include overall strategic planning, revenue generation, financial management, organizational development, staff management and program operations. Candidates should have knowledge about social sustainability and ethics and be skilled in communications and strategy development and execution.
- *Director, Sustainability Procurement Strategy*: This position is a specialist procurement role focused on sustainability and includes

developing and implementing procurement's strategy and policy on sustainability in relation to suppliers and their supply chains. Candidates should have knowledge about economic, social and environmental sustainability and ethics and be skilled in strategy execution, performance management and understanding the specific business elements of the industry in which the company operates.

- *Director of Environment, Health and Safety*: This position leads and directs the organization's EH&S processes and has company-wide responsibility for all EH&S-related functions with accountability for operational, administrative, technical, and financial components. Contributes to the development and execution of functional business plans and EH&S strategies and assesses operational risks that could affect EH&S in order to advise senior leadership on constructive plans and mitigation strategies. Candidates should have knowledge about environmental sustainability, stakeholder engagement and ethics and be skilled in strategy development and execution and risk management.
- *Director, Sustainability*: This position is responsible for developing a comprehensive sustainability strategy across all dimensions of sustainability that can be delivered through the tools of the practitioner, including issue monitoring, stakeholder consultation, materiality, risk analysis, transparency and reporting.

The activities under each of the directorships may be supported by steering committees and other processes for coordination and collaboration. For example, an EH&S steering committee might be responsible for proposing EH&S strategy and targets, overseeing the company's EH&S policies and performance and approving the company's EH&S audit program and reviewing the results of such audits to make recommendation to senior management. In many cases the activities of the EH&S steering committee are deemed to be of such significance that the CSO, as well as the EH&S director, will serve as a member, often as the chairperson.

Notes

1 C. Bader, "What Do Chief Sustainability Officers Actually Do?", *The Atlantic* (May 6, 2015), https://www.theatlantic.com/business/archive/2015/05/what-do-chief-sustainability-officers-actually-do/392315/ (accessed April 26, 2020).
2 http://corporatesustainabilityofficers.com/ (accessed April 26, 2020) Certain of the publications cited and relied upon in this chapter use different names for the position and the term "chief sustainability officer", or "CSO", has been substituted in the descriptions in this chapter for the sake of consistency.
3 *C-SUITE EXPECTATIONS: Understanding C-Suite Roles beyond the Core* (Washington, DC: National Association of Corporate Directors, 2013), 11.

4 A. Luijkenaar and K. Spinley, *The Emergence of the Chief Sustainability Officer: From Compliance Manager to Business Partner* (Chicago, IL: Heidrick & Struggles International, 2007), 6–7.

5 Id.

6 Heidrick & Struggles found that many companies were expanding EH&S, areas which had already been combined for a number of years, to include sustainability and corporate social responsibility and referring to the leader of activities in the expanded area as the CSO. Id. at 3.

7 K. Rangan, L. Chase and S. Karim, *Why Every Company Needs a CSR Strategy and How to Build It* (Cambridge, MA: Harvard Business School Working Paper 12-088, April 5, 2012), 21–22 (while the term "CSO" is used in the text, Rangan et al. preferred to refer to the position as "Chief Responsibility Officer" and focused on strategic management of corporate social responsibility).

8 Id. For further discussion of the model proposed by Rangan et al. for developing a corporate social responsibility strategy, see A. Gutterman, *Strategic Planning for Sustainability* (New York: Business Experts Press, 2020).

9 Corporate Responsibility Officers Association, *Structuring and Staffing Corporate Responsibility: A Guidebook* (2010), 22–23; and *C-SUITE EXPECTATIONS: Understanding C-Suite Roles beyond the Core* (Washington, DC: National Association of Corporate Directors, 2013).

10 Id. at 39–51.

11 A. Longsworth, H. Doran and J. Webber, "The Sustainability Executive: Profile and Progress" (PWC, September 2012), 15.

12 *C-SUITE EXPECTATIONS: Understanding C-Suite Roles beyond the Core* (Washington, DC: National Association of Corporate Directors, 2013).

13 Id.

14 Id. at 40.

15 A. Luijkenaar and K. Spinley, *The Emergence of the Chief Sustainability Officer: From Compliance Manager to Business Partner* (Chicago, IL: Heidrick & Struggles International, 2007), 9.

16 Id. at 11–12.

17 *C-SUITE EXPECTATIONS: Understanding C-Suite Roles beyond the Core* (Washington, DC: National Association of Corporate Directors, 2013), 12.

18 Id. at 13.

19 Adapted from A. Longsworth, H. Doran and J. Webber, "The Sustainability Executive: Profile and Progress" (PWC, September 2012), 18–29.

20 Id. at 34.

21 Id. at 34–35, 40.

22 *CSO Back Story: How Chief Sustainability Officers Reached the C-Suite* (San Francisco, CA: Weinreb Group, September 2011) and *CSO Back Story II: The Evolution of the Chief Sustainability Officer* (San Francisco, CA: Weinreb Group, Fall 2014).

23 Corporate Responsibility Officers Association, *Structuring and Staffing Corporate Responsibility: A Guidebook* (Northampton, MA: Corporate Responsibility Officers Association, 2010), 24.

24 Id. at 28–29.

7 Sustainable Leadership

While all leaders should have a vision and desire to inspire their followers to take collective action to make it happen, sustainability leaders can be distinguished as people who inspire and support action to identify and develop innovative sustainable solutions, business models and practices that will lead to a better world. Sustainable leadership focuses on bringing about dramatic changes and requires taking a long-term perspective in making decisions; fostering systemic innovation aimed at increasing customer value; developing a skilled, loyal and highly engaged workforce; offering quality products, services and solutions; engaging in ethical behavior and decision-making and establishing ethical values and standards throughout the organization.

In order to be effective, sustainability leaders must develop and practice several important habits including a systemic, interdisciplinary understanding; emotional intelligence and a caring attitude; values orientation that shapes culture; a strong vision for making a difference; an inclusive style that engenders trust; a willingness to innovate and be radical; and a long-term perspective on impacts. In addition, they must implement a number of initiatives to establish and maintain the foundation for sustainability throughout their organizations including training and staff development programs, proactively striving for amicable labor relations, development of strategies for staff retention, shifting compensation programs toward metrics that valued contributions to customer loyalty and to innovation, promoting environmental and social responsibility, initiating communications with multiple stakeholders and transparently taking into account and balancing their interests, and developing and embedding a shared vision for the goals of the business.

There is a considerable body of evidence that shows that sustainable leadership practices are more likely to enhance business performance over the long term than the traditional approach that puts the interests of shareholders first and focuses primarily on short-term financial metrics.[1] For example, companies that take a long-term perspective, and attract patient investors that share sustainability values, are able to reap benefits from investing in their people, innovative technologies and strong and enduring relationships with customers and suppliers. This allows those companies to build trust, accumulate and retain knowledge by working hard to train employees and retain them through development programs and finding ways to keep them during difficult economic times, and build an organizational culture that is readily adaptable to change and new opportunities. Moreover, savings realized from recycling and improving the eco-efficiency of operational activities not only strengthens financial performance but also can be re-invested in other environmental and social initiatives. Companies also find that many of the practices associated with sustainable leadership, such as focusing on staff retention and development, ultimately turn out to be important sources of competitive advantage.[2]

Cambridge Sustainability Leadership Model

After surveying the theories of leadership and observing specific practices of leadership relating to sustainability, Visser and Courtice proposed a sustainability leadership model that included three basic components: the external and internal context for the leader's actions; the traits, styles, skills and knowledge of the individual leader; and the internal and external leadership actions taken by the leader.[3] They pointed out that none of the elements of the model were unique to sustainability leaders, nor was the model static: context influenced the characteristics of the individual leader; those characteristics determined the actions taken by the leadership; and the actions impacted and changed both the context and leader's characteristics. However, while the skills, knowledge, styles and action of sustainability leaders evolved in response to changes in context, Visser and Courtice believed that seven core characteristics and habits of effective sustainability leaders remained in place: a systemic, interdisciplinary understanding; emotional intelligence and a caring attitude; values orientation that shapes culture; a strong vision for making a difference; an inclusive style that engenders trust; a willingness to innovate and be radical; and a long-term perspective on impacts.[4]

Traits

Visser and Courtice believed that a sustainability leader typically embodied a number of traits, which they described as distinguishing attributes, qualities or personal characteristics which are generally seen as being enduring, and discussed the following traits that were included in their sustainability leadership model based on evidence of their strong correlation with leadership for sustainability[5]:

- *Caring/morally-driven:* Sustainability leaders demonstrate care for the well-being of humanity and all other forms of life and are guided by a moral compass that incorporates the moral case for sustainable development (i.e., equity today, environmental justice, intergenerational equity and stewardship).

- *Systemic/holistic thinker:* Sustainability leaders are "systems think-ers" with the ability to appreciate the interconnectedness and inter-dependency of the whole system, at all levels, and to recognize how changes to parts of the system affect the whole. Effective sustain-ability leaders are able to simultaneously see and balance an array of issues such as business opportunity, customer satisfaction, job creation, pollution reduction and public policy.
- *Enquiring/open-minded:* Sustainability leaders actively seek new knowledge and diverse opinions, including challenges to their own opinions, and are willing to question received wisdom, traditional models of economic growth and the value of their organization's product or service to society.
- *Self-aware/empathetic:* Sustainability leaders have high levels of "emotional intelligence", including the ability to understand their own emotions and those of others, sincerity, personal humility and ability to listen to others, and the ability to see their own place in and influence on a situation.
- *Visionary/courageous:* Sustainability leaders bring inspiration, cre-ativity, optimism and courage to bear in their roles, are driven to produce results, and possess the ability to balance passion and ideal-ism with ambition and pragmatism. Sustainability leaders must also be courageous to seize opportunities and pursue them in the face of great difficulties and with no map to follow other than the one they draw on their own and no absolute knowledge about what the end destination will be.

Styles

Visser and Courtice noted that a clear distinction should be made be-tween the traits of sustainability leaders and their leadership styles, which were described as the manner and approach that the leader used to provide direction, motivate people and implement plans. Leadership styles have been categorized in a number of different ways including au-tocratic, democratic, laissez-faire charismatic, participative, situational, transactional, transformational, quiet, and servant, and researchers have observed that leaders often use a mix of styles that incorporate varying levels of concern for people and tasks.[6] While sustainability leaders have a number of styles to choose from, ultimately they need to rely on the style that is most effective form them and fits with their own unique set of traits and values. Styles that Visser and Courtice believed would be most effective for sustainability leaders included the following:

- *Inclusive:* Sustainable leaders are inclusive and encourage collab-oration and participation as a means for building commitment. The practice of inclusive leadership includes dialogue and con-sensus, democratic approaches, coaching and affiliative behavior (i.e. promoting harmony among followers, helping to resolve conflict and making sure followers feel connected to each other)[7] and building a climate of peer support and accountability.

- *Visionary:* Visser and Courtice explained that: "the visionary style of leadership brings passion and charisma into the mix. It focuses on challenging and transforming people's perceptions and expectations and motivating them to transcend narrower forms of self-interest".[8]
- *Creative:* Sustainable leaders need to be creative and willing and able to apply that creativity to a number of different roles in the transformation change process: designer, architect, innovator, game changer and systems transformer.
- *Altruistic:* Sustainability leaders are focused on transcending self-interest and focusing their attentions and activities on the collective good, characteristics that are in line with altruistic leadership styles such as servant or "quiet" leadership.
- *Radical:* Radical, or "missionary", leadership is an approaches that differs significantly from quiet leadership and was described by Visser and Courtice as involving taking risks, acting like a revolutionary or activist and challenging the status quo.

Skills

Leaders need a variety of specialized skills in order to effectively direct their businesses and followers in a sustainable economy[9]:

- *Manage complexity:* Visser and Courtice advised that sustainability leaders must be skilled at analyzing, synthesizing, and translating complex issues, responding to risk, uncertainty and dilemmas, recognizing and seizing opportunities and resolving problems and conflicts.
- *Communicate vision:* Effective sustainability leaders have good communication skills and are able to share a long-term vision and facilitate dialog that inspires action and change and creates shared meaning. Relevant techniques include active listening, emotional intelligence and reflection.
- *Exercise judgement:* According to Visser and Courtice, sustainability leaders are skilled to make good and decisive decisions in a timely fashion, including prioritizing, making difficult choices and handling dilemmas. Good judgment is particularly important in times of crisis when leaders must inspire their followers, set expectations and communicate effectively and in a timely manner with stakeholders.
- *Challenge and innovate:* Sustainability leaders need to be good at imagining possible solutions/futures or alternatives, bringing creativity into their thinking and practice and "thinking outside the box". Among other things, sustainability leaders must have the

creativity and insight to develop business models for their companies that allow them to grow in a sustainable way and which involve their full value chain.

- *Think long term:* Since sustainability involves balancing the present and the future, it is not surprising that sustainability leaders are expected to be able to envision and use strategic long-term thinking and planning in order to take into account the needs of future generations.

Knowledge

Visser and Courtice noted that prospective sustainability leaders need to have sufficient knowledge about sustainability in order to translate it into successful business strategies and effectively communicate on issues of sustainability to their followers and the stakeholders of their companies. Among the most important areas of knowledge for sustainability leadership are the following[10]:

- *Global challenges and dilemmas:* Sustainability leaders need to have knowledge about the key pressures on the world's social and ecological systems and the connections between those systems and economic and political forces. Specifically, sustainability executives need to know about the important social and environmental challenges around the globe (e.g., poverty and income inequality, education, pollution, infectious diseases, global warming and climate change) and the role that businesses like theirs can play in addressing those challenges, either on their own or in collaboration with others.
- *Interdisciplinary connectedness:* Sustainability leaders understand that sustainability in business involves multiple dimensions—economic, environmental and social actions and performance—and that they must be mindful of relevance and interconnectedness of a number of knowledge areas including physical sciences, social sciences, technology, business and other disciplines. Knowledge of these areas allows the sustainability leader to critically connect his or her company's financial, human, natural, social and technological assets.
- *Change dynamics and options:* Visser and Courtice noted that sustainability leaders are adept at understanding how complex systems work and are able to deploy a range of options for promoting beneficial change in them (e.g. financial markets, policy options and trends, technology options, consumer behavior and attitudes, organizational dynamics, change models and metrics).
- *Organizational influences and impacts:* Sustainability leaders generate and analyze knowledge about the full impact of their organization's activities as a means for identifying and developing opportunities for value creation and new markets. The key to unlocking this type of

information is creating environmental and social impact matrices and committing to full transparency in reporting on economic, environmental and social performance.

- *Diverse stakeholder views:* Visser and Courtice argued that sustainability leaders are open to different world views and belief systems, both within their communities and across geographic, cultural and political divides, and look for ways to incorporate these appropriately into the organization's overall sustainability initiatives.

Leadership Actions

Visser and Courtice argued that the biggest challenge for sustainability leaders was going beyond saying the right words about sustainability to actually "walking the talk" by taking the actions necessary to execute on the sustainability plans of their organizations. Among the problems that must be overcome are entrenched values and practices within the organization that would be upset by the sustainability strategies, and progress by sustainability leaders will depend on them taking certain internal actions such as providing managers and employees with a compelling vision and strategic goals, creating incentives for integrating sustainability into day-to-day practices, empowering people throughout the organization and providing opportunities to learn about sustainability and its place in the business context. At the same time, sustainability leaders must also look outward and take external actions such as incorporating sustainability principles into customer-oriented activities such as sales and marketing, involving their organizations in cross-sector partnerships and implementing stakeholder engagement and transparent reporting programs.[11]

Avery and Bergsteiner's Sustainable Leadership Practices

Avery and Bergsteiner argued that the best way to understand sustainable leadership practices was to contrast them directly with their polar opposite: "the typical shareholder-first approach, which business schools, management journals, the media, and many practitioners continue to promote".[12] During the course of several studies involving organizations from all around the world, they collectively identified and distinguished two diametrically opposed sets of 23 leadership practices, principles and/or attitudes that formed self-reinforcing systems and which they referred to as the "sustainable 'honeybee' leadership approach" and the "shareholder-first or 'locust' approach".[13] Avery and Bergsteiner arranged the 23 practices in the form of a pyramid with four ascending levels in order to provide guidance for intervention: foundational practices at the bottom, higher-level practices above them, key performance drivers at the third level and, finally, a top level that did not include specific practices but which described performance outcomes that their research showed contributed to sustainability.

Foundation Practices

The 14 "foundation practices" placed at the lowest level of the pyramid could be introduced at any time that the leadership of the organization decided. These leadership elements are included in the table below and contrasted to the approach generally taken by leaders following the shareholder-first philosophy.[14] Implementation of the foundational practices includes a number of different initiatives such as training and staff development programs, proactively striving for amicable labor relations, development of strategies for staff retention, shifting compensation programs toward metrics that valued contributions to customer loyalty and to innovation, promoting environmental and social responsibility, initiating communications with multiple stakeholders and transparently taking into account and balancing their interests, and developing and embedding a share vision for the goals of the business.

Leadership elements	*Sustainable leadership*	*Shareholder-first philosophy*
Developing people	Develops everyone continuously	Develops people selectively
Labor relations	Seeks cooperation	Acts antagonistically
Retaining staff	Values long tenure at all levels	Accepts high staff turnover
Succession planning	Promotes from within whenever possible	Appoints from outside whenever possible
Valuing staff	Is concerned about employees' welfare	Treats people as interchangeable and a cost
CEO and top team	CEO works as top team member or speaker	CEO is decision maker and hero
Ethical behavior	"Doing the right thing" as an explicit core value	Ambivalent, negotiable, an assessable risk
Long- or short-term perspective	Prefers long term to short term	Short-term profits and growth prevail
Organizational change	Change is an evolving and considered process	Change is fast adjustment, volatile, can be *ad hoc*
Financial markets orientation	Seeks maximum independence from others	Follows its masters' will, often slavishly
Responsibility for environment	Protects the environment	Is prepared to exploit the environment
Social responsibility (CSR)	Values people and the community	Exploits people and the community
Stakeholders	Everyone matters	Only shareholders matter
Vision's role in the business	Shared view of future is essential strategic tool	The future does not necessarily drive the business

Higher-Level Practices

Once the foundational practices have been put into place, leaders can begin to introduce one or more of the six higher-level practices placed at the second level of the pyramid. These practices address the leadership elements in the table below and generally involve difficult and time-consuming changes to many key aspects of how business is done on a day-to-day basis.[15] Notably, effective implementation of the higher-level practices requires that related foundational practices already be embedded into the operations and culture of the firm. For example, employees cannot reasonably be expected to become more self-managing unless they have received adequate training and career development and a have a clear sense of the vision for the firm that can be referenced when making decisions during the course of carrying out their job responsibilities and interacting with outside stakeholders such as customers and community groups. Self-management is also supported by long-term relationships with the firm during which employees gain a better understanding of the firm's culture and the networks within the firm that are available for support in resolving issues and launching innovative activities. Development of trust, another one of the higher-level practices, depends on consistent long-term application of the foundational principals such that employees and other stakeholders can rely on the actions that will be taken by the leader and the values that the leader will apply to decisions, operational activities and strategic goals.

Leadership elements	Sustainable leadership	Shareholder-first philosophy
Decision-making	Is consensual and devolved	Is primarily manager-centered
Self-management	Staff are mostly self-managing	Managers manage
Team orientation	Teams are extensive and empowered	Teams are limited and manager-centered
Culture	Foster an enabling, widely-shared culture	Culture is weak except for a focus on short-term results that may or may not be shared
Knowledge sharing and retention	Spreads throughout the organization	Limits knowledge to a few "gatekeepers"
Trust	High trust through relationships and goodwill	Control and monitoring compensate for low trust

Key Performance Drivers

The third level of the pyramid includes three key performance drivers: strategic, systemic innovation; staff engagement; and quality. According to Avery and Bergsteiner, these elements, which are compared and contrasted with the shareholder-first philosophy in the table below, "essentially provide what end-customers experience and so drive organizational performance".[16] Avery and Bergsteiner pointed out that each of the key performance drivers depend on elements lower in the pyramid. For example, they referred to research showing that enhancement of quality occurred when organizations had a team orientation, skilled and empowered employees, and a culture that supported knowledge sharing and the development and maintenance of trust.[17]

Leadership elements	Sustainable leadership	Shareholder-first philosophy
Innovation	Strong, systemic, strategic innovation evident at all levels	Innovation is limited and selective; buys in expertise
Staff engagement	Values emotionally committed staff and the resulting commitment	Financial rewards suffice as motivators, no emotional commitment expected
Quality	Is embedded in the culture	Is a matter of control

Performance Outcomes

At the top of their pyramid, Avery and Bergsteiner placed five performance outcomes that they believed created sustainable leadership, noting that the elements at the lower levels of the pyramid collectively drove organizations to these outcomes[18]:

- Integrity of brand and reputation.
- Enhanced customer satisfaction.
- Solid operational finances (all firms have to survive financially including in the short term).
- Long-term shareholder value.
- Long-term value for multiple stakeholders.

Using the Pyramid

Avery and Bergsteiner advised that their pyramid was intended to be dynamic in all directions and that the interactions between the elements not only flowed bottom-up and top-down, but practices on the same level also influenced each other.[19] They illustrated their point by focusing on trust, one of the higher-level practices, and pointing out that trust would not develop unless and until various other practices had been implemented and embedded including amicable labor relations, development of people, empowered decision-making, and focus on long-term retention of staff and caring for people. Other practices related to development and maintenance of trust include ethical behavior, taking a long-term perspective, practicing environmental and social responsibility, developing honest and trusting relationships with multiple stakeholders and defining and communicating a share vision. Relations and reinforcements among elements can also be seen at the top level of the pyramid: long-term shareholder value is enhanced and protected when companies protect their brands and reputation, keep their customers and investors satisfied.

Avery and Bergsteiner recommended that aspiring sustainable leaders begin with an audit of the perceptions of the current members of their organization as to how the organization is performing with respect to implementation and support of the 23 leadership practices included in the pyramid.[20] The goal is to determine what is working and which areas, particularly at the foundation level, need immediate attention. It is important for all or most of the foundational practices to be in place before moving too aggressively on the higher-level practices and key performance drivers and, in fact, without a solid foundation the leader will find that his or her directives will either be ignored or will face large challenges with respect to implementation. For example, becoming more innovative is not just a matter of increasing research and development spending, it also requires a focus on foundational practices such as taking a long-term vision and training and valuing employees who must cope with innovation in the form of changing job responsibilities and new systems and processes. Innovation also requires higher-level practices such as effective teamwork and collaboration, employees who are willing and able to become more autonomous in managing their jobs and making decisions, and knowledge sharing. The key performance drivers are related and success with innovation will mean better quality in products and services and strengthened staff engagement; however, Avery and Bergsteiner urged patience and counseled that building a successful innovation culture can take as long as ten years.

Ethical Leadership

An ethics-based organizational culture is essential for a sustainable business; however, surveys have repeatedly found that the "tone at the top", the actions and behaviors of organizational leaders, is possibly the greatest influencer of organizational ethics. Everyone throughout the organization, managers and employees, follows the actions of the chief executive officer (CEO) and quickly hears of ethical lapses. As such, it is essential for the CEO and the other members of his or her executive team to make a public commitment to ethical behavior and decision-making and proactively communicate with others in the organization on ways in which they can and should act to further the organization's ethical values and standards. In addition, organizational leaders should create and rigorously administer evaluation and reward systems that take into account ethical goals and standards when decisions are made regarding compensation and promotion. At the same time, codes of ethics should be vigorously enforced and it should be clear to everyone in the organization that failure to act in an ethical manner will lead to swift and severe disciplinary action.[21] Setting the right tone means not only visible positive actions such as supporting local charities but also consciously avoiding actions and behaviors that send the wrong message such as ostentatious use of company airplanes, if there are any; expensive "retreats" for members of the executive team; gaudy refurbishing of the personal offices of executives; excessively large severance packages for executives; and spending lavish amounts of company funds on entertainment and recreation.[22]

While direct responsibility for the "tone at the top" lies with the CEOs and others on the front lines of the company's daily business operations, the board of directors also has a fiduciary and ethical duty to the shareholders and other stakeholders of the company to be mindful of actions and transactions that may be perceived as being ethically unsound. In fact, to the extent that one of the traditional, albeit arguably narrow, duties of the board is to protect and enhance shareholder value, knowingly countenancing acts and contractual relationships with officers that reflect poorly on the company's reputation may rightly be construed as a fiduciary failure on the part of directors. For example, shareholders, employees and other stakeholders might reasonably look askance on directors who have approved gaudy severance packages for CEOs who oversaw extended periods of poor performance and who appear to sit idly by as the media releases embarrassing reports of CEO expenses and/ or unethical practices in the company supply chain come to light.

Notes

1 G. Avery and H. Bergsteiner, "Sustainable Leadership Practices for Enhancing Business Resilience and Performance", *Strategy and Leadership*, 39(3) (2011), 5, 11 (citing S. Ghoshal, "Bad Management Theories are Destroying Good Management Practices", *Academy of Management Learning & Education*, 4(1) (2005), 75).

2 Id. at 12 (citing C. Ichniowski, K. Shaw and G. Prennushi, "The Effects of Human Resource Management Practices on Productivity: A Study of Steel Finishing Lines", *American Economic Review*, 87(3) (1999), 291; B. Pfau and S. Cohen, "Aligning Human Capital Practices and Employee Behavior with Shareholder Value", *Consulting Psychology Journal*, 55(3) (2003), 169; W. Cascio, *Responsible Restructuring: Creative and Profitable Alternatives to Layoffs* (San Francisco, CA: Berrett-Koehler, 2002); R. D'Souza, L. Strazdins, M. Clements, D. Broom, R. Parslow and B. Rodgers, "The Health Effects of Jobs: Status, Working Conditions, or Both?", *Australian & New Zealand Journal of Public Health*, 29(3) (2005), 222; B. Pfau and S. Cohen, "Aligning Human Capital Practices and Employee Behavior with Shareholder Value", *Consulting Psychology Journal*, 55(3) (2003), 169.

3 W. Visser and P. Courtice, *Sustainability Leadership: Linking Theory and Practice* (Cambridge: University of Cambridge Institute for Sustainability Leadership, 2011), 3–4.

4 W. Visser, "The 7 Habits of Effective Sustainability Leaders", CSR International Inspiration Series, No. 12 (2013).

5 W. Visser and P. Courtice, *Sustainability Leadership: Linking Theory and Practice* (Cambridge: University of Cambridge Institute for Sustainability Leadership, 2011), 5–7.

6 Id. at 8 (including citations to sources for each of the leadership styles listed in the text). For further discussion of leadership styles, see A. Gutterman, *Practicing Leadership* (New York: Business Expert Press, 2018).

7 D. Goleman, R. Boyatzis and A. McKee, *Primal Leadership* (Boston, MA: Harvard Business Press, 2002).

8 W. Visser and P. Courtice, *Sustainability Leadership: Linking Theory and Practice* (Cambridge: University of Cambridge Institute for Sustainability Leadership, 2011), 9.

9 Id. at 10–12.

10 Id. at 13–16.

11 Id. at 16–21.

12 G. Avery and H. Bergsteiner, "Sustainable Leadership Practices for Enhancing Business Resilience and Performance", *Strategy and Leadership*, 39(3) (2011), 5–6.

13 Id. at 7 (citing M. Albert, *Capitalism vs Capitalism: How America's Obsession with Individual Achievement and Short-term Profit Has Led It to the Brink of Collapse* (New York: Four Walls Eight Windows, 1993); G. Avery, *Leadership for Sustainable Futures: Achieving Success in a Competitive World* (Cheltenham and Northampton, MA: Edward Elgar, 2005); G. Avery and H. Bergsteiner, *Sustainable Leadership: Honeybee and Locust Approaches* (London: Routledge, 2011); P. Hall and D. Soskice, "An Introduction to Varieties of Capitalism" in P. A. Hall and D. Soskice (Eds.), *Varieties of Capitalism: The Institutional Foundations of Comparative Advantage* (Oxford: Oxford University Press, 2001), 1; W. Hutton, *The World We're in* (London: Little, Brown, 2002); A. Kennedy, *The End of Shareholder Value: The Real Effects of the Shareholder Value Phenomenon and the Crisis It Is Bringing to Business* (London: Orion Business Books, 2000)).

14 Id. Original source for the information in the table was G. Avery and H. Bergsteiner, *Honeybees and Locusts: The Business Case for Sustainable Leadership* (Sydney: Allen & Unwin, 2010), 36–37.

15 Id. at 7.

16 Id. at 7 and 9.

17 See e.g. C. Lakshman, "A Theory of Leadership for Quality: Lessons from TQM for Leadership Theory", *Total Quality Management*, 17(1) (2006), 41; and J. Tarı' and V. Sabater, "Human Aspects in a Quality Management Context and Their Effects on Performance", *International Journal of Human Resource Management*, 17(3) (2006), 484.

18 G. Avery and H. Bergsteiner, "Sustainable Leadership Practices for Enhancing Business Resilience and Performance", *Strategy and Leadership*, 39(3) (2011), 5, 8–9.

19 Id. at 9–10.

20 Id. at 11–12.

21 R. Daft and D. Marcic, *Understanding Management* (5th ed.) (Mason, OH: South-Western Publishing Co., 2006), 141.

22 M. Kelly, J. McGowen and C. Williams, *BUSN* (Independence, KY: South-Western Publishing Company, 2014), 56.

8 Management Systems

A management system refers to what an organization does to manage its structures, processes, activities and resources in order that its products or services meet the organization's objectives, such as satisfying the customer's quality requirements, complying with regulations and/or meeting environmental objectives. Elements of a management system include policy, planning, implementation and operations, performance assessment, improvement and management review. By systemizing the way it does things, an organization can increase efficiency and effectiveness, make sure that nothing important is left out of the process and ensure that everyone is clear about who is responsible for doing what, when, how, why and where. While all organizations should benefit from some form of management system, they are particularly important for larger organizations or ones with complicated processes. Management systems have been used for a number of years in sectors such as aerospace, automobiles, defense and health care.

Organizations implement management systems for a variety of reasons such as achieving business objectives, increasing understanding of current operations and the likely impact of change, communicating knowledge, demonstrating compliance with legal requirements and/or industry standards, establishing "best practice", ensuring consistency, setting priorities or changing behavior. Organizations often have more than one management system to deal with different activities or assets and integrate several related operational areas. For example, a customer relationship management system might be launched to manage relationships with customers. Preventive maintenance management and financial management systems may be used to preserve the value of organizational assets and human resource management systems merge and integrate the principles of human resource management with information technology. Other management systems focus on managing all relevant areas of operation in relation to a specific aspect such as quality, environment, health and safety, information technology, data security, corporate social responsibility, risk management and business continuity.

Even though they may not realize it, all organizations have some sort of management system—"the way things get done"—in place. Elements of the system may be documented in the form of policies and checklists, but much of the system is based on unwritten rules and customs. The interest of organizational leaders in management systems is based not only on the desire to understand how things are currently done but also to find out how "things should be done" in order to improve organizational performance. Fortunately, reference can be made to management system standards, such as those promulgated by the International Organization for Standardization (ISO) (www.iso.org), which are intended to provide all organizations with easy access to international "state-of-the-art" models that they can follow in implementing their own management systems. Management systems standards are concerned with processes, meaning the way that organizations go about carrying out their required work— they are not product and service standards, although processes certainly impact the quality of the organization's final products and services.

Many of the ISO standards are intended to be generic, which means that they can be applied to any organization, large or small, whatever its product or service; in any sector of activity; and whether it is a business enterprise, a public administration or a government department. The standards specify the requirements for a management system (e.g., objectives, policy, planning, implementation and operation, performance assessment, improvement and management review); however, the actual format of the system must be determined by the organization itself taking into account its specific goals and the environment in which it operates. The first ISO standard for many organizations is ISO 9001, which is one of the best known and widely used ISO standards and provides a structure (i.e., a "quality management system") to help organizations develop products and services that consistently ensure customer satisfaction and continuously improve their products, services and processes to fulfill the customer's requirements.[1] ISO standards are available for management systems covering a broad range of additional topics including environment (ISO 14001), medical device quality (ISO 13485), medical devise risk (ISO 14971), information security (ISO 27001 and ISO 27002), business continuity (ISO 22301), supply chain security (ISO 28000), corporate risk (ISO 31000), food safety (ISO 22000), management auditing (ISO 19011) and environmental, health and safety (ISO 45001). Well-known ISO 26000, which can be used by organizations interested in improving their practices with respect to social responsibility, is actually not a management system standard and does not contain requirements.

Implementing any management system, regardless of the system's particular focus (e.g., quality, environment, risk etc.), is a challenging task. In many cases, reference can be made to published management systems standards available from ISO and others; however, there are certain key activities that should always be considered[2]:

* Identifying and understanding the organizational context
* Ensuring that senior management provides leadership in developing and implementing the system

- Developing a plan for the system that incorporates the risks and opportunities that could influence the performance of the system
- Ensuring that the organization is committed to support the system with the necessary internal and external resources
- Developing, planning, documenting, implementing and controlling the organizations' operational processes
- Planning in advance for monitoring, measuring, analyzing and evaluating the performance of the system

While not a requirement of standards such as ISO 9001, organizations may, and often do, seek and obtain certification by independent outside parties that their management systems conform to the requirements of ISO standards. Certification, known in some countries as registration, means that an independent, external body conducts an audit of the organization's management system and verifies that it conforms to the requirements specified in the applicable ISO standard. While organizations often implement and benefit from management systems based on ISO standards without incurring the additional expense of going through the certification process, they may be driven to pursue certification for important business reasons such as satisfying contractual, regulatory or market requirements; meeting customer expectations and preferences; strengthen a risk management program; and/or motivating managers and employees by establishing clear performance goals and objectives.

ISO itself does not carry out certification and does not issue or approve certificates. It is important that the certification body be accredited, which means that a specialized accreditation body has formally endorsed the certification body as being competent to carry out ISO certification in specified business sectors. In lieu of certification, or in preparation for a certification audit, organizations should conduct formal self-assessments on a regular basis that cover quality management system requirements; management responsibility requirements; resource management requirements; product realization requirements (e.g., planning, determination of customer requirements, design and development, purchasing, production and service provision); and measurement, analysis and improvement requirements.[3]

ISO 26000

Organizations interested in improving their practices with respect to social responsibility, including engagement with their stakeholders, may refer to ISO 26000. ISO 26000 defines "social responsibility" as the responsibility of an organization for the impacts of its decisions and activities (i.e., products, services and processes) on society and the environment through transparent and ethical behavior that contributes to sustainable development, including the health and welfare of society; takes into account the expectations of stakeholders; is in compliance with applicable law and consistent with international norms of behavior, and is integrated throughout the organization and practiced in its relationships, which includes all of the organization's activities within its sphere of influence (i.e., relationships through which the organization has the ability to affect the decisions or activities of others).

It is important to remember that although ISO 26000 draws on principles included in management systems developed by the ISO, it is not itself a management system standard and does not contain requirements. Instead, ISO 26000 sets out certain core principles and explains the core subjects and associated issues relating to social responsibility including organizational governance, human rights, labor practices, the environment, fair operating practices, consumer issues and community involvement and development. For each core subject, information is provided on its scope, including key issues; its relationship to social responsibility; related principles and considerations; and related actions and expectations. For example, with respect to labor practices, one of the core subjects, organizations are reminded to integrate consideration of the following issues into their policies, organizational culture, strategies and operations: employment and employment relationships; conditions of work and social protection; social dialogue; health and safety at work; and human development and training in the workplace.[4] ISO 26000 also emphasizes the importance of "stakeholder identification and engagement" as being central to addressing an organization's social responsibility.

Recommended steps for using ISO 26000 include the following:

- Setting the direction from the top by building social responsibility into governance and procedures and integrating social responsibility throughout the organization by using mission and vision statements to define values
- Identifying relevant social responsibility issues, determining relevance and significance of the identified issues and establishing priorities such as gap analysis (i.e., identify gaps between current and desired position)
- Assessing the organization's responsibilities and potential impact in its sphere of influence (e.g., decisions regarding product design can impact suppliers and the resources/raw materials that are used in the manufacturing process)
- Performing "due diligence" (i.e., the process of identifying the actual and potential negative social, environmental and economic impacts of an organization's decisions and activities, with the aim of avoiding and mitigating those impacts) by reviewing the legal requirements and context of activities and involving relevant stakeholders throughout the organization's sphere of influence
- Setting short-term and long-term goals and applying social responsibility to decisions on purchasing, investing, hiring and promoting, advertising, community relations etc.

- Identifying current weaknesses and the causes behind them; identifying the resources needed to overcome the weaknesses (i.e., personnel, time, money, partners etc.); and developing a timeline and action plan to bridge the gaps
- Incorporating transparency and accountability at all levels through reporting and other communications with stakeholders that describe the organization's activities on relevant issues within each of the seven core subjects and establish a continuing dialogue based on honest disclosure and meeting the specific needs of each stakeholder group with respect to the tone and content of communications
- Continuously reviewing and improving social responsibility performance through monitoring and measuring and making improvements in the reliability of information and management processes

There is no certification process for ISO 26000; however, organizations have communicated, if accurate, their effective use of the standard in a variety of ways including public declarations such as the following: "We have **used/applied** ISO 26000 as a **guide/framework/basis** to **integrate/ implement** social responsibility into our values and practices" and "We recognize ISO 26000 as a reference document that provides guidance for integration/implementation of social responsibility/socially responsible behavior". It is not appropriate to use wording such as "certified according to ISO 26000" or "meets the requirements of ISO 26000".[5]

ISO 14001 and Environmental Management Systems

ISO 14001 is an internationally agreed standard that sets out the requirements for a structure (i.e., an environmental management system (EMS)) to help organizations manage and minimize their environmental impacts, conform to applicable legal requirements and improve their environmental performance through more efficient use of resources and reduction of waste, thereby gaining a competitive advantage and the trust of stakeholders.[6] An EMS helps organizations identify, manage, monitor and control their environmental issues in a holistic manner and also includes the need for continual improvement of an organization's systems and approach to environmental concerns. ISO 14001 is suitable for organizations of all types and sizes, be they private, not-for-profit or governmental, and requires that an organization consider all environmental issues relevant to its operations, such as air pollution, water and sewage issues, waste management, soil contamination, climate change mitigation and adaptation, and resource use and efficiency. While an EMS may be adopted as a standalone system, it is often added to an existing management system (e.g., a system based on quality, such as ISO 9001).

Organizations that have adopted and implemented ISO 14001 standards have reported that it has helped demonstrate compliance with current and future statutory and regulatory requirements; increase leadership involvement and engagement of employees; improve company reputation and the confidence of stakeholders through strategic communication; achieve strategic business aims by incorporating environmental issues into business management; provide a competitive and financial advantage through improved efficiencies and reduced costs; and encourage better environmental performance of suppliers by integrating them into the organization's business systems. There is no requirement that organizations seek and obtained accredited certification to ISO 14001 and there are many benefits from using the standard without going through the accredited certification process. However, third-party certification has been found to be an excellent way for organizations to assure their stakeholders that the standards have been implemented correctly and may also be necessary for organizations to fulfill regulatory or contractual requirements.

In general, an EMS that is to be based on ISO 14001 standards should include the following elements[7]:

- Development and establishment of an appropriate environmental policy that is documented and communicated to employees and also made available to the public and which includes a commitment to continual improvement and pollution prevention, regulatory compliance and a framework for setting policy objectives
- A planning phase that covers the identification of the environmental aspects of the organization's activities, identification and access to legal requirements, establishment and documentation of objectives and targets consistent with the and establishment of a program for achieving said targets and objectives (including the designation of responsible individuals, necessary means and timelines)
- Implementation and operation of the EMS including the definition, documentation and communication of roles and responsibilities, provision of appropriate training, assurance of adequate internal and external communication, written management system documentation as well as appropriate document control procedures, documented procedures for operational controls, and documented and communicated emergency response procedures
- Checking and corrective action procedures, including procedures for regular monitoring and measurement of key characteristics of the operations and activities, procedures for dealing with situations of non-conformity, specific record maintenance procedures and procedures for auditing the performance of the EMS
- Periodic management reviews of the overall EMS to ensure its suitability, adequacy and effectiveness in light of changing circumstances

A report prepared by consultants from the Rand Corporation on the keys to successfully implementing environmental management found that it was important for organizations to integrate its environmental management program with the management system it uses to plan and execute its core missions and functions. In this way, managers would view environmental issues as being just one more relevant context in which they pursued the core values of the organization.[8] The report suggested that insights gained from surveying the best commercial practices indicated that successful and effective integration could be achieved by taking the following steps:

- Identify how environmental issues affect its key stakeholders and how these issues relate to stakeholder goals
- Develop and sustain senior leadership support for proactive treatment of environmental issues
- Identify champions who can take day-to-day responsibility for managing environmental issues to satisfy the specific stakeholder goals that the senior leadership has endorsed
- Make environmental principals in the organization effective partners in coalitions in the organization to align environmental interests with other specialized interests
- After identifying the organization's position in the value chains that it services, work with other elements of these value chains to achieve common goals
- State specific environmental goals in simple terms that help individual decision makers relate them to broader corporate goals without much ambiguity
- For specific decisions or projects, use teams that include representatives of all the relevant functions, including environmental representatives when appropriate
- Promote routine use of databases and analytic tools that help decision makers see how environmental decisions affect all parts of the organization
- Balance centralization and decentralization to align environmental concerns with the most closely related core activities

Companies often implement several different, but interrelated, environmental management programs as part of their overall environmental strategy. Common areas of focus include product design, which involves continuous efforts of design teams to locate new materials and technologies to ensure that future products are at the leading edge of commercial environmental product design and recognition of specific design considerations such as environmentally oriented materials selection, design to facilitate cleaner production, design for durability and extended product life, design for refurbishment and reuse and design for disassembly and recycling; supply chain management, which involves routine dialog with supply chain members about their efforts to create and maintain a sustainable production system and adhere to environmental requirements through continuous improvement actions; operations, including certification of the company's EMS; product stewardship, including a robust and practical end-of-life management approach that maximizes environmental and economic value; and communications with internal and external stakeholders regarding sustainability.[9]

Environmental, Health and Safety Management Systems

Experts have identified essential elements for an effective environmental, health and safety (EH&S) management system as including management leadership, commitment and accountability; risk planning, assessment and management; facility/site and equipment/tool safety management; EH&S regulatory management, information and documentation; EH&S planning and procedures; personnel and organizational competence and training; emergency management and community awareness; incident investigation, analysis and management; management of change; third party services; and EH&S performance monitoring, measurement, reporting and improvement.[10]

An important tool for companies seeking to implement EH&S management systems was introduced by ISO in 2018 when the new ISO 45001 standard on occupational health and safety (OH&S) management systems was finalized and published. ISO 45001 is intended to help organizations reduce the burden of occupational accidents and illnesses by providing a framework to improve employee safety, reduce workplace risks and create better, safer working conditions, all over the world. ISO 45001 follows other generic management system approaches such as ISO 14001 and ISO 9001 and also takes into account other relevant internal standards such as OHSAS 18001 (an international standard that has provided a framework to identify, control and decrease the risks associated with health and safety within the workplace), the International Labour Organization's ILO-OSH Guidelines, various national standards and the ILO's comprehensive international labor standards and conventions. The ISO has explained that an effective OH&S management system enables organizations to provide safe and healthy workplaces, prevent work-related injury and ill health, and continually improve its OH&S performance.[11]

Illustrative Framework for a CSR/CG Management System

An illustration of how a sustainability-focused management system might be designed and implemented was provided by Castka et al., who described a Corporate Social Responsibility/Corporate Governance (CSR/CG) management system intended to be compatible with other management system standards, particularly ISO 9001 and ISO 14001.[12] The key elements of their system include defining the organization's CSR/CG policy; identifying the expectations of stakeholders; identifying and evaluating the organization's environmental and social impacts and risks; strategic planning and establishing the organization's CSR/CG objectives, targets and indicators; establishing and discharging the responsibilities of the board of directors and senior management with respect to managing the system; disclosure and reporting activities; monitoring, measuring and analyzing the processes included in the system; and managing change and ensuring continual improvement of the system.

CSR/CG Policy

According to Castka et al., one of the first steps to be taken is for the board of directors and senior management to define the CSR/CG policy of the organization and ensure that the policy[13]:

- Is appropriate to the nature, scale and business impacts of the organization's activities, products or services
- Specifies expected organizational ethics policies pertaining to bribery and corruption
- Includes a commitment by the organization and its personnel to comply with relevant national and other laws that are applicable, and with other requirements (e.g., voluntary standards) to which the organization subscribes
- Includes a commitment by the organization and all of its personnel to conform to all requirements of the management system
- Includes a commitment to continual improvement and prevention of adverse social and environmental impacts of the organization
- Is effectively documented, implemented, maintained, communicated and accessible in an appropriate way to all stakeholders and the general public

Stakeholder Expectations

Castka et al. emphasized that when an organization is developing and implementing the management system, it is important to identify and understand the needs of its stakeholders. As such, the organization must ensure that there is a process to ensure meaningful inclusion of stakeholders, which includes identifying them and describing the organization's relationship with each individual group, demonstrating inclusive engagement of stakeholders on issues of significant concern to them and demonstrating that an appropriate approach has been used to enable stakeholders to express their views and opinions.[14]

Identification and Evaluation of Impacts and Risks

Once stakeholder identification and engagement has been launched, Castka et al.'s view was that stakeholder expectations should be evaluated in light of the aspects of the "Triple Bottom Line" (i.e., economic, environmental and social). They advised that part of this process should be an evaluation of the social and environmental impacts of the activities (including business relationships), products and services that the organization can control and influence. Records of that evaluation should be maintained and should include, but not necessarily be restricted to, financial health, corporate governance and business ethics, workplace health and safety, human rights issues, individual supply chains and the overall supply web, business partners and communications. Castka et al. called on organizations to also identify the business risks to the organization, including regulatory risks, risks identified through stakeholder involvement, damage to the reputation of the organization, risks that can affect the market position of the organization and product/service failure. Risks related to CSR/CG can be identified and evaluated in the context of the organization's existing formalized approaches to risk management using systems and programs that have come to be known as "enterprise risk management", or "ERM". ERM has been conceived as a comprehensive solution to risk management that requires that all strategic, management and operational tasks of an organization be enabled through projects, functions, and processes so that those tasks are aligned to a common set of risk management objectives. Many organizations have created a separate chief risk officer position and board-level risk management committees. If that is the case, the activities of the position and committee should be carefully coordinated with those of the chief sustainability officer and his or her support group.

Strategic Planning

Castka et al. counseled that once the impacts and risks have been identified in the manner described above, it is time for the organization to assess the likelihood and consequences of identified adverse impacts and risks and transform the most salient of those impacts and risks into an overall CSR/CG strategic plan that includes objectives, targets and indicators. The plan should not only address the areas of greatest risk to the organization through preventative measures, but should also include strategies and tactics to take advantage of opportunities in the organization's environmental and social context that are suited to its core competencies. For example, many companies have re-designed their products to incorporate sustainability into inputs, processes, design and recycling, actually reducing costs and fulfilling the demands and expectations of consumers want to do business with environmentally and socially responsible firms. The strategic plan should provide for adequate financial support and personnel deployment, establishment of control mechanisms and maintenance of records. The CSR/CG objectives, targets and indicators should be documented and reviewed at determined intervals.[15]

Managing the CSR/CG System

Castka et al. admonished organizations to implement their strategic plan with respect to CSR/CG objectives and targets through an appropriate management system and related processes that is monitored by the board of directors and supported by adequate resources.[16] The organization should manage and improve the processes of its CSR/CG system in order to run the business profitably and ethically and determine, provide and optimize resources to manage and continually improve the CSR/CG system; the relationship of the organization with the stakeholders; the infrastructure, work environment and staff relations of the organization; and the supply web and partnerships of the organization. Castka et al. suggested the following list of board and management responsibilities and actions with respect to managing the organization's CSR/CG system:

- The board/management should ensure that roles, responsibilities and authorities are defined, documented and communicated within the organization to facilitate an effective CSR/CG management system
- The board/management should appoint a member or members of the board/management with adequate influence or status within the organization who, irrespective of other responsibilities, would ensure that processes needed for the CSR/CG management system were established, implemented and maintained; report to the board/management on the performance of the CSR/CG management system for review and any need for improvement; and ensure the promotion of awareness of stakeholder expectations throughout the organization
- The organization should allow non-management personnel to choose a representative from their own group to facilitate effective communication with the board/management on matters related to the CSR/CG management system
- The organization should establish and maintain compliance with legal and other regulatory requirements relevant to its activities, products or services
- The board/management should ensure that appropriate communication processes are established with all of the organization's stakeholders and that communication takes place between the various employee levels and functions of the organization regarding the effectiveness of the CSR/CG management system
- The organization should identify training needs of all personnel who are involved in managing, auditing, improving and controlling elements of the CSR/CG management system, and ensure that they receive appropriate training and continually develop their competence
- The organization should identify and ensure compliance with all rules and regulations of the jurisdiction in question and with relevant international norms pertaining to CG, CSR, environmental and

consumer law, fair labor standards, human rights, health and safety protection and similar, as required by law or agreed upon through effective stakeholder engagement

Disclosure and Reporting

An important and unique characteristic of a CSR/CG management system is the need to focus on disclosure and reporting activities. As such, Castka et al. called on organizations to ensure that timely and accurate disclosure is made on all matters relevant to stakeholders including, without limitation, the financial and operating results of the organization; organization objectives; major share ownership and voting rights; members of the board and key executives, and their remuneration; material foreseeable risk factors; material issues regarding employees and other stakeholders; governance structures and policies; and the status of legal and regulatory compliance relevant to operations. In addition, the organization should commit to preparation and dissemination of a social and ethical report at determined intervals. The information disclosed in these reports must be prepared in accordance with high quality reporting procedures or as agreed with stakeholders receiving this information and the reports should clearly explain how the performance of the organization relates to its CSR/CG objectives, targets and indicators; provide a comparison of these over time and across organizations; credibly address issues of concern to stakeholders; include information about the performance of the organization measured against its CSR/CG objectives, targets and indicators; describe responsibilities and activities of an audit committee; and present a balanced and reasonable contribution of the organization to sustainable development.[17]

Monitoring and Measurement

As with any management system, it is the responsibility of the organization, through the leadership of its board of directors, to plan, monitor, measure, analyze and continually improve its CSR/CG management system. Castka et al. noted that, among other things, this means establishing methods for measuring stakeholder satisfaction and development; financial health; access to capital; operational efficiency; environmental performance; intellectual capital; brand value and reputation; potential for innovation; risk profile; performance of the board; improvement of organizational systems; and compliance with legal and regulatory requirements of the organization. The measurement process should be overseen by an internal audit committee and audit function and the organization should demonstrate the credibility of its CSR/CG management system through third-party verification and/or external audit including verification of its annual reports.[18]

Continuous Review and Improvement

Castka et al. made it clear that the board of directors and senior management should be expected to review the CSR/CG management system at pre-determined intervals to ensure its adequacy, suitability, and continuing effectiveness. In order for the review process to be meaningful, the directors and senior managers must have access to the results of audits and results from an audit committee; feedback from stakeholders; data on the performance of the CSR/CG management system; the status of preventive and corrective actions; and follow-up from previous board/management reviews. The board/management review for the CSR/CG management system can be incorporated into other reviews such as board meetings, quality management reviews or similar reviews. Based on these reviews, the board of directors and senior management should be able to make recommendations for improvement, including changes to policy, objectives and other elements of the CSR/CG management system. In addition, the organization should investigate, address and respond to the concerns of it stakeholders and to any non-conformances in the CSR/CG management system (i.e., take actions to eliminate the causes of non-conformance of the CSR/CG management system and/or prevent their re-occurrence). According to Castka et al., the overriding goal should be to establish effective ways for the organization to continually improve its CSR/CG management system and develop an organizational culture that is responsive to continual change and the pursuit to responsible corporate behavior.[19]

Notes

1 ISO 9001 gives the requirements for what the organization must do to manage processes affecting the quality of its final products and services; however, ISO 9001 is not a product or service standard, nor does it specify what the objectives of the organization should be with respect to "quality" or "meeting customer requirements", each of which must be defined by organizations on their own. See the ISO publications "Overview of ISO 9001 and ISO 14001" and "ISO 9001:2015", each of which is available at the ISO website (www.iso.org).
2 "ISO 9001 2015—Plain English Outline" Retrieved from http://www.praxiom.com/iso-9001-outline.htm.
3 See http://cw.routledge.com/textbooks/eresources/9781856176842/Requirement_checklist.pdf.
4 ISO 26000, *Guidance on Social Responsibility: Discovering ISO 26000* (Geneva: International Organization for Standardization, 2014) and *Handbook for Implementers of ISO 26000, Global Guidance Standard on Social Responsibility by Small and Medium Sized Businesses* (Middlebury, VT: ECOLOGIA, 2011). The discussion of ISO 26000 in this section is adapted from ISO 26000 Basic Training Manual (ISO 26000 Post Publication Organization, March 15, 2016). ISO 26000 is available for purchase from ISO webstore at the ISO website (www.iso.org) and general information about ISO 26000 can be obtained at www.iso.org/sr.

5 See ISO 26000 Communication Protocol, https://www.iso.org/files/live/sites/isoorg/files/standards/docs/en/iso_26000_comm_protocol_n15.pdf.

6 The summary discussion of ISO 14001 herein is adapted from "Introduction to ISO 14001: 2015" prepared and distributed by the International Organization for Standardization in 2015.

7 ISO 14001, *Environmental Management System Self-Assessment Checklist* (Washington, DC: Global Environmental Management Initiative, November 2000), 2. While the guidelines in the text are based on a prior version of ISO 14001, they remain relevant as an overview of how organizations should approach the process of fulfilling the ISO 14001 standards.

8 F. Camm, J. Drezner, B. Lachman and S. Resetar, *Implementing Proactive Environmental Management: Lessons Learned from Best Commercial Practice* (Arlington, VA: National Defense Research Institute/RAND, 2001), xii–xiii.

9 *Sustainable Business: A Handbook for Starting a Business* (New Zealand Trade and Enterprise).

10 Adapted from Statement of Environment, Health and Safety Policy issued by Kenny Ogilvie, CEO of EHS Support, on August 24, 2012, http://www.ehs-support.com/wp-content/uploads/EHSMS-Manual.pdf.

11 https://www.iso.org/obp/ui/#iso:std:iso:45001:ed-1:v1:en.

12 P. Castka, C. Bamber and J. Sharp, *Implementing Effective Corporate Social Responsibility and Corporate Governance: A Framework* (London: British Standards Institution and the High Performance Organization Ltd., 2005).

13 Id. at 7. See also Chapter 10 (Internal Sustainability-Related Codes and Policies) in this volume.

14 Id. at 11.

15 For detailed discussion of strategic planning relating to sustainability and CSR, see A. Gutterman, *Strategic Planning for Sustainability* (New York: Business Expert Press, 2020).

16 P. Castka, C. Bamber and J. Sharp, *Implementing Effective Corporate Social Responsibility and Corporate Governance: A Framework* (London: British Standards Institution and the High Performance Organization Ltd., 2005), 7–10 and 13–15.

17 Id. at 6–8.

18 Id. at 15–18.

19 Id. at 19–20.

9   Ethical Management

Sustainable management is ethical management, and businesses seeking to act in a sustainable manner need to take ethics seriously and establish and enforce ethical standards for current and future workers. However, defining "ethics" and identifying "ethical behavior" are not easy tasks. It is has been said that, in general, ethics can be defined as a set of beliefs about right and wrong, good and bad, and that business ethics is the application of right and wrong, good and bad in a business setting.[1] Daft and Marcic defined ethics as "the code of moral principles and values that governs the behaviors of a person or group with respect to what is right or wrong" and explained that ethics can be seen as setting the standards for what is good or bad in conduct and decision-making when the conduct or decision may harm or benefit others.[2]

The concept of "ethics management" has been described as a managerial function to regulate the conduct or behavior of the employees from top to bottom through written code or unwritten code and as a managerial tool to enforce integrity of employees where codified rules and regulations are absent yet it is necessary for employees and the company to follow reasonable ethical standards or well-founded standards of right and wrong that prescribe what humans ought to do.[3] Managerial ethics include principal-based ethics about what is considered fair and ethical in the scope of the workplace (e.g., department boundaries and the use of company equipment), policy-based ethics that cover responses to various situations that arise in the course of day-to-day workplace activities such as conflicts of interest and responding to gifts from vendors and other business partners and strategic-based ethics which includes decisions made with regard to the plans that the company intends to pursue in order to achieve its financial goals and objectives (e.g., deciding whether to outsource manufacturing activities to reduce costs even though taking such an action would mean laying off workers in the community in which the company is headquartered).[4]

Ethics and ethical behavior has always been a concern for managers; however, ethical issues have become even more important over the years beginning in the early 2000s when news of corporate scandals based on fraud, financial dishonesty and personal greed of senior executives emerged from major US corporations such as Enron, Arthur Andersen, Adelphia, WorldCom and Tyco, In the aftermath of the distressing events at these companies and many others, surveys showed that large numbers of Americans believed that questionable business practices were widespread and that the honesty of chief executive officers (CEOs) should be questioned. A significant percentage of survey respondents reported that they had personally observed their managers making false or misleading promises to customers, discriminating in hiring or promotions and violating employees' rights.[5] Another factor that has made business ethics even more complex and challenging is the accelerating globalization of business activities that has pushed executives, managers and employees to interact with counterparts in foreign countries where the answers to questions about what constitutes ethical behavior may be quite different. For example, numerous surveys have shown that a number of countries continue to consider bribery an acceptable, even necessary, practice in order to conduct business.

Daft and Marcic suggested that ethics and ethical standards can be understood by reference to a continuum of human behavior that crosses three categories or domains.[6] At one extreme is the domain of "codified law", which includes the legal standards for conduct formally set out in statutes, regulations and court decisions. In the business context, these standards include requirements such as obtaining licenses to engage in certain business activities, paying corporate taxes, refraining from anti-competitive activities prescribed under antitrust laws and fully and truthfully disclosing all material facts about a company's business and financial condition. At the opposite end of the continuum is a second domain, referred to as "free choice", which includes behavior that is not covered by any legal standard as to which individuals and companies have complete freedom, at least in the eyes of the law, and are only accountable to themselves. In the middle of the continuum, between law and free choice, is the domain of ethics. No specific laws apply in this domain; however, individuals and companies are not free to act only in their own interest, ignoring the interests of others, but are instead expected to engage in conduct and make decisions based on shared principles and values about moral conduct that guide an individual or company and take into account the interests of the larger community.

Developing an ethical corporate culture reinforced by codes of ethical conduct is a way for companies to intelligently bridge the gap between the domains of codified law and free choice. Compliance with the rule of law is necessary for companies to avoid fines and other sanctions that can cripple their businesses, and sometimes put them out of business altogether. However, it is a mistake to assume that if a law does not apply then companies have a free choice to act as they wish. Ethically focused companies recognize the middle domain and the role that ethics plays in contributing to the greater social good. A well-written code of ethics supported by a strong ethical corporate culture eliminates the need for writing more formal laws and reduces the dangers associated with allowing executives, managers and employees to make choices based solely on their personal interests.[7] That said, while laws stipulate what is right or wrong—legal or illegal—a code of ethics cannot fully resolve an ethical dilemma on its own and at best provides individuals and companies with tools to identify and understand the dilemma and guidelines for coming to ethical decisions.

The Manager's Personal Moral Development

Each manager brings his or her own specific personality and behavioral traits to the job and a manager's value system is shaped by his or her personal needs, family influence, social group and religious background, as well as the societal culture in which he or she lives and works.[8] Daft and Marcic argued that a manager's ability to make ethical decision depends heavily on certain personal characteristics including ego strength, self-confidence, a strong sense of independence and the level of personal moral development. With respect to personal moral development, they suggested that people could be placed within a model that had three levels[9]:

- Pre-conventional level: At this basic level, individuals are concerned with external rewards and punishments and obey authority to avoid detrimental personal consequences. The leadership style associated with this level is autocratic or coercive and employees are primarily focused on dependable accomplishment of the specific tasks that have been assigned to them.
- Conventional level: At this next level, people have learned to conform to the expectations of good behavior set by their colleagues, family, friends and society in general and place greater importance on meeting their social and interpersonal obligations. The preferred leadership style is guiding, encouraging and team-oriented and employees prefer work group collaboration to accomplish organizational goals.
- Post-conventional level: The highest level, also referred the principled level, finds individuals guided by an internal set of values and standards regarding justice and right and may disobey rules or laws that violate these principles and/or defy the expectations of others inside or outside the organization. At this level, an individual acknowledges that people hold different values and seeks creative solutions to ethical dilemmas that balance concern for the individual and concern for common good. Transforming or servant leadership is the preferred leadership style and employees are empowered and fully participating in decision-making.

Managers should feel a duty and obligation to strive to achieve the highest level of personal moral development. Daft and Marcic opined that the great majority of managers operate at level two, a few have not advanced beyond level one and only about 20% of all adults in the United States reach the post-conventional, or principled, level of personal moral development. An individual's aspirations to act in an ethical fashion will inevitably be challenged by basic fears and other emotions that can cloud their judgement at any particular moment. For example, the pressure to behave unethically can become intense when a person is concerned about losing his or her job, feeling pressure from time and management to produce results, pursuing his or her personal ambitions for attainment of career goals or acting out a revenge for a perceived wrong inflicted upon him or her by a person or the company itself.[10]

Moreover, not only must managers discipline themselves to act in an ethical manner—adhering to standards of fairness and acting properly and ethically in their dealings with others—they must also be prepared and able to encourage the moral development of other members of the organization and provide encouragement, guidance and support for the ethical behavior of all employees.[11] Companies have begun including ethical factors in the performance review criteria used for managers, such as gauging how well managers treat their employees and otherwise live up to the standards set out in the company's code of ethics.

Ethical Organizational Culture

While individual integrity and ethical values play a large role in any one person's behavior and decisions, executives, managers and employees are inevitably influenced by the values, attitudes, beliefs, expectations and behavior patterns of the organizational culture in which they operate.[12] This is particularly true given that, as discussed above, most people are at level two of personal moral development and thus feel a strong duty to fulfill the obligations and expectations of others including the persons in their specific social networks within their organization. A strong corporate culture can be an important tool in helping executives, managers and employees make ethical decisions in a continuously shifting business environment that brings changes on a daily basis and creates new problems for which solutions have yet to be developed. While hopefully the obligations and expectations embedded in the organizational culture are ethically sound, if a person works within a team, department or an entire organization where unethical behavior is tolerated or even encouraged it is more likely that he or she will be socialized into thinking that it is necessary to follow suit. In fact, a person working in that type of culture may became fearful about losing his or her job if she does not go along with the unethical behavior.

Common elements of organizational culture can be used to create and enhance an ethical mindset among executives, managers and employees. Daft and Marcic suggested that high ethical standards can be affirmed and communicated through public awards and ceremonies and that people can be recognized and celebrated as organizational heroes, and thus role models, based on their ethical decision-making practices.[13] Kelly et al. reported on research carried out by the Ethics Resource Center (ERC) that suggested that organizational culture has more influence than any other variable on the ethical conduct of individual employees and that, in fact, organizations with a strong ethical culture had significantly lower levels of observed misconduct.[14] Kelly et al. noted that the ERC found that the key elements of a strong organizational culture included displays of ethics-related actions at all levels of an organization and accountability at all levels for acting in a manner that conforms to company standards (i.e., the company proactively and consistently confronts misconduct and establishes and enforces a rigorous system of sanctions and remedial actions to reduce the likelihood of recurrences).[15]

Code of Ethics

One of the elements of a strong ethically-focused organizational culture is formal documents that provide concrete guidelines for ethical behavior and making ethical decisions. Companies of all sizes have taken to creating formal ethics programs and the centerpiece of these programs is a written code of ethics that serves as a formal statement of the organization's values concerning ethics and social issues.[16] The code of ethics explicitly announces the company's intent to act in an ethical manner in furtherance of its core values and lays out overriding principals and specific rules and procedures that employees are expected to follow when confronted with an array of common situations that raise ethical dilemmas. The code of ethics should be supported by continuous communications to employees and appropriate training programs.[17]

Codes can be presented using several different approaches and formats. For example, the code of ethics for some organizations is essentially a list of core principles, accompanied by a brief description of each, intended to define fundamental values that organizational leaders hope to infuse into the organization's culture such as integrity, quality, safety, diversity and inclusion, trust and respect, corporate citizenship and stakeholder success.[18] Other organizations implement codes of ethics or conduct that are based on setting out policies and procedures that members of the organization are expected to follow in specific ethical situations. As is the case with the principle-based approach, the intent is that the code will serve as a foundation for the workplace culture and a guide for conducting business affairs in an ethical manner. For example, the code of ethics or conduct may require that employees:

- Not engage in any activity that might create a conflict of interest for the employee or the organization and inform his/her management of

potential conflicts of interests that may give the impression of influence over his/her judgment and actions
- Not take advantage of their organizational position to seek personal gain through the inappropriate use of organizational or non-public information or abuse such position
- Observe fair dealing in all of my transactions and interactions
- Protect all organizational, customer and supplier assets and use them only for appropriate organization approved activities
- Without exception, comply with all applicable laws, rules and regulations
- Promptly report any illegal or unethical conduct to management or other appropriate authorities

While the specifics in the code of ethics will vary substantially among organizations, certain steps must always be taken in order to ensure that efforts to create a meaningful and impactful code of ethics are successful. For example, the board of directors and members of the senior management team must enthusiastically and visibly buy-in to the code and commit to following through on enforcing the ethical principals in the code. These organizational leaders must not only communicate repeatedly about the importance of ethics, but must also prioritize leading by example. Expectations regarding ethical behavior should apply to all levels of the organization and to outside parties such as suppliers, distributors and customers. If the company has operations in foreign countries, the code should be customized so that it is applicable both globally and locally, which often means translating the code into multiple languages and conducting training that addresses unique situations that might arise in a particular country. Finally, in order to retain employee trust, the company must enforce the code of ethics so that everyone knows that there will be consequences to violating ethical norms.[19]

Compliance Programs

Since laws can form the boundaries and a basis for human and corporate conduct, and laws and ethics together define acceptable behavior, companies should implement compliance programs as a fundamental aspect of their overall ethics initiatives.[20] Compliance programs build awareness among executives, managers and employees of the specific legal requirements that are applicable to the company's activities and which need to be considered when taking actions within the company (e.g., actions and decisions subject to laws and regulations relating to the employment relationship) and in dealings with customers, suppliers, regulators and other external stakeholders.

Organizational Structure

Organizations striving to improve their ethical profile create various organizational structures and systems to help put values into practice and shape and influence ethical behavior throughout the organization. One structural move is the creation of an ethics committee and the appointment of a chief ethics officer. The role of the ethics committee, which is composed of executives from different functional areas, is to oversee the company's ethics and this includes interpreting, clarifying and communicating the codes of ethics, resolving thorny ethical issues and, quite importantly for the signals sent to other managers and employees, disciplining wrongdoers.

The ethics committee is led by the chief ethics officer, who is an executive of the company with responsibility for overseeing all aspects of ethics including[21]:

- Establishing and broadly communicating ethical standards
- Developing and maintaining policies and procedures for the general operation of the ethics program, including standards of ethical conduct and related activities
- Overseeing the ongoing operation of the ethics program
- Collaborating with other departments to ensure that there are reasonable and appropriate channels for reporting, investigating and resolving ethical issues
- Responding to alleged violations of rules, regulations, policies, procedures, and standards of ethical conduct
- Identifying potential areas of vulnerability and risk, developing plans for resolution and providing guidance on how to avoid similar situations in the future
- Advising senior managers as they make ethical decisions and providing counseling for employees faced with ethical dilemmas
- Regularly reporting to executives and board members on the operation and progress of compliance efforts
- Developing and maintaining an ethics communication program for the organization, including ethics/compliance, awareness of standards of ethical conduct, and understanding of new and existing ethics issues
- Working with the human resources department and others as appropriate to develop a corporate ethics training program
- Establishing and administering confidential hotlines that managers and employees can use to report behavior they believe to be unethical or otherwise questionable

Reporting channels for the chief ethics officer should be carefully considered. In general, the position reports to the CEO with a dotted-line reporting structure to the chair of the committee of the board of directors responsible for overseeing ethics issues, which may be the audit committee or a separate ethics committee that also has authority over related areas such as compliance and/or corporate governance. If an ethics issue arises with respect to the CEO and/or other members of the executive team, the chief ethics officer should report the matter directly to the appropriate board member and seek guidance from the relevant board committee as to the steps that should be taken with respect to notifying the CEO.

Ethics Training

Ethics training is one of the most important activities for the chief ethics officer and his or her staff and companies implement training programs as a means for assisting executives, managers and employees in identifying ethical issues and applying the principles of the code of ethics to their day-to-day activities. Ethics must play a role in new employee orientation and in all ongoing training. Larger companies typically require all employees to participate in ethics training at least annually and many firms, large and small, have training events more frequently (e.g., weekly or monthly meetings to discuss workplace ethics and role play the proper steps for assessing commonplace ethical dilemmas). Specialized training should be made available for employees who face more temptation (e.g., purchasing agents, overseas sales reps).[22] Of course, a training program will only be effective if organizational leaders support and practice the principles that are covered in the program.

Whistleblower Procedures

One area where the law has moved over the soft line between the legal and ethical domains is "whistleblowing", which is disclosure by managers or employees of illegal, immoral, illegitimate, dangerous or unethical practices by or on behalf of their employer. For a long time, whistleblowers had no practical internal path for reporting wrongdoing and often made their disclosures to outside parties such as regulators, legislators or reporters. This was often done because whistleblowers feared that internal reporting would not be taken seriously and/or would jeopardize their positions with the company. Recently, however, companies have begun to see that whistleblowing is a benefit to the company and have established procedures to make it easier for reports to be filed and, quite importantly, protect whistleblowers from retaliation. While these steps have been positive, and protection from retaliation is now mandated by federal and state laws, whistleblowing remains a risky proposition for employees, and persons reporting issues are still often seen as simply being disgruntled troublemakers. Nonetheless, creating an atmosphere in which employees feel free to come forward with ethical concerns using a clear, trusted reporting structure is essential for an effective ethics program since there will always be mistakes and/or people who simply are not interested in following the ethical path.

Board Oversight of Ethical Management Systems

While the chief ethics officer can and should be the C-suite officer with primary responsibility for drafting and proposing a code of ethics, the members of the board of directors are ultimately accountable for the contents of the code, committing the resources necessary to provide education and training regarding ethical matters throughout the organization and ensuring that everyone in the organization has access to tools for reporting suspected ethical wrongdoing without fear of retribution. The board also needs to set the appropriate "tone at the top" with respect to ethics, as it should with other sustainability-related issues, and communications between the board and chief ethics officer regarding the code of ethics should be extensive and interactive rather than a quiet acceptance of proposals by the board without challenges or questions.[23]

One of the primary roles of the chief ethics officer is ensuring that board members receive certain information on a regular and timely basis including a complete and regularly updated code of ethical behavior that has been customized to the company's specific needs, but also inclusive of recent internal and external trends and events; updates on recently reported violations, resulting responses and activities, and plans to ensure violations decline over time; information on internal and external ethics trends and plans to mitigate potential risks and reports on ongoing training on ethical behavior customized to specific corporate subsets (e.g., onboarding of new employees, managers, recently merged/acquired organizations, etc.).[24] A publication prepared by the National Association of Corporate Directors (NACD) also recommended that board members conduct regular meetings with the CEO to go through questions relating to the following topics[25]:

- The adequacy and quality of the current code of ethics, training, and reporting/hotline programs in maintaining the highest level of ethical behavior
- How the code of ethics, as well as programs built to support it, might be improved
- How well top executives are engaged in personally modeling desired ethical behaviors
- Examples of how the chief ethics officer is proactively engaged in risk assessment, training, and counseling around ethics issues
- How well the chief ethics officer is customizing programs to address the needs of distinct subsets of the corporation (new employees, managers, recently merged/ acquired organizations, etc.).

In addition, while the chief ethics officer has primary responsibility for ethical standards, issues and training, his or her success will clearly be influenced by the actions of the company's CEO, a position that obviously has its own unique set of ethical obligations and expectations. Ethical missteps by the CEO can cripple even the best internal programs and expose companies and their directors to harsh criticism, legal liability and tarnished reputations. As such, directors have an obligation to assume responsibility for monitoring the actions of the CEO including the CEO's adherence to the ethical standards that the board has established.

While every issue coming before the board should be viewed through an ethical lens, a formal evaluation on a regular basis, generally as part of the board's annual performance assessment, should be placed on the board's agenda and ethics should be emphasized in education and training programs that board members are required to complete. The NACD guide recommended that directors ask themselves about these topics as reviews of overall board performance and the performance of individual directors are conducted[26]:

- Their familiarity with the organization's code of ethical behavior
- How well the directors are modeling ethical behavior
- The adequacy of the ethics information that they are receiving and its value in supporting major decisions
- The clarity of the company's understanding of its key values at all levels of the organization and across all geographies
- The roles the board can play and the additional "value add" that the board can provide with regard to ethical behavior
- The integration of the company's ethical values into decision-making

Many companies have supplemented their organization-wide codes of conduct with codes of conduct and ethics for the board of directors that include specific rules for directors relating to legal compliance, prohibition of unethical behavior and reporting and investigation of unfair dealing and unethical behavior that comes to their attention. In addition, directors should take appropriate steps to ensure that the company follows recommended principles and practices of high quality ethics and compliance programs including making ethics and compliance central to business strategy; creating and supporting systems to ensure that ethics and compliance risks are identified, owned, managed, and mitigated; placing leaders at all levels across the organization who are willing and able to build and sustain a culture of integrity; encouraging, protecting and valuing the reporting of concerns and suspected wrongdoing and taking action and holding itself accountable when wrongdoing occurs.[27]

Notes

1 M. Kelly, J. McGowen and C. Williams, *BUSN* (Independence, KY: South-Western Publishing Company, 2014), 53–54.

2 R. Daft and D. Marcic, *Understanding Management* (5th ed.) (Mason, OH: South-Western Publishing Co., 2006), 120.

3 J. Thangasamy, *Meaning of Ethics Management*, http://www.academia. edu/4152189/Meaning_of_Ethics_Management.

4 A. Burke, *What Are Managerial Ethics*, http://smallbusiness.chron.com/ managerial-ethics-36425.html.

5 R. Daft and D. Marcic, *Understanding Management* (5th ed.) (Mason, OH: South-Western Publishing Co., 2006), 120.

6 Id. at 120–121.

7 Id. at 121.

8 Id. at 126.

9 Id. at 126–127 (citing L. Kohlberg, "Moral Stages and Moralization: The Cognitive-Developmental Approach" in T. Lickona (Ed.), *Moral Development and Behavior: Theory, Research, and Social Issues* (New York: Holt, Rinehart, and Winston, 1976), 31; and J. W. Graham, "Leadership, Moral Development and Citizenship Behavior", *Business Ethics Quarterly*, 5(1) (January 1995), 43).

10 Notes on "Chapter 9: Management Ethics and Social Responsibility", http:// www2.ivcc.edu/aleksy/Fall14/Fall14Mgmt/Plunkett10Ch09.pdf.

11 R. Daft and D. Marcic, *Understanding Management* (5th ed.) (Mason, OH: South-Western Publishing Co., 2006), 141.

12 Id. at 129–130.

13 Id. at 131.

14 M. Kelly, J. McGowen and C. Williams, *BUSN* (Independence, KY: South-Western Publishing Company, 2014), 57 (citing National Business Ethics Survey: How Employees View Ethics in Their Organizations, 1994–2005, Ethics Resource Center, October 12, 2005, http://www.ethics.org/research/ 2005-press-release.asp; and Ethics Resource Center, 2009 National Business Ethics Survey, http://www.ethics.org/nbes/files/nbes-final.pdf).

15 For further discussion of organizational culture, see Chapter 11 (Organizational Culture and Sustainability) in this volume.

16 R. Daft and D. Marcic, *Understanding Management* (5th ed.) (Mason, OH: South-Western Publishing Co., 2006), 142.

17 For further discussion of codes of conduct, see Chapter 10 (Internal Sustainability-Related Codes and Policies) in this volume.

18 http://www.boeing.com/principles/vision.page (accessed July 27, 2016).

19 M. Kelly, J. McGowen and C. Williams, *BUSN* (Independence, KY: South-Western Publishing Company, 2014), 58.

20 R. Daft and D. Marcic, *Understanding Management* (5th ed.) (Mason, OH: South-Western Publishing Co., 2006), 131.

21 Certain of the items in the list are adapted from *C-SUITE EXPECTATIONS: Understanding C-Suite Roles beyond the Core* (Washington, DC: National Association of Corporate Directors, 2013), 13–14.

22 M. Kelly, J. McGowen and C. Williams, *BUSN* (Independence, KY: South-Western Publishing Company, 2014), 58.

23 *C-SUITE EXPECTATIONS: Understanding C-Suite Roles beyond the Core* (Washington, DC: National Association of Corporate Directors, 2013), 16.

24 Id.

25 Id.

26 Id.

27 *Principles and Practices of High-Quality Ethics & Compliance Programs* (Arlington, VA: Ethics and Compliance Initiative, 2016) (also including extensive lists of best practices that should be consulted when designing an ethics and compliance program). See also *Director Essentials: Strengthening Compliance and Ethics Oversight* (Washington, DC: National Association of Corporate Directors, 2018).

10 Internal Sustainability-Related Codes and Policies

Effective sustainability governance and management requires a structure through which the objectives of the company are set, the means of attaining those objectives and monitoring performance are determined, and the company and its people are held accountable.[1] In order for their governance procedures to be effective, companies must establish and maintain the appropriate "control environment" (i.e., the mindset and philosophy that drives decisions and attitudes throughout the organization). One of the first steps in establishing the appropriate control environment is the adoption and dissemination of internal governance codes, policies and procedures, which are consistent with the long-standing regulatory approach to corporate governance, sustainability and corporate social responsibility (CSR) based largely on voluntary codes and self-regulation. These instruments provide guidance to everyone inside and outside the company about the principles that should be applied when decisions are made about strategy and operational matters; however, they must be more than just words on paper and the directors and executive officers of the company must commit to support and enforce them. Companies must also be prepared to regularly report to all of their stakeholders on the effectiveness of the instruments and the steps that have been taken to put them into practice.

The scope and contents of a company's internal governance codes, policies and procedures will be strongly influenced by whether or not the company's securities are listed on public securities exchanges, which have adopted stringent requirements covering a wide range of topics; however, many of the larger private companies use the same governance instruments as public companies, often at the insistence of their stockholders and in recognition of the fact that their operations can be extensive and involve contact with a variety of different stakeholders. At a minimum, the corporate governance instruments for public companies should include a code of business conduct for directors, officers, employees and contractors; corporate governance principles; guidelines for director qualifications and evaluations; in situations where the board has appointed a "lead independent director", a description of the duties and responsibilities associated with that role; a code of ethics for directors and the company's chief executive and senior financial officers; and charters for each of the committees established by the board (e.g., audit, governance and nominating and compensation committees).

The principles and specific guidelines in each of the corporate governance instruments referenced above are essential for effective sustainability governance and management and reference should be made to extensive guidance and commentaries on each of them that is readily available from the securities exchanges, regulators and other sources.[2] In this chapter, attention is placed on codes, policies and other communications specifically focused on topics that are foundational to sustainability-related management topics. For example, codes of conduct and ethics should include sustainability commitments that are supported by a related instrument that lays out in detail the company's adoption and commitment to overriding principles of corporate responsibility. A supplier code of conduct should also be implemented to provide guidance on overseeing the actions of supply chain partners with respect to key sustainability issues such as working conditions and environmental and community impacts and demonstrate commitment to sustainability across the value chain and comply with emerging disclosure and reporting requirements (e.g., California Transparency in Supply Chains Act). Companies often supplement their corporate governance principles and ethics codes with additional policies on specific topics and issues. For example, the board of directors, either directly or through the lead of one of its committees, may implement policies relating to work environment, political contributions, anti-bribery, conflicts of interest and/or health and safety practices. In addition, companies often adopt statements of mission, purpose and values to provide context for the various governance and sustainability instruments.

Code of Conduct

Adopting and adhering to ethical behavior is a core principle and characteristic of a sustainable business and the foundation of any sustainable governance and management framework is a code of conduct that sets the basic internal standards to be observed by all directors, officers, employees and contractors of the company in order to establish, maintain and strengthen the business ethics and compliance systems throughout the company. The code of conduct is intended to serve as a guide for everyone acting on behalf of the company to make good decisions and conduct business ethically. In addition to legal and regulatory compliance standards, the code of conduct should also state the company's intention to engage in ethical business practices with respect to such areas as labor standards, respect for human rights, safety of products and services, environmental conservation and information disclosure, all subjects that may be addressed in greater detail in separate, yet related, principles of corporate responsibility discussed below.

When preparing a code of conduct, it is customary to include a description of the legal requirements that apply to the company business and operations; examples of specific types of conduct that will actually or potentially violate those requirements; and a description of the methods that the company intends to use to ensure that the code is followed, including specific penalties that the company may apply. This information may be included in the code itself, or the drafter may elect to cover the topics in separate appendices such as a summary description of the relevant laws and regulations pertaining to the company's business activities. Beyond specific examples, the code may also include a statement of certain core company values and principles which may serve as a guide for employees to select appropriate and lawful behavior in situations that have not been discussed in advance as part of the code.[3]

Principles of Corporate Responsibility

In general, the topics that are typically covered in the code of conduct described above are primarily focused on compliance with existing laws and regulations as opposed to the "beyond the law" standards and aspirations associated with sustainability and CSR. There are obviously very good reasons, notably the requirements of the US Sentencing Guidelines and the securities exchanges, for having such a code of conduct; however, more and more companies are supplementing those codes by laying out a set of principles necessary for them to operate as responsible companies which include, at a high level, the company's corporate responsibility policies and operating guidelines related to stakeholder relations and otherwise acting as a responsible business.[4] These principles of corporate responsibility are an opportunity for a company to lay out the rules that it has elected to establish for itself in order to embed their environmental and social principles and values systematically into the operations and culture of the company.[5]

There is no "standard" for the contents of the principles of corporate responsibility, and variations are likely due to size of operations and factors unique to the sectors in which the company operations; however, the principles generally should address, at a minimum, legal compliance, financial responsibility, fair competition, prohibitions on bribery and corruption, conflicts of interest, customer relationships, supply chain relationships, workplace conditions and employee wellbeing, environmental responsibility and community relations; environmental policies; human resources policies and principles of responsible purchasing.[6] In many cases, the code will incorporate by reference applicable principles from external standards and instruments such as the International Labor Organization's core labor standards, the principles of the United Nations Global Compact and/or the Universal Declaration of Human Rights.

Suppliers' Code of Conduct

Few companies are self-sufficient—able to create all the resources needed for their products and services and distribute them on their own and provide support to customers without the assistance of others. As such, companies are typically dependent on the members of their supply chain, many of which operate in different legal and cultural environments throughout the world. Companies striving to be environmentally and socially responsible must commit to ensuring that all of their suppliers and their facilities adhere to the same standards that the company has set for itself in its internal code of business conduct. In turn, each supplier must also guarantee to the company that it will hold their own supply chain, including subcontractors and third party labor agencies, to the same high standards.

Supplier accountability begins with a strong suppliers' code of conduct which is tightly and formally linked to the legal contracts which form the basis for the relationship between the company and its suppliers. Perhaps the most common and significant topic in a suppliers' code of conduct is human rights and labor practices. Suppliers should be required to conduct their activities in a manner that respects human rights and in accordance with wide-recognized global standards, such as the United Nations Universal Declaration of Human Rights. Suppliers should expect to be obligated to submit to audits by the company to assess supplier compliance with the code including facility inspections, employee interviews and a review of the supplier's books and records and business practices. In order to facilitate the audit process, suppliers will be required to maintain accurate and transparent books, records and accounts to demonstrate compliance with applicable laws and regulations and the supplier's code of conduct. Suppliers should also be required to be familiar with the company's general code of conduct, discussed above, applicable to all of the company's employees and create and maintain reporting systems (and accompanying protection for whistleblowers) that can be used to report violations of laws, regulations or any of the company's codes of conduct and related policies.[7]

Environmental Policy

Formal laws and regulations pertaining to environmental issues have become a fixture and companies have experience in understanding and complying with requirements that have been imposed by legislators and regulators. In fact, compliance with environmental laws and regulations is an important part of any company's compliance and risk management activities. However, sustainability and environmental responsibility calls on companies to take additional voluntary steps toward caring for and safeguarding the environment and balancing environmental considerations with successful pursuit of the company's business goals. One important step is the thoughtful development and adoption of an environmental policy. Companies can face a variety of environmental challenges and a specific policy should take into account the unique issues raised by the company's operational activities. Development of an environmental policy should begin with an audit and assessment of the environmental impact of the company's activities throughout its own operations and those of its major supply chain partners. The results of this assessment can be used to develop an environmental strategy and establish benchmarks for measuring progress against internal goals and the performance of peer companies in the industry.

The environmental policy should identify and describe the key goals and objectives and the strategies that the company intends to undertake with respect thereto. For example, a company's environmental policy might focus on waste reduction and recycling (i.e., helping to preserve the environment by using the principles of reducing, reusing and recycling); and resource conservation, which can be pursued in a number of different ways including improving energy efficiency in building design and construction, implementing energy conservation best practices in existing and future facilities, reducing energy costs through environmental controls and identifying opportunities in new and innovative programs offered through utility companies and with local, state and national agencies. Consideration should be given to include specific actions that the company will be taking in connection with its environmental goals and objectives such as recycling office paper, modifying procurement policies to ensure that vendors are in compliance with the company's environmental standards, recycling hazardous materials in accordance with regulatory guidelines, implementing a centralized energy management system to encourage energy conservation, installing equipment and technology that facilitate water conservation, modifying logistics practices to reduce overall fuel use and dependence on high carbon modes of transportation and utilizing energy saving designs in new building construction. As referred to above, the company's major supply chain partners should be covered by the environmental policy and should be required to submit to regular audits of their operational activities to determine whether they are, at a minimum, upholding the relevant environmental laws, regulations and policies of the countries in which they do business.[8] In addition to environmental policies, companies may also promulgate issue-specific policies covering topics such as climate change.

Social Responsibility Policy

Various countries in Europe, in the course of making recommendation in their national corporate governance codes, have recommended that companies adopt policies on CSR that include a determination and statement of the company's values and ethical guidelines to be followed in accordance with such values; include information about the environment and its impact on financial performance in their financial reports; disclose various risk factors, including environmental risks; establish risk management systems that cover ethical risks; involve stakeholders in the development and implementation of CSR practices; establish requirements that candidates for board membership should have adequate personal integrity and business ethics; and adopt ethical policies and continuously train employees on the principles in those policies.[9] Many US-based public companies have adopted social responsibility policies as part of their overall sustainability governance frameworks and use such policies as reference points when setting out the duties and responsibilities of the board of directors and any CSR committee of the board.

A basic social responsibility policy should include the definition of CSR that has been adopted by the board of directors and include a statement of the basic commitments and goals of the company with respect to social responsibility and the key steps that will be taken to fulfill those commitments and achieve the goals. Focus areas commonly mentioned in social responsibility policies include corporate governance (i.e., ensuring that the business is conducted through fair business practices and according to rigorous ethical, professional and legal standards and that all stakeholders are treated in a fair, open and respectful manner); environment, particularly striving to reduce the impact of the company's activities on the environment; human rights (i.e., support and respect for the protection of internationally proclaimed human rights and observation of international human rights norms in the workplace and the supply chain); and ethical trading and procurement, which includes implementation of procedures for ensuring that goods and services obtained from the supply chain have been created in an ethical and sustainable manner.[10]

Human Rights Policy

Respect for human rights and proactive and public embrace of universally recognized principles of human rights is a fundamental principal of CSR and sustainability. While human rights will be covered in other company codes and policies, notably the company's code of conduct, further details are often included in a separate human rights policy. It is common to begin a human rights policy with references to, and acceptance of, the UN Guiding Principles on Business and Human Rights and the principles of the Universal Declaration of Human Rights, including those contained within the International Bill of Rights and the International Labor Organization's 1998 Declaration on Fundamental Principles and Rights at Work. The policy will continue with specific commitments for topics such as community and stakeholder engagement, diversity and inclusion, freedom of association and collective bargaining, safe and health workplace, workplace security, forced labor and human trafficking, child labor, work hours, wages and benefits and land rights and water resources.

The human rights policy should extend throughout the entirety of the company's internal operations and to the activities of major supply chain partners, each of which will be obligated to submit to audits and assessment of their human rights practices. Each of the aspects of the policy should be covered regularly in employee training and employees, as well any other parties with a relationship to the company, should have access to procedures for reporting potential violations of the policy. The policy should be posted on the company's website and the company's human rights-related commitments and activities should be reported on as part of the company's annual sustainability report.[11]

Human Resources Policy

While employee rights are often covered in the code of conduct and a separate human rights policy, companies often choose to adopt a more specific human resources, or employment, policy that recognizes the importance of talented and dedicated employees to the overall performance of the company and the achievement of its environmental, social and economic goals. Human resources policies are generally built on a foundation of explicit support for the United Nation's Principles on Business and Human Rights and the various Fundamental Conventions of the International Labor Organization relating to elimination of forced and compulsory labor, abolition of child labor, elimination of discrimination in respect of employment and occupation and freedom of association and collective bargaining. Human resources policies are intended to set forth uniform minimum standards for all of the company's business units and employees, as well as the company's major supply chain partners.

A responsible company's human resources policy should set out the key principles and objectives of human resources management and describe how the company will discharge its ethical obligations to act responsibly in its personnel relationships. A company that treats its employees with respect and with attention to their personal wellbeing can expect to enjoy greater productivity, higher morale and reduced turnover, all of which contribute to better financial performance. The human resources policy should address compliance with applicable legal and regulatory requirements and then expand outward to include occupational wellbeing and job satisfaction, workplace safety and health, discrimination and harassment in the workplace, performance assessment, compensation and benefits and training and development.[12]

The human resources policy is also an opportunity for the company its own basic expectations regarding the actions of its employees beginning with a commitment by employees to respect the company's corporate values and principles and act as an ambassador of the company and its brand when interacting with fellow employees, customers, business partners, members of the local communities in which the company operates and other stakeholders. Employees should be expected to behave ethically and within the law, handle confidential information of the company with due care and skill, treat other employees with mutual trust and respect, adhere to the letter and principles of the company's code of conduct, principles of corporate responsibility and other policies, and conduct the company's business with honesty and integrity and in a professional manner that fosters the company's reputation.

Stakeholder Engagement and Community Development Policy

Stakeholder engagement is one of the bedrock principles of sustainability and CSR and directors and members of the executive team must be committed to participating in continuous dialogue with all of the company's stakeholders, not just stockholders, to seek their input on, and keep them informed about, the company's environmental, social and economic goals and activities.[13] Engagement with stockholders, employees, customers and suppliers has been commonplace for many years; however, companies now realize that they must also engage with the local communities that are often most impacted by the company's operational activities. Communicating with local communities allows companies to identify and manage expectations and avoid conflicts that may delay projects and reduce their value. Community engagement facilitates "buy in" by those closest to what the company is doing, particularly if the company includes a social investment in the community as part of the project.

Companies have begun to adopt formal policies relating to stakeholder engagement and community development, particular in those instances where the company's operations can reasonably be expected to have a significant environmental impact on the surrounding communities (e.g., oil and gas production and other extractive industries). These policies grow out of the realization that while the business activities are regulated, and the company is expected to adhere to the requirements imposed by law, dialogue with and support from local communities is just as essential to the overall success of the enterprise as being legally compliant. Engagement with the community as a key stakeholder also provides opportunities for the company to participate in the improvement of conditions within the community and overall economic development and wellbeing in the area.

A variety of ideas and principles may be expressed in a stakeholder engagement policy. First and foremost should be the concept of transparency and a commitment by the company to disclose the material terms of its operational activities in the community and the environment, social and economic objectives that the company is pursuing through those activities. Another essential guiding principle for this type of policy is, of course, a commitment to engaging and consulting with community representatives, and all stakeholders, as part of the process of deciding whether or not to proceed with material activities that might have a material impact on the community and/or one or more other stakeholders. The goal of consultation should be to assess and, where necessary and practicable, implement measures to avoid or mitigate adverse environmental or social impacts. The company should commit to keeping abreast of the concerns and perspectives of stakeholders and keeping them informed of plans in order to ensure continuous engagement and open communications. Other topics that should be addressed in the policy include managing impacts, social investment priorities, supplier performance and local content, procedures for addressing complaints and grievances, and accountability and review.[14]

CSR Manual

The principles of corporate responsibility and the various policies described above are often accompanied by and integrated within a comprehensive CSR manual or handbook. Typical elements of a CSR manual would include an introduction, which would provide an overview of the purposes and contents of the manual and a message from the chairperson of the board of directors and/or managing director/CEO of the company; a lengthy section that include chapters or parts on each of the core subjects of the CSR with respect to the company such as corporate governance, staff welfare and human rights, labor practices, the environment, fair operating practice, consumer issues, supply chain partner relationships and community involvement and development; a section that describes how the company will engage with each of its key stakeholder groups; a section that describes how CSR performance will be monitored, reviewed and reported on to stakeholders; and a final section that guides readers on where they can obtain additional resources regarding the company's CSR activities and how they can ask questions and raise concerns in a manner that is safe and free from risk of retaliation. The manual itself is often supplemented by the various issue-specific policies and procedures discussed above relating to the core subjects (e.g., environmental management systems, policies and procedures and corporate governance guidelines that address compliance with laws, ethics and bribery/corruption).

Notes

1 http://www.governanceinstitute.com.au/knowledge-resources/governance-foundations/more-thoughts-on-governance/.

2 Further discussion of each of these corporate governance instruments by the author of this publication (including references to guidance for preparation and use of such instruments) can be found in A. Gutterman, *Sustainability and Corporate Governance* (New York: Routledge, 2020).

3 For further discussion of codes of ethics, see Chapter 9 (Ethical Management) in this volume. See also A. Gutterman, *Sustainability and Corporate Governance* (New York: Routledge, 2020).

4 Finnish Textile & Fashion, *Corporate Responsibility Manual* (Helsinki: Finnish Textile & Fashion, 2016), 18.

5 *Handbook on Corporate Social Responsibility (CSR) for Employers' Organizations* (Ankara, Turkey: European Union CSR for All Project, April 2014), 29.

6 Id.

7 For further discussion of supply chain management and policies and procedures for suppliers by the author of this publication, see A. Gutterman, *Business and Human Rights* (Chicago, IL: Business Law Section of the American Bar Association, Forthcoming 2021). In addition, for examples of suppliers' codes of conduct and additional commentary on preparation of such codes, see "Governance Codes and Policies" in the management tools available as part of "Governance: A Library of Resources for Sustainable Entrepreneurs" prepared and distributed by the Sustainable Entrepreneurship Project (www.seproject.org).

8 For examples of environmental policies and additional commentary on preparation of such policies, see "Governance Codes and Policies" in the management tools available as part of "Governance: A Library of Resources for Sustainable Entrepreneurs" prepared and distributed by the Sustainable Entrepreneurship Project (www.seproject.org).

9 D. Szabó and K. Sørensen, "Integrating Corporate Social Responsibility in Corporate Governance Codes in the EU", *European Business Law Review*, 2013(6), 1, 20–32.

10 For examples of social responsibility policies and additional commentary on preparation of such policies, see "Governance Codes and Policies" in the management tools available as part of "Governance: A Library of Resources for Sustainable Entrepreneurs" prepared and distributed by the Sustainable Entrepreneurship Project (www.seproject.org).

11 For further discussion of the preparation of human rights policies by the author of this publication, see A. Gutterman, *Business and Human Rights* (Chicago, IL: Business Law Section of the American Bar Association, Forthcoming 2021).

12 Finnish Textile & Fashion, *Corporate Responsibility Manual* (Helsinki: Finnish Textile & Fashion, 2016).

13 For detailed discussion of stakeholder engagement, see A. Gutterman, *Stakeholders and Stakeholder Engagement* (Oakland, CA: Sustainable Entrepreneurship Project, 2019), available at www.seproject.org.

14 For examples of stakeholder engagement policies and additional commentary on preparation of such policies, see "Governance Codes and Policies" in the management tools available as part of "Governance: A Library of Resources for Sustainable Entrepreneurs" prepared and distributed by the Sustainable Entrepreneurship Project (www.seproject.org).

11 Organizational Culture and Sustainability

It is clear that over the last several decades organizations have continuously expanded the application of the principles of sustainable development to the business world and that companies have increasingly focused efforts on introducing or changing policies, products and/or processes to address pollution, minimize resource use, and to improve community and stakeholder relations.[1] However, while these initiatives are laudable, some critics have argued that they are often largely superficial and not conducive to the creation and maintenance of authentically sustainable organizations and industries.[2] For them, the only way that an organization can truly and fully respond to environmental and social challenges and become sustainable is to undergo a significant cultural change and transformation that leads to the development and maintenance of a sustainability-oriented organizational culture.[3] In fact, studies have indicated that there is a strong relationship between organizational culture and corporate sustainability and that sustainability initiatives are more likely to be successful if they are defined and implemented in a way that is aligned with the organizational culture.[4]

The concept of organizational culture began to emerge in the 1970s when researchers in the US and Europe were particularly interested in understanding the sources of the comparatively higher performance of Japanese companies including the question of whether or not the organizational culture in those firms provided a specific competitive advantage.[5] A number of definitions of organizational culture have been offered; however, if managers and employees are consulted, they may simply respond that culture is "how we do things around here". There is obviously truth to such a statement but it would be a mistake to ignore the breadth and scope of the issues that are influenced by cultural norms and values—how activities within the organization are carried out, how members communicate with one another, who is accepted into the organization and who is ostracized, and what is the organization's overall morale. The culture of a particular organization is created and maintained by its members, particularly the founders and senior managers, based on a variety of influencing factors and they are also the ones who can change and transform the culture when they are convinced that such actions are necessary in light of the then-current environment that the organization is facing.

A Taxonomy of Organizational Cultures Based on Integration of Sustainability

It has been suggested that it was possible and useful to recognize four types of organizational cultures and then distinguished them based in large part by the degree to which they have integrated sustainability values and principles and the practices they use in approach and managing sustainability-related issues[6]:

- *Reactive/Obstructionist*: Reactive/Obstructionist organizations do not generally approach items regarding sustainability in their day-to-day work activities and are more concerned with traditional goals such as maximizing the value their stockholders. The focus on economic performance that accrues to the benefit of stockholders and incumbent executives often causes these types of organizations to take what has been referred to as an "obstructionist stance", which means that they try to block and stop what is going on and avoid corporate social responsibility (CSR). For example, such an organization may crack down on workers striking for better wages and working conditions rather than see their actions as a signal for the need to engage with employees to forge a mutually beneficial working arrangement.[7]
- *Defensive*: Defensive organizations take actions relating to sustainability only after it finds it to be necessary as a response to legislative and/or community pressures. Defensive organizations are not particularly responsible with respect to social responsibility and sustainability and typically limit their actions to what is required of them by law and nothing more. For example, tobacco companies, after fighting proposed regulations to place warning on cigarette packaging, eventually agreed to provide the warnings; however, their goal was to simply fend off legal problems and they generally did little more in terms of providing information to consumers about the dangers of their products.
- *Adaptive/Accommodative*: Adaptive/Accommodative organizations have begun the process of integrating sustainable development principles into their management processes, but have yet to establish clear goals and objectives with respect to sustainability. These types of organizations believe that social responsibility is important, perhaps just as important as making a profit, and have exceeded legal minimums in their commitments to groups and individuals in its social environment and publicly accepted responsibility for certain problems and embarked on specific initiatives to develop solutions for those problems.[8]
- *Sustainable/Proactive*: Sustainable/Proactive organizations have successfully integrated duties to the environment and the community

into their goals and actions. A proactive approach means acting in advance of a future situation rather than responding, or reacting, to a situation or probably that has already happened. Sustainable/ Proactive organizations sincerely embrace the arguments in favor of social responsibility and view themselves as citizens in a society with a duty to seek out opportunities to contribute. Proactive strategies are frequently seen in areas such as supply chain management, waste reduction and support for innovative programs to benefit the communities in which the organization is operating.

Competing Values Framework: Organizational Culture and Sustainability

Linnenluecke and Griffith set out to explore and discuss the relationship between corporate sustainability and organizational culture using the widely-recognized "competing values" framework of organizational culture that has been used to identify and describe the four types or models of organizational culture (i.e., human relations, open systems, internal process and rational goal), each with its own set of valued outcomes and a coherent managerial ideology about how those outcomes could be achieved. They put forward the following theoretical propositions with respect to each of the four cultural types with respect to how the ideological underpinnings of the applicable organizational culture were likely to influence how sustainability will be implemented and the outcomes that can be achieved from the sustainability initiatives.[9]

Organizations that are dominated by *human relations values* promote cohesion and morale through training and development, open communication and participative decision-making. These types of organizations, which emphasize social interaction and interpersonal relations, rely more heavily on internal staff development, learning and capacity building in their pursuit of corporate sustainability. Organizations with a strong focus on social or human relations values are likely to support or attract social entrepreneurship and leaders of these organizations will likely invest significant time and energy, often at the expense of neglecting business goals and objectives, in advocating corporate sustainability principles within the organization. The challenge for pursuing sustainability within organizations with an embedded human relations model will be resolving the tensions between creating a business venture and pursuing a social purpose.

Organizations that are dominated by *open systems values* promote growth and resource acquisition through adaptability and change, visionary communication and flexible decision-making. Organizations dominated by the open systems model place greater emphasis on innovation for achieving ecological and social sustainability as they pursued corporate sustainability. In this instance, innovation is applied not merely to attain higher levels of eco-efficiency, but rather to develop products, systems and practices that "move beyond pollution control or prevention and allow the organization to operate within the carrying capacity of the natural environment by minimizing their resource use and ecological footprint". As for social sustainability, the assumption is that the organization must recognize and embrace its responsibilities toward various stakeholder groups and the community in which they operate.

Organizations that are dominated by *internal process values* promote stability and control through information management, precise communication and data-based decision-making. Organizations dominated by the internal process model have a preference for pursuing economic sustainability and thus place greater emphasis on economic performance, growth and long-term profitability in their sustainability initiatives. The key aspects of this approach would be maximizing production and consumption of the organization's products and services in order to increase profits and achieving economic efficiency through the simplification of products, services and processes in order to achieve costs reductions, maximize product and pursue economic outcomes; however, realization of economic sustainability (i.e., the maximization of profits, production and consumption) alone is not sufficient for overall organizational sustainability.

Organizations that are dominated by *rational goal values* promote efficiency and productivity through goal-setting and planning, instructional communication and centralized decision-making. These types of organizations emphasize resource efficiencies in their pursuit of corporate sustainability. There is no doubt that there are operational and sustainability advantages to implementing policies and practices that reduce costs and operational efficiencies, and many organizations have implemented human resources and environmental policies focused on reducing and eliminating waste; however, efficiency should not be pursued in isolation, since it is also necessary to consider the impact that the steps taken to achieve efficiency may have on the environment and society. Moreover, efficiencies may be of limited competitive advantage to organizations if they can be easily copied and implemented by competitors.

The propositions for each of the cultural types championed by Linnenluecke and Griffith are important for sustainability leaders in the way they serve as reminders that there is no single best type of sustainability-oriented organizational culture and that organizational culture is best viewed as a fundamental influencer on how corporate sustainability is implemented and the types of outcomes that can be expected. Can sustainability leaders make the changes in organizational culture necessary to facilitate a shift toward different sustainability-related ends? Organizational rigidity and multiple subcultures make the task more difficult; however, Linnenluecke and Griffith suggested that certain changes can be made to the elements of an organization's observable culture (i.e., at the surface level) to provide a conducive context for the changes in the values, beliefs and core assumptions of organizational members necessary to pursue sustainability: publication of corporate sustainability reports, the integration of sustainability measures in employee performance evaluation and employee training.

NBS Framework for Embedding Sustainability in Organizational Culture

Bertels prepared a report that was distributed through the Network for Business Sustainability (NBS) that proposed a framework for embedding sustainability in organizational culture that was designed for executives and senior human resources and sustainability managers and also included a portfolio of 59 practices that had either been shown to be effective by research or that showed potential but remained untested.[10] The framework grouped the practices into four different categories: fostering commitment; clarifying expectations; building momentum for change and instilling capacity for change. Bertels and the NBS recommended that sustainability leaders employ a selection of practices from each of the framework's four categories, thus creating a change program that simultaneously included practices for delivering on the organization's current sustainability commitments, affecting values and behaviors inside the organization, establishing rules and procedures that could be followed by organizational members to advance sustainability initiatives and moving the organization further along the path to sustainability.

Fostering Commitment

Sustainability leaders need to implement informal practices to build and reinforce the importance of sustainability for the organization and to support and encourage employees who are making efforts to embed sustainability. Five categories of practices relating to fostering commitment were identified by Bertels and the NBS: engaging (i.e., support, educate, link, challenge, leverage, capture quick wins and recognize), signaling (i.e., model, allocate resources, commit, self-regulate, adhere to standards, accommodate work-life balance and invest in the community), communicating (i.e., telling stories and customizing), managing talent (i.e., recruit, allocate people and promote) and reinforcing (i.e., inform, repeat and follow up).

Clarifying Expectations

Sustainability leaders can employ formal practices for delivering on current sustainability commitments by establishing rules and procedures that clarify employee expectations regarding sustainability. Bertels and the NBS suggested seven categories of practices: codifying (i.e., creating policies, setting goals and operationalizing); integrating (i.e., integrating sustainability into product design and life cycle; mission, vision and values; strategy and business plans; business processes and systems; and existing roles); assigning responsibility to senior leaders and creating roles; training; incentivizing; assessing (i.e., inventory, development and tracking of metrics and reporting); and verifying and auditing. The objective of these practices is to integrate sustainability into the core of the organization's strategies and processes; equip and encourage employees via training and incentives; and measure, track, and report on the organization's progress toward its sustainability goals.

Building Momentum for Change

Sustainability leaders need to implement informal practices to build momentum for change in the organization and support a culture of sustainable innovation by developing new ideas needed to bring your organization closer to its long term sustainability goals. The goal in this area is to inspire and reassure employees so that they can experiment, try new things, and build on each other's ideas. Bertels and the NBS suggested six categories of practices: raising awareness through framing sustainability; championing; inviting (i.e., ask, listen and seeking external help from industry experts, guest speakers and suppliers and customers); experimenting; re-envisioning by defining sustainability and back-casting (i.e., imagining a desired future in which the organization is "sustainable", working backwards from the future vision to determine the necessary steps to get there and setting distinct milestones to construct the path to the desired future); and sharing knowledge internally and externally and collaborating.

Instilling Capacity for Change

Sustainability leaders need to implement formal practices—rules and procedures—that can serve as structures and supports for a foundation for innovation and other future changes in the organization. The focus of these efforts fall into two categories: learning (i.e., scanning, benchmarking, piloting, learning from failure and reflecting) and developing, which includes both new products and services and new business processes and systems. Bertels and the NBS suggested several different practices that sustainability leaders could use to instill capacity for change in their organizations:

- Scanning: Attend industry and environmental conferences; join a sustainability group in which members share information and best practices; observe your competitors' sustainability activity; develop diverse internal and external knowledge and networks; research stakeholder needs and values; and scan for changes in legislation and upcoming regulatory requirements

- Developing New Products and Services: Develop new products and services with minimal negative impacts on the natural environment; and develop new products and services that meet unmet sustainability needs
- Pilot Projects: Adopt initiatives that originated at the grassroots level as formal pilot projects; welcome suggestions and follow through by allocating resources to piloting the best ideas; and set internal targets for finding and executing pilot projects
- Benchmarking: Select sustainability metrics used by others to facilitate benchmarking; decide which information you will make public so your performance can be compared with that of other companies; and consider benchmarking internally between divisions, business units or locations

Embedding Sustainability in Organizational Culture using the Star Model

The NBS also collaborated with Canadian Business for Social Responsibility (CBSR) on a workshop involving sustainability and human resources professionals that involved the exchange of information on best practices for embedding sustainability into organizational culture. The workshop led to the creation of a framework that was based on the five elements of organizational design in the well-known "Star Model" developed and popularized by Galbraith and included strategic planning (e.g., incorporating sustainability into mission and vision statements), organizational structure (e.g., creating an executive position with responsibility for sustainability), human resource management (e.g., providing sustainability training to employees), processes (e.g., collecting and reporting data on sustainability performance) and employee rewards and incentives (e.g., incorporating sustainability into financial and non-financial rewards programs). This framework included certain "best practices for embedding sustainability in organization culture" which are briefly described in the following paragraphs.[11]

Strategy

Recommended best practices for "strategy" included establishing an agreed-upon definition of sustainability that is relevant to the company's business and its success. Feedback should be gathered from internal and external stakeholders in order to understand the many faces of sustainability and CSR. Experts should be recruited to provide information to various internal stakeholders, such as employees, so that they have a better understand of the types of innovation that are involved in sustainability programs. Experts can also facilitate dialogue with external stakeholders on setting a sustainability agenda and establishing reporting mechanisms. Once a definition has been agreed upon, sustainability should be integrated into the corporate vision and linked to the company's mission, values, corporate beliefs and goals. When selecting sustainability projects, companies should focus first on developing their strengths and choose projects that are aligned with their core competencies. This makes it easier for companies to establish a leadership position in particular areas and secure executive support for expanding the initiative. Additional projects work best when developed with the input and support of employees and they should be allowed to participate in the restructuring of their jobs as needed to pursue the sustainability goals.

Structure

With respect to structure, key recommendations included making senior executives responsible, establishing accountability and using partners and collaborators to leverage the company's capabilities and achieve greater outcomes. Companies were urged to establish a CSR executive position that reported directly to the board of directors or the CEO and have that executive work regularly with a cross-functional CSR team that oversaw the sustainability initiative. In addition to support and formal structure at the top of the organization, other people from all around the company should be given sustainability roles and goals. Senior managers throughout the organization should "own" the performance metrics for the sustainability programs they oversee, which requires them to establish processes within their units for setting and tracking goals, and each manager and employee should have their CSR-related responsibilities formally incorporated into their roles. At the same time, however, employees should be invited to participate in defining their roles and setting their individual targets and the manner in which their performance will be measured and reported. Collaborations with NGOs and other community organizations are a good and efficient way to engage external stakeholders in sustainability initiatives.

People

NBS and CBSR explained that the "people" element in organizational design includes influencing and building the organization's human resources through recruitment, promotion, rotation, training and development. Positive training that motivates employees to want to "do the right thing" is essential and should be incorporated into explanations of the business case for the initiative. Sustainability and human resources leaders should develop teachers and associates throughout the organization—"sustainability champions"—who can help generate grassroots energy among the workforce for sustainability programs. Perhaps most importantly, organizations need to engage their employees about issues that are fundamental to them such as pay, work-life balance and the overall working environment. Effective engagement includes giving employees permission to voice their concerns about sustainability goals and offer suggestions for improving the programs. Training and education should be used to ensure that employees are aligned about the sustainability goals and how they should be achieved so that decisions in the field can be made more efficiently and consistently.

Processes

Designing and implementing organizational processes for sustainability should begin by asking big, and difficult, questions about what the organization should look like in the future and the role that sustainability will be playing. Companies need to go beyond product characteristics to include the entire customer experience. The key recommendation for companies was to be proactive. Once a vision has been created, companies should publish targets to the outside world that include public commitments to sustainability-focused processes and objectively measurable outcomes. It is best if commitments are developed with input from the relevant stakeholders and stakeholders should be afforded an opportunity to comment and critique the company's commitments and the proposed methods for achieving those commitments. Results of the company's efforts should be shared internally and externally and should be accompanied by thoughtful analysis of why things went well and how processes can be improved. When reporting results, information should be collected directly from stakeholders about how they were impacted by the sustainability initiatives.

Rewards

Rewards are essential for motivating executives, managers and employees and aligning the personal goals of the workforce to the sustainability targets of the organization. Companies are encouraged to link compensation to CSR performance, typically in the form of bonus payments that can easily and objectively be computed after analysis of metrics on specific sustainability targets. While most incentives are monetary, other tools can be used to reward good work including recognition and celebration of ideas and successes and support, such as grants and prizes, for new projects that are suggested by employees. Companies may also motivate by committing to making charitable donations to worthy causes selected by employees and often allow employees to provide services to those charities during work hours while being compensated by the company.

Understanding Organizational Change to Become a Sustainable Company

Eccles et al. observed that even though there was empirical support for the view that adoption of sustainability-related strategies was necessary in order for companies to be competitive and that "high sustainability" companies significantly outperformed counterparts that had not adopted environmental and social policies, relatively few companies exhibited a broad-based commitment to sustainability on the basis of their original corporate DNA.[12] Because of this Eccles et al. argued that most companies needed to make a conscious and continuing effort to formulate and execute a sustainable strategy and embed sustainability into their strategy and operations. Based on their research comparing the organizational models of "sustainable" and "traditional" companies, they concluded that companies needed to be prepared to embark on large-scale change in two stages: the first stage involves reframing the company's identity through leadership commitment and external engagement, and the second stage involves building internal support for the new identity through employee engagement and creating and codifying mechanisms for execution.[13]

Eccles et al. argued that the first stage in becoming a sustainability company—reframing the company's identity—requires both leadership commitment and external engagement. Transformation of the company's organizational culture requires the strong and focused guidance of the leadership team and the organizational leaders are the people who are best situated to drive the necessary engagement relating to sustainability between the company and the diverse range of external stakeholders including investors, community members, regulators, activists and members and representatives of civil society. The goal at this stage is to strengthen the commitment to sustainability at the top of the organization and redefine the company's identity to the world as being an organization that has embraced the principles of sustainability and embedded them in its organizational culture, strategy, operational processes and relations with stakeholders. As the organizational leaders begin to reach out to external stakeholders they gather the information necessary to formulate and execute the company's sustainability strategy. As the engagement process expands in the second stage to include employees their interaction with external stakeholders creates opportunities for learning that can be used to make the company more innovative and committed to creating value for itself and society in general. Leadership commitment and external engagement should continue during the second stage of the process as parallel drivers of the company's new identity.

The second stage of the process of creating a sustainable company involves building internal support for the new identity developed during the first stage through employee engagement and creating and codifying mechanisms for execution. Eccles et al. defined employee engagement as the actions that the company takes in order to secure the interest and attention of its employees in the company's sustainability efforts and the roles that employees are asked to play. In most cases the transition to become a sustainable company will require that employees change their behaviors and behavioral change will not occur unless the employees believe that it will be worth it. Employees will also need to understand and accept the reasons for the company's decision to make changes and have a clear picture of the specific individual role that they are expected to play and how their performance will be measured. The process of employee engagement will not be easy; however, Eccles et al. pointed out that engaged employees are emotionally connected to their work and to their workplace and thus tend to be more productive and more willing to engage in discretionary efforts to achieve company goals.[14]

Eccles et al. pointed out that the transformation would be extremely challenging and companies with an established organizational culture that included strong capabilities for change, a commitment to innovation and high levels of trust would have a significant advantage.[15] They found strong differences between sustainable and traditional companies with regard to the level of change readiness in the corporate culture, noting that almost all of the sustainable companies had a strong track record of implementing large-scale changes successfully. This is important because transformational change can take years, if not decades, to accomplish and the company must be comfortable with setting its direction, calibrating the risk and then pushing forward even without a precise plan. Innovation was found to be another core cultural capability for becoming a sustainable company and the sustainable companies surveyed by Eccles et al. were able to identify and focus on the innovations in processes, products and business models that were necessary to improve financial performance along relevant environmental, social and governance dimensions. A third key element of the organizational culture for a sustainable company is trust on the part of every employee, which means that employees believe that organizational leaders and everyone else in the organization can be taken at their word and will do their best to deliver on commitments and processes. Without trust, employees will be reluctant, if not completely unwilling, to take the risks associated with the level of innovation required in order to achieve the transformational changes associated with sustainability.

Notes

1 M. Linnenluecke and A. Griffiths, "Corporate Sustainability and Organizational Culture", *Journal of World Business*, 45 (2010), 357 (citing A. Crane, "Corporate Greening as Amoralization", *Organization Studies*, 21(4) (2000), 673).
2 See, e.g., S. Hart and M. Milstein, "Creating Sustainable Value", *Academy of Management Executive*, 17(2) (2000), 56; and P. Senge and G. Carstedt, "Innovating Our Way to the Next Industrial Revolution", *MIT Sloan Management Review*, 42(2) (2001), 24.

3 A. Crane, "Rhetoric and Reality in the Greening of Organizational Culture", *Greener Management International*, 12 (1995), 49; J. Post and B. Altman, "Managing the Environmental Change Process: Barriers and Opportunities", *Journal of Organizational Change Management*, 7(4) (1994), 64; and W. Stead and J. Stead, *Management for a Small Planet: Strategic Decision Making and the Environment* (Newberry Park, CA: Sage, 1992) (as cited in M. Linnenluecke and A. Griffiths, "Corporate Sustainability and Organizational Culture", *Journal of World Business*, 45 (2010), 357).

4 M. Tatarusanu, A Onea and A. Cuza, *Organizational Culture and Values for Corporate Sustainability* (Romania: University of Iasi), http://docplayer.net/11003116-Organizational-culture-and-values-for-corporate-sustainability.html (accessed May 1, 2020). See also L. Abbett, A. Coldham and R. Whisnant, *Organizational Culture and the Success of Corporate Sustainability Initiatives: An Empirical Analysis Using the Competing Values Framework*, https://www.researchgate.net/publication/282195341_Organizational_Culture_and_the_Success_of_Corporate_Sustainability_Initiatives_An_Empirical_Analysis_using_the_Competing_Values_Framework (if there is greater congruence between organizational culture and the sustainability initiative, the initiative will be more successful, and the greater the congruence the greater the success of the initiative).

5 Id.

6 Adapted from M. Tatarusanu, A Onea and A. Cuza, *Organizational Culture and Values for Corporate Sustainability* (Romania: University of Iasi); D. Steege, *Powerpoint Presentation*, Retrieved from Colorado Technical University Online, Virtual Campus, MGM110-0803A-12: Principles of Business; http://docplayer.net/11003116-Organizational-culture-and-values-for-corporate-sustainability.html; and Approaches to Social Responsibility (Wednesday, May 1, 2013), http://tafes.blogspot.com/); and B. Kanobi, "What Are the Four Basic Approaches to Social Responsibility?" (1999), http://www.ehow.com/info_8254493_four-basic-approaches-social-responsibility.html (accessed May 1, 2020).

7 B. Kanobi, "What Are the Four Basic Approaches to Social Responsibility?" (1999), http://www.ehow.com/info_8254493_four-basic-approaches-social-responsibility.html (accessed May 1, 2020).

8 J. VanBaren, *Accommodative Social Responsibility* (2010), https://bizfluent.com/info-8017302-accommodative-social-responsibility.html (accessed August 29, 2020).

9 The article itself can be found at M. Linnenluecke and A. Griffiths, "Corporate Sustainability and Organizational Culture", *Journal of World Business*, 45 (2010), 357. For further discussion and description of the competing values framework of organizational culture, see R. Quinn, *Beyond Rational Management: Mastering the Paradoxes and Competing Demands of High Performance* (San Francisco, CA: Jossey-Bass, 1988); R. Quinn and J. Kimberly, "Paradox, Planning, and Perseverance: Guidelines for Managerial Practice" in J. Kimberly and R. Quinn (Eds.), *Managing Organizational Translations* (Homewood, IL: Dow Jones-Irwin, 1984), 295; and R. Quinn and J. Rohrbaugh, "A Spatial Model of Effectiveness Criteria: Towards a Competing Values Approach to Organizational Analysis", *Management Science*, 29(3) (1983), 363. See also the chapters on "Dimensions of Organizational Culture" and "Typologies of Organizational Culture" in A. Gutterman, *Organizational Culture: Research and Management* (Oakland, CA: Sustainable Entrepreneurship Project, 2019) Retrieved from www.seproject.org.

10 S. Bertels, *Embedding Sustainability in Organizational Culture: A How-to Guide for Executives* (London and Ontario: Network for Business Sustainability, 2010). A longer version of the report, which includes more discussion of academic research, including 179 studies conducted over 15 years, and detailed information on the practices discussed in this section (including case studies), was published as S. Bertels, *Embedding Sustainability in Organizational Culture: A Systematic Review of the Body of Knowledge* (London and Ontario: Network for Business Sustainability, 2010) and is available for downloading at http://nbs.net/knowledge/topic-culture/culture/systematic-review/ (accessed May 1, 2020).

11 Network for Business Sustainability and Canadian Business for Social Responsibility, Embedding Sustainability in Organizational Culture: Framework and Best Practices. For further discussion of the "Star Model", see A. Gutterman, *Organizational Design: Creating an Effective Design for Your Business* (Oakland, CA: Sustainable Entrepreneurship Project, 2019) Retrieved from www.seproject.org. See also J. Galbraith, *Organization Design* (Reading, MA: Addison-Wesley, 1977).

12 R. Eccles, K. Perkins and G. Serafeim, "How to Become a Sustainable Company", *MIT Sloan Management Review*, 53(4) (Summer 2012), 43–44.

13 See "About the Research" on page 45 in the article for an extended discussion of the methodology used by the researchers and the scope of the companies surveyed.

14 Id. at 47.

15 Id. at 44.

12 Sustainable Human Resources Management

As discussed elsewhere in this volume, International Standard 26000 (ISO 26000) released by the International Organization for Standardization in November 2010 provides internationally recognized guidance on the underlying principles of the social responsibilities of organizations, the core subjects and issues pertaining to social responsibility and ways to integrate socially responsible behavior into organizations.[1] Article 6.4 of ISO 26000 addresses "labor practices" of organizations, which are defined as including "all policies and practices relating to work performed within, by or on behalf of the organization, including subcontracted work". The precise words of the definition are important because the scope is explicitly intended to extend beyond the relationship of an organization with its direct employees or the responsibilities that an organization has at a workplace that it owns or directly controls. Among the labor practices covered by ISO 26000 are recruitment and promotion of workers; disciplinary and grievance procedures; the transfer and relocation of workers; termination of employment; training and skills development; health, safety and industrial hygiene; recognition of worker organizations and representation and participation of both worker and employer organizations in collective bargaining, social dialogue and tripartite consultation to address social issues related to employment; and any policy or practice affecting conditions of work, in particular working time and remuneration.

The prescriptions in ISO 26000 regarding labor practices are based on the fundamental principles that labor is not a commodity and should not be treated as a factor of production and subjected to the same market forces that apply to commodities and that everyone has a right to earn a living by freely chosen work and the right to just and favorable conditions of work. Article 6.4.1.2 of ISO 26000 describes the important relationship between an organization's labor practices and social responsibility:

> The creation of jobs, as well as wages and other compensation paid for work performed, are among an organization's most important economic and social contributions. Meaningful and productive work is an essential element in human development; standards of living are improved through full and secure employment. Its absence is a

primary cause of social problems. Labor practices have a major impact on respect for the rule of law and on the sense of fairness present in society: socially responsible labor practices are essential to social justice, stability and peace.

The social responsibilities of businesses with respect to their labor practices can be found at the core of the evolving discipline of "sustainable" human resources management (HRM), which has been defined as "strategies and activities to achieve a company's balanced objectives of social accountabilities and economic profits through acquiring, developing and attaining human resources".[2] Sustainability has transformed HRM thinking such that employees are no longer seen as simply tools to be used to achieve financial goals but also as resources to be valued and preserved so that they can continue to make contributions to their companies, families and the general community. As a result, HRM professionals are beginning to see HRM as both a "means" for achieving an organization's sustainability-based strategic objectives and an "end", or objective, in its own right. Specifically, HRM professionals are expected to train and direct employees in carrying out their individual roles and responsibilities with respect to sustainability (i.e., HRM as a "means") and initiate and administer programs and practices that enhance the long-term physical, social and economic well-being of employees (i.e., HRM as an "end").[3]

There has been a significant amount of research and literature on the relationship between sustainability and HRM. For example, surveys of 1,000 organizations across eight countries on the key subject areas of sustainable HRM found that the most frequently mentioned areas were human resource development—training and development, re-training, license and certification, and career development—and employee characteristics, such as employee motivation, flexibility, reliability and volunteerism for performance.[4] Other researchers have emphasized social responsibility, in line with ISO 26000; however, some prefer an economically rational explanation for sustainability in organizations and conceive of sustainable HRM as being the actions that companies should take in their environments in order to have durable access to skilled human resources. Another strand of HRM research and literature, referred to as "strategic HRM", is grounded in business strategy scholarship and sees sustainability as a means, or strategy, for achieving a "sustainable competitive advantage" necessary for a company to maintain long-term economic competitiveness.[5]

ISO 26000 and Socially Responsible HRM

The minimum obligation of companies to their employees is to abide by applicable legal standards in key areas and activities such as recruiting and hiring (i.e., equal opportunity laws), compensation and benefits (i.e., minimum wage and overtime requirements), job design and placement (i.e., laws pertaining to reasonable accommodation for disabilities), protection from discrimination and harassment, workplace safety, family and medical leaves, union relations, performance evaluation and promotion, and prohibitions on unlawful termination.[6] However, socially responsible HRM is based on the proposition that employers have an obligation to exceed legal standards when forging relationships with their employees and take steps to ensure that employees are treated with dignity and value and that their contributions and hard work brings both financial and non-financial rewards. When deciding how to effectively integrate social responsibility into their labor practices and relationships with employees and other workers, companies should refer to Article 6.4.3 of ISO 26000, which describes and lays out related actions and expectations for five core labor practices issues: employment and employment relationships; conditions of work and social protection; social dialogue; health and safety at work; and human development and training in the workplace. While primary responsibility for ensuring fair and equitable treatment of workers lies with governments, the content and enforcement of laws vary from country to country and ISO 26000 is based on the premise that organizations should always adhere to the standards contained in recognized international agreements relating to human rights and labor standards such as the International Labour Organization Tripartite Declaration of Principles Concerning Multinational Enterprises and Social Policy and the UN Guiding Principles on Business and Human Rights.[7]

Article 6.4.6.1 of ISO 26000, which addresses health and safety at work, is particularly important and relevant given the outbreak of the global pandemic at the time of the publication of this volume and the difficult challenges that businesses must address in safeguarding their workers during a public health crisis and an uncertain aftermath. According to ISO 26000, health and safety at work concerns the promotion and maintenance of the highest degree of physical, mental and social well-being of workers and prevention of harm to health caused by working conditions, and also relates to the protection of workers from risks to health and the adaptation of the occupational environment to the physiological and psychological needs of workers. Article 6.4.6.2 of ISO 26000 calls for organizations to

- Develop, implement and maintain an occupational health and safety policy based on the principle that strong safety and health standards and organizational performance are mutually supportive and reinforcing
- Understand and apply principles of health and safety management, including the hierarchy of controls: elimination, substitution, engineering controls, administrative controls, work procedures and personal protective equipment
- Analyze and control the health and safety risks involved in its activities
- Communicate the requirement that workers should follow all safe practices at all times and ensure that workers follow the proper procedures

- Provide the safety equipment needed, including personal protective equipment, for the prevention of occupational injuries, diseases and accidents, as well as for dealing with emergencies
- Record and investigate all health and safety incidents and problems in order to minimize or eliminate them
- Address the specific ways in which occupational safety and health (OSH) risks differently affect women (such as those who are pregnant, have recently given birth or are breastfeeding) and men, or workers in particular circumstances such as people with disabilities, inexperienced or younger workers
- Provide equal health and safety protection for part-time and temporary workers, as well as subcontracted workers
- Strive to eliminate psychosocial hazards in the workplace, which contribute or lead to stress and illness
- Provide adequate training to all personnel on all relevant matters
- Respect the principle that workplace health and safety measures should not involve monetary expenditures by workers

In addition, organizations should base health, safety and environment systems on the participation of the workers concerned and recognize and respect the rights of workers to:

- Obtain timely, full and accurate information concerning health and safety risks and the best practices used to address these risks
- Freely inquire into and be consulted on all aspects of their health and safety related to their work
- Refuse work that is reasonably considered to pose an imminent or serious danger to their life or health or to the lives and health of others
- Seek outside advice from workers' and employers' organizations and others who have expertise
- Report health and safety matters to the appropriate authorities
- Participate in health and safety decisions and activities, including investigation of incidents and accidents
- Be free of the threat of reprisals for doing any of these things

ISO 26000 recommends the formation of joint labor-management health and safety committees in order to ensure that workers are involved in the development of occupational health and safety programs. Among other things, such committees can gather information; develop and disseminate safety manuals and training programs; report, record and investigate accidents; and inspect and respond to problems raised by workers or management. Worker representatives on these committees should be elected by the workers themselves rather than being appointment by management and membership in these committees should be equally divided among management and worker representatives and should include both men and women, whenever possible. Committees should be large enough to allow all shifts, sections and locations of the organization to be represented.

Role of the HR Function with Respect to Sustainability Initiatives

Core organizational commitments with respect to labor practices such as those that might be adopted from ISO 26000 should be approved at the top of the organizational hierarchy by the board of directors and the members of the senior executive team; however, implementation is generally assigned to the human resources (HR) function. Ideas about the role of the HR function with respect to sustainability initiatives can be found in surveys such as the one conducted by Wirtenberg et al., who analyzed the role that HR leaders and the HR function played with respect to sustainability initiatives at nine large, public, multinational companies that had been recognized as being among the world leaders in handling environmental, governance, social responsibility, stakeholder management and work environment issues.[8] In general, HR leaders were strongly positioned for strategic influence at these companies, meaning that they regularly participated on board- and executive-level committees that discussed and oversaw major initiatives; however, in only a few instances were HR leaders proactive initiators of sustainability-related initiatives. Wirtenberg et al. found that the greatest contributions by the HR function to sustainability effectiveness among the studied companies occurred in the following areas:

- Leadership Development: A number of the companies placed a strong emphasis on creating a "culture of development" and offered unlimited leadership development opportunities for high potential employees that reinforced a core of sustainability as one of the overarching corporate goals.
- Training and Development: The HR function was frequently cited as an essential element of the company's efforts to educate employees about sustainable development. For example, HR personnel created examples for employees not involved in the technology area (i.e., accountants, administrators and floor workers) to help them see the relationship between their job tasks and sustainable development. The HR function can also leverage its learning management systems to build employee knowledge about sustainability and allow employees to continuously upgrade their competencies with an easy-to-use program that can also track individual performance and engagement.
- Diversity and Multiculturalism: The HR function played an active role in addressing a number of challenges and issues relating to diversity and multiculturalism including transparency and metrics in diversity policies and procedures; achieving a "winning inclusive culture strategy" and "cognitive diversity"; workplace practices in the

global context; and compensation schemes, such as providing workers in developing countries with a living wage.

- Ethics and Governance: HR leaders were heavily involved in ethics and compliance oversight committees, development and implementation of policies and performance standards that often exceed local laws and regulations and which are consistent with the UN Global Compact, self-assessments, design and administration of mandatory ethics and compliance training programs that also covered sustainability and values, and e-learning programs.
- Talent Management: HR leaders created value to their companies through their efforts with respect to recruiting and staffing and providing companies with the right people and right mental models, as well as the requisite functional expertise. An emphasis on sustainability also provided companies with a competitive advantage when attempting to attract and retain talent (i.e., the more talented workers tend to be attracted to firms that have been branded as a company that is sustainable and "doing the right thing").
- Workforce Engagement: HR was an important player in getting employees engaged and involved in a company's journey to sustainability and high levels of employee engagement were also found to be positively related to company sustainability, customer satisfaction and business growth. Wirtenberg et al. noted that workforce engagement may be the domain that best epitomized the "people" element of the "triple bottom line" and workforce engagement follows from building a sense of commitment among employees who become passionate about making a difference.

Bäbler surveyed the relevant literature and conducted case studies in order to identify the HRM practices most relevant to corporate environmental initiatives (CEI)[9]:

- Training and Development: Training and development focuses on general training plans and guidelines useful for the entire organization as opposed to training programs specifically tailored to individual employees. Training is an important tool in bringing about the changes in skills, knowledge and behavior of employees that is necessary for the success of any CEI.
- Policies: The HR department plays an important role in developing policies and rules that guide employees on how they are expected to act with respect to critical aspects of the employment relationship. With regard to any CEI, the HR department will be involved in creating codes of conduct and behavioral guidelines for environmental matters and relevant societal or legal issues.
- Recruiting: Recruiting involves the key question of "who will be hired" and the HR department will be tasked with identifying the qualities, competencies and abilities that employees will need in

order for the CEI to be successful and recruiting candidates for employment that will strengthen the CEI-related human capital skills of the organization.

- Compensation and Performance Appraisals: Compensation practices and performance appraisals impact motivation and skill development among the individual employees of the organization and can and should be tied to the overall goals and objectives of the CEI. In particular, compensation decisions can be tied to achievement of personal performance targets that align with the tasks and other activities required for the success of the CEI.
- Talent Management: In general, talent management focuses on identifying and nurturing high performing employees who appear to have the potential for promotion to higher positions within the organization. In the context of a CEI, the role of the HR department is to define the specific skills and personal attributes that organizational leaders are expected to have and incorporate those skills and attributes into talent searches and talent development programs.

Bäbler noted that three of the practices described above—training and development, policies and recruiting—could be considered as "macro-level" activities of the HR function that are primarily concerned with the organization as a whole, and the remaining two practices—compensation and performance appraisals—while requiring general know-how and experience from the HR department, are most often practiced at the "micro-level" where the focus is on the performance and development of individuals within the organization. Other key roles and responsibilities for HR professionals with respect to any CEI included acting as a "change facilitator" to anticipate the need for organizational changes in connection with any CEI, prepare the organization for change through clear and thoughtful communication of the necessary changes, oversee execution of the necessary changes, and energize others to accept and embrace the changes; serving in a collaborative role across internal and external organizational boundaries to share information in order for the CEI to be successful; proactively developing new approaches to managing people and helping the organization create an environment that supports continuous learning and creativity; and understanding and attempting to align the concerns of multiple stakeholders, including employees, customers, shareholders and the society at large, and educating managers about the value of HR and the consequences of managing people effectively (or ineffectively).[10]

Notes

1 For further discussion of ISO 26000, see Chapter 8 (Management Systems) in this volume.
2 S. K. Kim, *Sustainable Management and Future of Human Resource Management*, http://docplayer.net/14543650-Sustainable-management-and-future-of-human-resource-management.html (accessed May 7, 2020).

3 See M. Huselid, B. Becker and R. Beatty, *The Workforce Scorecard: Managing Human Capital to Execute Strategy* (Boston, MA: Harvard Business School Press, 2005) and S. Taylor, J. Osland and C. Egri, "Guest Editors' Introduction: Introduction to HRM's Role in Sustainability: Systems, Strategies and Practices", *Human Resources Management*, 51(6) (2012), 789.

4 S. K. Kim, *Sustainable Management and Future of Human Resource Management*, http://docplayer.net/14543650-Sustainable-management-and-future-of-human-resource-management.html (accessed May 7, 2020).

5 B. Mazur, "Sustainable Human Resource Management in Theory and Practice", *Economics and Management*, 6(1) (January 2014), 158159. See also, B. Mazur, "Linking Diversity Management and Corporate Social Responsibility", *Journal of Intercultural Management*, 5(3) (2013), 39.

6 M. Kelly, J. McGowen and C. Williams, *BUSN* (Independence, KY: South-Western Publishing Company, 2014), 58–59.

7 ISO 26000 Article 6.3.10 requires organizational commitment to "fundamental principles and rights at work", which are described by reference to the fundamental rights at work identified by the International Labour Organization including freedom of association and effective recognition of the right to collective bargaining (i.e., workers must have the right to establish and, subject only to the rules of the organization concerned, to join organizations of their own choosing without previous authorization and representative organizations formed or joined by workers should be recognized for purposes of collective bargaining); the elimination of all forms of forced or compulsory labor (i.e., the organization should not engage in or benefit from any use of forced or compulsory labor and should not condone work or service being exacted from any person under the threat of any penalty or when the work is not conducted voluntarily); the effective abolition of child labor (i.e., organizations should not engage in or benefit from any use of child labor, although organizations may employ a child for light work that does not harm a child or interfere with school attendance or with other activities necessary to a child's full development (such as recreational activities)); and the elimination of discrimination based on race, color, gender, religion, national extraction, social origin, political opinion, age, or disability regarding employment and occupation (i.e., hiring policies and practices, earnings, employment conditions, access to training and promotion and termination of employment should be based solely on the requirements of the job). For further information on international standards and instruments addressing labor practices, see A. Gutterman, *Sustainability Standards and Instruments* (New York: Business Experts Press, 2020) and A. Gutterman, *Business and Human Rights* (Chicago, IL: American Bar Association, Forthcoming 2021).

8 J. Wirtenberg, J. Harmon, W. Russell and K. Fairfield, "HR's Role in Building a Sustainable Enterprise: Insights from Some of the World's Best Companies", *Human Resource Planning*, 30(1) (2007), 10. The companies included Alcoa, Bank of America, BASF, The Coca Cola Company, Eastman Kodak, Intel, Novartis AG, Royal Philips and Unilever. Id. at 12.

9 S. Bäbler, *Human Resource Management and Environmental Sustainability* (Zurich: Institut für Strategie- und Unternehmensökonomik at University of Zurich, 2010), 30–31.

10 Id. at 33–34.

13 Sustainable Technology Management

Technology plays a big role in the pursuit of sustainability and economic development. Sustainable technologies include technologies that use durable, low-maintenance, recyclable and economic materials and technologies, including materials and technologies that can be locally sourced to reduce transportation costs. Sustainable technologies may be incorporated into sustainable design practices for products that are focused on designing products to leverage materials and technologies that will reduce product life cycle environmental impacts. An effective sustainable technology will facilitate improvements in the appearance, performance, quality, functionality and ecological, social and economic value of the products. From a technology management perspective, companies may consider investing in the development of new technologies that provide alternatives to traditional technologies that have been shown to be being damaging to the health of members of the community and to the environment.

Sustainable technology management is based on the premise that individual companies can and do make an impact on sustainable development through the decisions they make as part of their technology management programs: what products should they manufacture and what technologies should be included in those products; what process technologies should be used; what types and amounts of resources should be used in the manufacturing process; how much should be invested in research and development (R&D) and which R&D projects should be given the highest priority; and can the company deploy technologies that do not harm the environment and improve the overall quality of life of their employees, customers and members of society in general.

While sustainable technology management obviously impacts the traditional economic "bottom line" that is relevant to investors, it also is important to many of the other key stakeholders of the company[1]:

- Many customers are concerned about whether or not sourced components have been manufactured to meet certain environmental standards and may require that supplier provide the results of audits of their manufacturing processes to verify compliance.

- Employees are concerned about the health and safety aspects of participating in the manufacturing process such as air quality and exposure to harmful materials in the workplace.
- Local communities are concerned about the environmental impact of manufacturing activities including emissions, odors and noise and it is often necessary and prudent to providing information to community members about standards and performance.
- Regulators will be concerned about a company's compliance with applicable environmental laws and regulations as well as progress being made on effort to improve energy efficiency and reduce harmful emissions beyond the levels otherwise permitted by law.
- Consumer action groups will monitor various impacts of the company's finished products such as greenhouse gas emissions and may engage in adverse publicity campaigns to force the company to take steps to improve its performance.

Areas and Issues Relating to Sustainable Technology Management

Developing and implementing a sustainable technology management initiative begins with identifying and understanding when and how the operational activities of businesses can have an adverse environmental impact. A good starting point would be to think about the following areas and issues[2]:

- *Air Pollution*: Companies should consider and implement technological solutions that increase the efficiency of energy supply and energy use. An effort should be made to reduce dependence on fossil fuels and when such fuels are used it should done in a manner that reduce pollution. Companies can help reduce air pollution, promote climate protection, and save money, by employing energy-efficient technology in their business operations and implementing strategies to reduce the environmental impacts from commuting, fleet and business air travel.
- *Renewable Energy*: Companies should consider embracing renewal energy initiatives, sometimes referred to as "green power" or "clean energy", which involve reliance on energy sources that are continuously renewed (e.g., wind, solar, geothermal, hydro and biomass).
- *Infrastructure*: Companies make decisions relating to technology-based public infrastructure all the time and consideration must be given to selecting communications and transportation solutions that are the most efficient in terms of cost and which have the most modest environmental impact. When companies are identifying sites for manufacturing, R&D and other activities, consideration should be given to ease of access for personnel.

- *Water*: Companies often engage in activities that raise issues regarding excess water usage and pollution and it is incumbent upon them to operate in a manner that does not harm their surrounding communities. Technologies are available for controlling many types of pollutants and manufacturing processes should be modified to minimize water consumption.

- *Product Design and Manufacturing*: One of the tenets of sustainable development is to create industrial ecosystems that imitate natural ones and companies have been drawn to finding ways to reduce, reuse, and recycle materials and products. The most innovative companies have used technology to aggressively redesign their products and processes and have formally embraced environmental issues as being just as important as the cost and quality of their products and the safety of their workers. In the manufacturing area, consideration should be given to energy and water use, water generation, emissions, noise and odors, logistics and operations.

- *Materials*: Companies need to consider the environmental impact of the materials that they manufacture and/or use in their products. New technologies have revolutionized the properties of widely-used materials such as steel, concrete and plastic and can also be used by scientists and engineers to design new materials that facilitate the development of products that are more energy efficient, consume less mineral resources for their manufacture, and are lighter, stronger and recyclable.

- *Green Building Design*: Companies realize substantial benefits from applying green design principles to their design and construction projects at their facilities, both new building projects and major renovations of existing buildings. Green building design includes both selecting energy efficient equipment and using natural sources for energy needed to power activities within the facility. Companies can seek LEED (Leadership in Energy and Environmental Design) certification to benchmark their efforts with respect to resource efficiency in their facilities.

- *Paper Usage*: Paper manufacturing consumes a significant amount of energy and natural resources and companies can contribute to reducing these harmful impacts on the environment by reducing the amount of paper they use in day-to-day activities (e.g., two-sided copying and emphasis on electronic distribution and use of documents), selecting paper with a high recycled content and recycling paper products.

- *Recycling and Waste Management*: All companies can find ways to reduce waste and improve their overall efficiency and productivity while enhancing their public image. Waste reduction begins by tightening up purchasing practices for raw materials, office supplies and equipment including purchasing environmentally preferable products.

When designing products and packaging, companies should look for ways to reduce the amount of materials. Companies should also mandate participation by all personnel in recycling initiatives.

- *Environmentally Preferable Purchasing*: Environmentally preferable purchasing (EPP) has become popular among governmental agencies and call for procurement of goods and services that have a reduced impact on human health and the environment as compared to other goods and services serving the same purpose. When practicing EPP, governmental agencies and companies must take into account numerous environmental considerations, such as post-consumer recycled content; energy and water efficiency; durability; low/zero air emissions and hazardous substances; easy, non-hazardous maintenance; end-of-life management that keeps materials out of landfills (e.g., reuse, recycling, return to manufacturers); low life-cycle cost and packaging and distribution efficiency.

- *Information Technology*: Companies must track advances in information technology and consider adopting new technologies that will allow them to exert better control over their industrial processes, thereby creating opportunities to make those processes more efficient, safer and less damaging to the environment. Information technology can also be used to collect and analyze data from the supply chain and thus make it easier for companies to manage suppliers and ensure they are acting in a socially responsible manner.

Addressing many of the areas and issues mentioned above will require the development of new processes and procedures, including implementation of environmental management systems and changes to existing compliance programs, and investment in new technologies and platforms; however, sustainable technology, for all of its anticipated benefits, is not the end goal. When making decisions about sustainable technology management, companies must be satisfied that the technology and processes will make them more productive and efficient can contribute to the overall success of the business. While it is possible to create customized technology solutions internally, it is easier and less costly to rely on the work of others. Companies must create a dedicated team to scan for new solutions and test them before they are seriously considered for full-scale implementation. Any new solution must be adequately supported and training must be available.

For most companies, management of "technology" involves both engineering/product development activities (i.e., incorporating technology into products and/or the processes used to manufacture products) and information technology activities that include internal and external communications and other projects and support. In some instances, these companies will create separate management structures for each of these functions, although a single senior executive, who is generally referred to as either the "chief information officer" (discussed below) or the chief technology officer, will still retain ultimate responsibility and the leaders of each function will report to that executive.[3] The activities and responsibilities of the technology executive will vary depending on the size and business focus of the company and the skills, experience and job descriptions of the other members of the senior management group; however, the executive should expect to be involved in the development and implementation of a technology strategy for the company, including identification and implementation of sustainable technology initiatives and solutions; planning and coordinating R&D activities to support the company's technology strategy; coordinating the technology strategies and activities of divisions and business units; acting as the functional manager of the activities of the technology managers for each of the company's divisions and business units; overseeing technology sales, purchases and licensing activities; providing information and advice to the senior management group and other company managers regarding technology-related issues; and supporting new technology-based business initiatives launched by the company.[4]

Sustainable Product Design and Use

In addition to the manufacturing process, the environmental impact of the finished products themselves needs to be considered, a process that takes into account the composition of the finished products and how they are used and disposed. The quality of a company's product from the perspective of environmental impact can influence the reputation of the company's business, inspire and motive employees in their day-to-day activities and decisions and define the terms of engagement between the company and key stakeholders such as supply chain partners and customers. Some of the ways that companies can make their products more "green", and the potential benefits from taking those steps, including the following[5]:

- Substituting recycled/renewable materials for non-renewables saves material cost and creates a more attractive product for some buyers
- Reducing hazardous substances in products lowers the cost of monitoring, treatment and disposal and makes them appear to be safer and more desirable to consumers
- Improving the recyclability or biodegradability of products enhances the value of material inputs and reduces disposal costs
- Lowering the energy requirements for products reduces the cost of use, improves product desirability and anticipates regulatory requirements and future standards
- Improving product durability lessens the need for non-renewable materials and increases product value

Environmental issues and opportunities should be considered early in the product development process, at the design phase, and normally include the composition of the materials to be used in the product and whether they comprise recycled, renewable or reused materials, or are non-renewable or hazardous; the need for the product to be disposed or recycled at the end of its useful life; the intensity of energy consumption and greenhouse gas emissions of the product; and the potential ability of the product to help customers and consumers reduce their own environmental impact by the way that they use the product throughout its life.[6] Measurement tools and performance indicators should be developed for each of the key indicators of the environmental performance and impact of products such as recycled/reused content of products; recyclability of products; renewable materials content of product; non-renewable materials intensity over product lifetime; restricted substances content of products; and intensity of energy consumption and greenhouse gas emissions associated with products.[7] Tools, such as the Cradle to Cradle® product design framework, are available to help companies integrate sustainability into their product development and design processes and showcase their efforts to prospective customers.

Sustainable Manufacturing

Many companies have recognized sustainable manufacturing techniques as an important part of their overall strategies for optimizing their businesses. Among the commonly cited benefits of "greening" manufacturing activities are reducing energy consumption reduces energy costs; reducing waste generation and emissions reduces the cost of monitoring, treatment and disposal and reduces the loss of the economic value of materials; reprocessing and/or remanufacturing end-of-life materials will increase the value of material inputs; replacing or upgrading equipment and/or production lines will improve the efficiency of operations; and improving on-site biodiversity and the native habitat will reduce the need for watering, air conditioning and other maintenance.[8] Key areas for businesses to consider when looking to reduce the adverse environmental impact of their manufacturing activities and improve productivity and efficiency include energy and water use, water generation, emissions, noise and odors, logistics and operations.[9] Measurement tools and performance indicators should be developed for water consumption, energy consumption, use of renewal energy, greenhouse gas emissions, waste generation; emissions into the air and water and natural cover.[10]

Sustainable Information Technology Management

Sustainable, or "green", information technology (IT) has been broadly defined to include effort to manufacture, manage, use and dispose of IT equipment in a way that minimizes damage to the environment.[11] For IT manufacturers, sustainable IT includes the methods that care used to produce their products in ways that do not harm the environment (e.g., reducing the amount of harmful chemicals and toxic substances in the products, making the products more energy efficient and packaging the products in recycled materials). When the focus is management and use of IT assets in day-to-day business activities, consideration needs to be given to purchasing energy-efficient equipment, managing the power consumption during the use of the equipment and making sure that the equipment is disposed at the end of its life cycle in a manner that is not damaging to the environment.

In order for sustainable IT initiatives to be effective, appropriate business practices must be embedded in business operations such that sustainability is no longer seen as a separate initiative but as part of the essence of how things are done on a day-to-day basis within the company.[12] Many companies rely on a chief information officer (CIO) as the person and position ideally placed to assist in this process because he or she has experience in developing and implementing business systems and relationships that extend throughout the organization. Baya and Mathaisei, writing on behalf of PwC, suggested that the CIO's contributions to sustainability efforts could be described in three dimensions that included activities that could be done almost entirely within the IT department and activities requiring collaboration with other departments within the organization and with business partners outside of the organization in its value chain[13]:

- **Embedding sustainability in IT:** Often referred to as "Green IT", this dimension includes the actions that can be taken by the IT department to measure, monitor, and manage the environmental and social footprint from the use of IT resources, both within and outside IT operations. Green IT is the cornerstone of CIO involvement, given that it is largely under his or her control, and provides the credibility needed in order to influence other departments and make contributions on the other dimensions.
- **Embedding sustainability in the enterprise:** This dimension focuses on how the IT department can assist in establishing the internal systems and processes needed to enable the rest of the enterprise to monitor, measure, and manage their environmental and social footprint. For example, internal systems and processes are commonly used to manage energy and water usage throughout the company and waste production across all facilities and internal operations.
- **Embedding sustainability in the value chain:** The IT department can collaborate with other to collect and analyze the data needed to measure, monitor and manage the environmental and social footprint in the company's value chains. Studies have shown that members of

the company's value chain have a substantial impact on the sustainability performance of the company and it is important to gain the support and cooperation of value chain members in order for the sustainability initiatives to be successful.

Specific sustainable technology activities and projects might include the following:

- IT equipment can be used to help companies design more eco-friendly products and databases created and maintained through the IT support function can make it easier for other department to assess and analyze information on materials and other inputs (i.e., data mining) that can be used to develop sustainable products.
- Within the IT department itself, the CIO can encourage personnel to engage in conservation activities including simple things like shutting off their computers and the lights when they leave the office for the day.
- Environmental impact should be a primary consideration when making IT investments and companies should take advantage of technologies and techniques that will reduce energy consumption.
- The IT department should be an active participant in developing tracking and reporting tools that the company needs in order to comply with its obligations under environmental regulations.
- The CIO should improve asset life cycle management by implementing a formal IT asset disposal policy and take advantage of "take back" programs offered by IT equipment manufacturers and engage with life cycle asset disposal companies.
- The CIO should work with the COO and other members of the executive team to create and implement programs that make operational activities more environmentally efficient (e.g., systems that reduce the amount of paper that employees need to use in order to print out documents and other records, deploying tracking systems to measure plant emissions and installing systems that save energy by controlling heat and air conditioning in the office).
- The CIO can mobilize the IT department to support the company's activities with respect to measuring and reporting performance on its sustainability activities by developing or acquiring the software and other technology that eases the process of monitoring and collecting data need for analysis of sustainability performance and the analytical tools can be used to identify opportunities and problems to be addressed in the company's sustainability strategies.
- The tools available from the IT department can also be deployed to contribute directly to the company's sustainability initiatives in a number of areas outside of environmental impact. For example, technology-based tools can be used to support compliance systems

(e.g., supply chain management, environment, health, safety, etc.), employee and customer satisfaction tracking systems, product safety programs, customer knowledge improvement systems, customer engagement via social media and mobile services.

- The CIO and other members of the IT department can collaborate with organizations outside of the company to promote sustainability. For example, the IT department can assist in the development of design tools for supply chain partners to ensure that design for inputs to the company's products meet its sustainability standards. Companies should also track and adopt relevant standards from industry groups that will enhance their ability to measure their own performance, and the performance of their suppliers, on use of hazardous materials, equipment and materials efficiency and socially responsible business practices.

Given the broad range of potential activities under each of the dimensions described above, the CIO will often create a program office under his or her scope of authority to specifically schedule and manage sustainability changes. Specialists in the program office would be responsible for developing the specific tools and processes necessary for the sustainability activities to be effective and the metrics required to assess the success of the initiatives. A dedicated program office is highly recommended when the sustainability initiatives are first launched; however, the need for such an office will hopefully diminish as sustainability becomes more embedded throughout all parts of the organization and other departments assume more responsibility for measurement.

While the IT department can and should play a leading role in implementing each of the principles described above, success will depend on the cooperation and support of other departments. The CIO will need to reach out to other departments to ensure that collaboration goes smoothly and that all relevant policies and procedures have been centrally vetted to identify and remove redundancies and clearly establish responsibilities and communications channels. The CIO should also champion socially responsible IT among the other members of the executive team and the board of directors and establish performance metrics that can be easily tracked and reported upon on a regular basis. The IT department should also be well represented in outreach efforts and other communications to the company's stakeholders: employees, customers, value chain partners, regulators and community members. Finally, the CIO should make socially responsible IT a positive and motivating endeavor the members of the IT department, helping them to feel that what they are doing is a valued contribution to the company's sustainability efforts, their colleagues in the workplace and society generally.

Planning and Implementing the Sustainable Technology Initiative

A company's efforts regarding sustainable technology management should be carried out in an organized manner to ensure that the principles and goals of the initiative are clearly understood and widely disseminated within the organization and among the company's important external stakeholders. The board of directors and members of the executive team, led by the executive with responsibility for technology management (i.e., the CIO or a chief technology officer), should prepare and adopt a mission statement that includes the guiding principles for the initiative, the goals of the initiatives and guidelines for the operational procedures that will need to be implemented in order for the initiative to be successful and for progress to be measured. The mission statement should be distributed to all employees and should be emphasized repeatedly by the top leaders of the organization.

As companies identify the areas of interest for their sustainable technology management initiative, they need to develop methods for measuring performance and commit to reporting the progress that the company is making against its performance goals. Metrics and benchmarks are the best way to ensure that everyone in the organization keeps the initiative at the top of their priority list and allows the company to quickly identify areas where more work is needed. Metrics for measuring performance on environmentally-related sustainability efforts are suggested elsewhere in this chapter and the leader of the initiative should ensure that information gathering tools are in place to generate those metrics. Performance reports, which include a clear statement of the goals and the means for measurement, should be prepared and published on a regular basis, no less frequently than annually, and should explain to readers what the company is doing and what effect the initiatives are having on the company's environmental impact, the traditional economic "bottom line" (i.e., reduction in costs) and the reputation of the company among its employees, customers and other stakeholders. Distribution should be broad and include all of the company's key stakeholders: employees, customers, suppliers, investors, regulators, environmental groups, industry associations and members of the communities in which the company operates and/or markets and sells its products.

Companies should proactively involve employees from all parts of the organization in the sustainable technology management effort by forming teams with members from different departments to coordinate certain activities such as reduction of waste, recycling and reducing/prevention pollution. These teams, sometimes referred to as "green teams", are a great way to roll out an initiative across the company and ensure that all departments are following similar guidelines and that best practices are shared quickly and disseminated throughout the organization. In order to be successful, however, green teams need to be given the same status as other important projects such as product development and provided with support from the top of the organization as well adequate financial and human resources and opportunities to communicate directly with employees and educate them about their responsibilities. When forming the teams, provision should be made for encouraging all employees, not just team members, to make suggestions about improvements that can be made about how the company goes about basic but important tasks such as using paper products, turning off lights and equipment, recycling and waste disposal and setting thermostats. Employees should also be asked to weigh in on how the company can be more energy efficient and environmentally conscientious when design and manufacturing products. Many companies expand their reward and bonus programs to include ideas from employees that lead to demonstrable financial and social benefits. Environmental activities should be one of many ways that companies provide opportunities for employees to live healthy lives and benefit from working with the company.

Another fundamental piece of an effective sustainable technology management initiative is training and education for executives, managers and employees. It is not only important for everyone to understand how they can participate in day-to-day activities that reduce the environmental impact of the company's operations, but an effort should be made to make sure that they have current information about the economic, environmental and social trends that are driving decisions about sustainability within the company. Well-informed employees will be more motivated to participate and will have a better idea of exactly what they are doing. Educating executives and managers makes them better prepared to engage with employees and other stakeholders of the company. In particular, when company representatives are armed with the most current thinking on sustainability issues and practices, they can have more effective engagements with supply chain partners, regulators, industry groups and local communities on the company's goals and activities relating to the environment. Education can include formal training classes, distribution of articles, webinars and videos and guest speakers. Another part of education is ensuring that there is a constant stream of communication on sustainability efforts including regular staff meetings, in-house newsletters and e-mail bulletins and managers who are accessible to employees with questions or suggestions.

Finally, while engaging and communicating with external stakeholders has been referred to several times already above, there are several specific issues that companies need to consider when developing plans for interacting with customers, community members and other important players in their industries and markets. First, the company should ensure that all company representatives are adequately educated and trained on how to communicate with customers and community members about the company's sustainability efforts and environmentally-related aspects of the company's products (e.g., how they are designed, what materials are used, how they operate and how they should be disposed). Second, companies can and should demonstrate their commitment to sustainability by getting involved with community activities including encouraging volunteerism by employees and making contributions to support local environmental groups and activities. Third, the leader of the sustainability technology management initiative, and other people from throughout the organization, should getting involved with industry groups working to develop best practices for socially responsible technology management. This is a great way to build a reputation as a leader in the field and tap into the expertise of other companies and consultants to develop ideas for improvements to the product design, procurement, manufacturing, waste management and assessment/reporting practices. Fourth, companies should continuously look for opportunities to partner with other organizations that have developed a reputation for being innovative contributors to sustainable technology.

Notes

1 OECD Sustainable Manufacturing Toolkit: Seven Steps to Environmental Excellence—Start-Up Guide (2011), www.oecd.org/innovation/green/toolkit, 16.
2 Examples in this section are adapted from National Research Council, "Pathways to Sustainability" in *The Role of Technology in Environmentally Sustainable Development* (Washington, DC: The National Academies Press, 1995).
3 S. Hart, "Inside the Minds—The Role of the CTO in a Technology Company" in *Achieving Success as a CTO: Leading CTOs on Building IT's Reputation, Capitalizing on Employee Strengths and Creating a Productive Environment* (Boston, MA: Thomson/Aspatore, 2008).
4 A. Gutterman, *Technology Management and Transactions* (Eagan, MN: Thomson Reuters, 2019), 707.
5 OECD Sustainable Manufacturing Toolkit: Seven Steps to Environmental Excellence—Start-Up Guide (2011), www.oecd.org/innovation/green/toolkit, 32.
6 Id. at 33.
7 Id. at 34.
8 Id. at 25.
9 Id. at 26.
10 Id. at 26–27.
11 K. Walsh, "Environmentally Sustainable IT: Definition and Solutions", CIO.com (October 29, 2007), http://www.cio.com/article/2437751/energy-efficiency/environmentally-sustainable-it-definition-and-solutions.html (accessed May 2, 2020).
12 V. Baya and B. Mathaisei, "The CIO's Next Leadership Opportunity: Sustainability", *PWC Technology Forecast*, Issue 4 (2011), 56, http://www.pwc.com/us/en/technology-forecast/2011/issue4/features/feature-sustainability-cio.html (accessed May 2, 2020).
13 Id.

14 Reporting and Communications

In order to know whether or not sustainability and corporate social responsibility (CSR) initiatives and their related commitments are actually improving the company's performance it is necessary to have in place procedures for reporting and verification, each of which are important tools for measuring change and communicating those changes to the company's stakeholders. Hohnen and Potts described reporting as "communicating with stakeholders about a firm's economic, environmental and social management and performance" and verification, which is often referred to as "assurance", as a form of measurement that involves on-site inspections and review of management systems to determine levels of conformity to particular criteria set out in codes and standards to which the company may have agreed to adhere.[1] Verification procedures should be tailored to the company's organizational culture and the specific elements of the company's CSR strategy and commitments; however, it is common for companies to rely on internal audits, industry (i.e., peer) and stakeholder reviews and professional third-party audits. Verification procedures should be established before a specific CSR initiative is undertaken and should be included in the business case for the initiative.

While, as discussed below, certain CSR and corporate sustainability disclosures have now become minimum legal requirements in some jurisdictions, in general such disclosures are still a voluntary matter and directors have some leeway as to the scope of the disclosure made by their companies and how they are presented to investors and other stakeholders. Some companies continue to limit their disclosures to those are specifically required by regulators; however, most companies have realized that they need to pay attention to the issues raised by institutional investors and other key stakeholders and make sure that they are covered in the disclosure program. At the other extreme, there are companies that have embraced sustainability as integral to their brands and have elected to demonstrate their commitment by preparing and disseminating additional disclosures that illustrate how they have woven sustainability into their long-term strategies and day-to-day operational activities. These companies understand that not only are investors paying more attention but that more and more people everywhere are considering environmental, social and governance (ESG) performance when deciding whether to buy a company's products and/or work for a particular company and that it is therefore essential to lay out their specific CSR and corporate sustainability goals and the metrics used to track performance and provide regular reports to all of the company's stakeholders on how well they are doing against those goals.[2]

The scope and sophistication of CSR reporting has come a long way since the idea first came up in the mid-1990s, when only a handful of companies reported on social responsibility issues and activities in addition to their regular financial reports. Today almost all of the largest global companies produce reports on their environmental policies and activities, often providing interested parties with a whole range of documents that can be accessed in a separate yet highly visible section of the company website. Other international standards, such as the UN Global Compact, explicitly incorporate reporting as a fundamental requirement for demonstrating a commitment to sustainability. Specifically, companies participating in the Compact are required to make an annual "Communication on Progress" that outlines the actions they have taken with respect to integrating the Compact's ten principles and to make the communication publicly available to stakeholders through annual financial, sustainability or other prominent public reports in print or on the company's website.

Legal and Regulatory Considerations

Cleveland et al. noted that when companies get started with sustainability reporting they have a number of basic questions: "What are we legally required to communicate?" "What are we permitted to communicate?" What can or should we say to stay competitive and protect business relationships, profitability and our social license to operation? "What standards should we use?"[3] They pointed out that many companies start down the path of sustainability reporting primarily as a marketing strategy, hoping to address the questions from customers and demonstrate social responsibility and philanthropy as part of an effort to build reputation. However, as the information is made available companies must be prepared to defend it by responding to demands for verification and "ratings" released by organizations that often do not seek input from the companies that they evaluate. At the same time investors are likely to have questions regarding the matters covered in sustainability reports and companies can expect that they will soon be asked to expand their reporting beyond their own activities to include their supply chains. Very quickly what may have begun as a project in the marketing department expands into a multi-disciplinary initiative that will require support from across the organization and development of a comprehensive communications program with all of the company's stakeholders to ensure that the sustainability reporting is addressing their needs and expectations.

Williams noted that to the extent that governments have regulated corporate responsibility *per se*, such regulation has focused on disclosure and during the period 2000–2015 over 20 countries enacted legislation to require public companies to issue reports including environmental and/or social information.[4] Many of these countries are in Europe and the EU has implemented a directive that requires nearly 7,000 large companies and "public interest organizations", such as banks and insurance companies, to "prepare a nonfinancial statement containing information relating to at least environmental matters, social and employee-related matters including diversity, respect for human rights, anti-corruption and bribery matters".[5] When preparing their reports companies are expected to describe their business model and the outcomes and risks of their policies. Larger companies are also required to include and evaluate information on their supply chains, which means that smaller companies that act as suppliers to the reporting companies will need to expand their own data collection and information reporting activities even though they are not directly subject to the public reporting requirements. In addition, several stock exchanges around the world require social and/or environmental disclosure as part of their listing requirements including exchanges in Australia, Brazil, Canada, India, Singapore, South Africa and the London Stock Exchange.[6] Also, pension funds in countries such as Australia, Belgium, Canada, France, Germany, Italy, Japan, Sweden and the UK are required to disclose the extent to which the fund incorporates social and environmental information into their investment decisions.[7] All things considered, surveys show that more and more jurisdictions are implementing mandatory ESG disclosure requirements and that "there is a clear trend towards an increasing number of environmental and social disclosure requirements around the world".[8]

The US, which has comprehensive reporting requirements relating to a broad range of corporate governance matters, has been a notable laggard with respect to establishing a comprehensive general ESG disclosure framework. However, while ESG- and CSR-related reporting is not yet specifically required for companies with shares listed on US exchanges, by 2013 more than half of the companies in the S&P 500 had voluntarily decided to report and disclose ESG and CSR information[9] and so-called sustainability reporting is well on its way to becoming an expected standard practice that must be added to oversight agenda of the entire board and the disclosure and reporting committee. In the US the federal Securities and Exchange Commission (SEC) has struggled in its attempts to prescribe requirements for reporting on sustainability-matters in filings that must be made by public companies. For example, with respect to climate change the SEC promulgated Release No. 33-9106, *Commission Guidance Regarding Disclosure Related to Climate Change* (February 2, 2010), which suggested that climate change disclosures might be provided in responses to certain disclosure items in Regulation S-K such as Description of Business (Item 101 of Regulation S-K), Legal Proceedings (Item 103 of Regulation S-K), Risk Factors (Item 503(c) of Regulation S-K), and Management's Discussion and Analysis of Financial Condition and Results of Operations (Item 303 of Regulation S-K). The Release called on companies to consider disclosures on the following matters relating to climate change: the impact of legislation and regulation regarding climate change, including the potential impact of pending legislation; when material, the impact on their business of treaties or international accords relating to climate change; whether legal, technological, political, and scientific developments regarding climate change will create new opportunities or risks, including reputational risks; and the actual and potential material impacts of the physical effects of climate change on their business, such as the effects of severe weather, sea levels, arability of farmland, and water availability and quality.[10]

Other sustainability-related areas in which the Congress, the SEC and state lawmakers have required disclosures include the sourcing of certain "conflict minerals"; payments to governments by resource extraction issuers; business with certain governments, persons, and entities subject to specific US trade sanctions; releases into the environment; management through recycling; median employee pay; and mine safety disclosure.[11] Directors need to be involved in decisions regarding placement of CSR and corporate sustainability disclosures including links in SEC filings to online sustainability reports and adding sustainability information to proxy statements as part of the company's investor-focused communication efforts. Companies can, and often do, rely on communications professionals to prepare sustainability reports; however, even when such reports are not included in the company's SEC filings they should be subject to the same level of scrutiny applied in procedures established by the board's disclosure committee.

In addition, companies may be subject to disclosure requirements under the laws of various provincial, state and local laws in the countries in which they operate. For example, under the California Transparency Supply Chains Act of 2010,[12] which went into effect on January 1, 2012, every retail seller and manufacturer doing business in California and having annual worldwide gross receipts that exceed $100 million is required to disclose its efforts to eradicate slavery and human trafficking from its direct supply chain for tangible goods offered for sale. The disclosures must be posted on the retail seller's or manufacturer's website with a conspicuous and easily understood link to the required information placed on the business' homepage. In the event the retail seller or manufacturer does not have a website, consumers must be provided the written disclosure within 30 days of receiving a written request for the disclosure from a consumer. At a minimum, the disclosures should disclose to what extent, if any, that the retail seller or manufacturer does each of the following:

- Engages in verification of product supply chains to evaluate and address risks of human trafficking and slavery. The disclosure must specify if the verification was not conducted by a third party.

- Conducts audits of suppliers to evaluate supplier compliance with company standards for trafficking and slavery in supply chains. The disclosure must specify if the verification was not an independent, unannounced audit.
- Requires direct suppliers to certify that materials incorporated into the product comply with the laws regarding slavery and human trafficking of the country or countries in which they are doing business.
- Maintains internal accountability standards and procedures for employees or contractors failing to meet company standards regarding slavery and trafficking.
- Provides company employees and management, who have direct responsibility for supply chain management, training on human trafficking and slavery, particularly with respect to mitigating risks within the supply chains of products.

The exclusive remedy for a violation of the disclosure obligations is an action brought by the California Attorney General for injunctive relief.

Scope and Format of CSR Reporting

The scope of the company's reporting and verification efforts will depend on various factors including the size of the company, the stage of development and focus of its CSR commitments, legal requirements, the financial and human resources available for investment in those activities and the degree to which companies want and are able to integrate sustainability indicators into their traditional reporting of financial results. As mentioned elsewhere in this publication, Ceres, a non-profit organization advocating for sustainability leadership (www.ceres.org), has developed and disseminated its Ceres Roadmap as a resource to help companies re-engineer themselves to confront and overcome environmental and social challenges and as a guide toward corporate sustainability leadership.[13] In the area of disclosure and reporting, Ceres stated that the overall vision was that companies would report regularly on their sustainability strategy and performance, and that disclosure would include credible, standardized, independently verified metrics encompassing all material stakeholder concerns, and details of goals and plans for future action. Specific expectations regarding disclosure were as follows:

- D1—Standards for Disclosure: Companies will disclose all relevant sustainability information using the Global Reporting Initiative (GRI) Standards as well as additional sector-relevant indicators.
- D2—Disclosure in Financial Filings: Companies will disclose material sustainability risks and opportunities, as well as performance data, in financial filings.

- D3—Scope and Content: Companies will regularly disclose trended performance data and targets relating to global direct operations, subsidiaries, joint ventures, products and supply chains. Companies will demonstrate integration of sustainability into business systems and decision-making, and disclosure will be balanced, covering challenges as well as positive impacts.
- D4—Vehicles for Disclosure: Companies will release sustainability information through a range of disclosure vehicles including sustainability reports, annual reports, financial filings, corporate websites, investor communications and social media.
- D5—Verification and Assurance: Companies will verify key sustainability performance data to ensure valid results and will have their disclosures reviewed by an independent, credible third party.

When establishing plans for reporting and verification it is useful to obtain and review copies of reports that have been done and published by comparable companies. Reports of larger companies are generally available on their corporate websites and extensive archives of past CSR-focused reports can be accessed through various online platforms such as CorporateRegister.com, a widely recognized global online directory of corporate responsibility reports. It is also important to have a good working understanding of well-known reporting and verification initiatives such as the GRI Standards; the International Integrated Reporting Framework; the Sustainability Accounting Standards Board framework; the AccountAbility AA1000 series; the UN Global Compact; and the International Auditing and Assurance Standards Board ISAE 3000 standard. Country-specific information is also available through professional organizations such as the Canadian Chartered Professional Accountants, which has published an extensive report on sustainability reporting in Canada.[14]

CSR Communications

In addition to formal reporting on corporate responsibility, companies should consider how their corporate responsibility activities can be integrated into their overall corporate communications strategies and activities and their marketing activities. Finnish Textile & Fashion, the central organization for textile, clothing and fashion companies in Finland, cautioned that CSR communications should be appropriate in light of the company's nature, size, operating methods and potential risks related to corporate responsibility, and recommended that companies focus their communications efforts on matters that are essential from the business perspective, are of interest to stakeholders and include potential operational and reputational risks. For example, since consumers are interested in the origin of the products that are marketed and sold by the company, communications should include transparent information on all stages of the value chain including a description of how the company monitors the environmental and social responsibility of supply chain partners and data on compliance by those partners with company requirements. Information on environmental and social responsibility aspects of the inputs to products should also be presented and corporate communications are a good opportunity for companies to describe the process that is followed in designing and manufacturing products including consideration of methods for managing the environmental footprint of products over their entire lifecycle of use and disposal.[15]

ISO 26000 also emphasized the important roles that internal and external communications play in social responsibility including[16]:

- Raising awareness both within and outside the organization on its strategies and objectives, plans, performance and challenges for social responsibility
- Demonstrating respect for social responsibility principles
- Helping to engage and create dialogue with stakeholders
- Addressing legal and other requirements for the disclosure of information related to social responsibility
- Showing how the organization is meeting its commitments on social responsibility and responding to the interests of stakeholders and expectations of society in general
- Providing information about the impacts of the organization's activities, products and services, including details of how the impacts change over time
- Helping to engage and motivate employees and others to support the organization's activities in social responsibility
- Facilitating comparison with peer organizations, which can stimulate improvements in performance on social responsibility
- Enhancing an organization's reputation for socially responsible action, openness, integrity and accountability, to strengthen stakeholder trust in the organization

Section 7.5.2 of ISO 26000 described the necessary and appropriate characteristics of information relating to social responsibility as including completeness, understandability, accuracy and verifiability, balance, timeliness and accessibility, and noted that organizations can select from a wide range of methods for communication including meetings, public events, forums, reports, newsletters, magazines, posters, advertising (including public statements to promote some aspect of social responsibility, letters, voicemail, live performance, video, websites, podcasts (website audio broadcast), blogs (website discussion forums), product inserts and labels, media activities (e.g., press releases, interviews, editorials and articles), submissions to government bodies or public inquiries, participation in social responsibility interest groups and articles in communications instruments aimed at peer organizations.[17]

When developing a communications strategy and program relating to social responsibility, each of the organization's key stakeholders should be considered and plans should be made to tailor communications with stakeholders to the social responsibility issues that are of greatest concern to them. For example, communications with employees should raise general awareness about and support for CSR and related activities; communications with suppliers should explain the organization's CSR-related procurement requirements; and communications with consumers relating products (e.g., product labelling and other product information) should address their expectations regarding how the company integrates safety and sustainability into the design and production of its products.

Since there is so much that any one organization might choose to communicate on with respect to CSR, difficult decisions need to be made about what information and message are disseminated since too much communication can confuse stakeholders as much as it informs and educates them. The UN Global Compact suggests that communications strategies by designed with a reference to materiality of particular issues or events to both stakeholders (as determined through engagement with stakeholders) and the business and overall sustainability of the organization itself. When using this framework, the most attention in communications should be given to those issues that are material to both stakeholders and the business of the organization and in those instances communications should be comprehensive and include a statement of the organization's policies and commitments, an assessment of potential impact and a description of relevant performance indicators and measures. As for issues that are considered to be important to its business by the organization but are which not that important to stakeholders, communications may be limited to impacts. In turn, when stakeholders have identified an issue as important, but the organization does not believe the issue is material to its business, communications may be limited, at least initially, to a description of the organization's approach and policies with respect to the issue.[18]

While organizations need to be proactive in allocating resources to communications and developing a formal communications strategy, it should not be forgotten that communication is a tool to be used as part of the broader and more important CSR activity and requirement of dialogue and engagement with stakeholders. In other words, effective CSR communications flow both ways and all of the communication methods mentioned above should include information on how recipients can provide feedback to the organization.[19] Among other things, organizations should leverage the communications process to gather important information from stakeholders regarding the adequacy and effectiveness of the content, media and the frequency and scope of communication, so that they can be improved as needed; set priorities for the content of future communication; and secure verification of reported information by stakeholders, if this approach to verification is used.[20]

The UN Global Compact endorsed the recommendations regarding communications included in ISO 26000 by calling on organizations to ensure that their communications strategies and content were based on the following characteristics[21]:

- Communications should be understandable to intelligent stakeholders and the organization must be careful to ensure that they are not too technical so as to be only understandable to some
- Communications should respond to the concerns of stakeholders
- Communications should be accurate, based on solid evidence and accountability, and should not descend into "PR-hype"
- Communications should be balanced and trustworthy and not only highlight what the organization does well but also outline areas where the organization has performed less well or has not met targets and objectives
- Communications should respond to issues and events as swiftly as possible and avoid reliance on outdated accounts of historical events that are not of great use to stakeholders
- Information should be easily accessible and retrievable.

In addition, the UN Global Compact has emphasized the important of stakeholder communications as a means for documenting the organization's performance on its material CSR issues and providing stakeholders with useful and credible information along with evidence to support the organization's progress toward its CSR commitments and targets. CSR communications should educate stakeholders about the relevant issues and build trust that becomes a foundation for continuing engagement and dialogue.[22]

Notes

1 P. Hohnen (Author) and J. Potts (Editor), *Corporate Social Responsibility: An Implementation Guide for Business* (Winnipeg: International Institute for Sustainable Development, 2007), 67.
2 Expansive disclosure of this type increases the risk of litigation and/or adverse market reaction in the event that the company fails to meet its stated CSR and corporate sustainability goals, even if the disclosures are accompanied by appropriate disclaimers and are not included in regulatory filings that typically are covered by anti-fraud standards. Disclosure of actual or potential links between CSR and corporate sustainability goals and compensation must also be handled carefully, similar to links between short-term financial goals and compensation.
3 N. Cleveland, D. Lynn and S. Pike, "Sustainability Reporting: The Lawyer's Response", *Business Law Today* (January 21, 2015).

4 C. Williams, "Corporate Social Responsibility and Corporate Governance" in J. Gordon and G. Ringe (Eds.), *Oxford Handbook of Corporate Law and Governance* (Oxford: Oxford University Press, 2016), 15, Retrieved from http://digitalcommons.osgoode.yorku.ca/scholarly_works/1784 (citing Initiative for Responsible Investment, Corporate Social Responsibility Disclosure Efforts by National Governments and Stock Exchanges (March 12, 2015), Retrieved from http://hausercenter.org/iri/wpcontent/uploads/2011/08/CR-3-12-15.pdf). These countries included Argentina, China, Denmark, the EU, Ecuador, Finland, France, Germany Greece, Hungary, India, Indonesia, Ireland (specific to state-supported financial institutions after the 2008 financial crisis), Italy, Japan, Malaysia, The Netherlands, Norway, South Africa, Spain, Sweden, Taiwan, and the UK.

5 See 6 of Directive 2014/95/EU of the European Parliament and of the Council of October 22, 2014, amending Directive 2013/34/EU as regards disclosure of non-financial and diversity information by certain large undertakings and groups, Official Journal of the European Union L330/1-330/9.

6 C. Williams, "Corporate Social Responsibility and Corporate Governance" in J. Gordon and G. Ringe (Eds.), *Oxford Handbook of Corporate Law and Governance* (Oxford: Oxford University Press, 2016), 16, Retrieved from http://digitalcommons.osgoode.yorku.ca/scholarly_works/1784 (citing Initiative for Responsible Investment, Corporate Social Responsibility Disclosure Efforts by National Governments and Stock Exchanges (March 12, 2015), Retrieved from http://hausercenter.org/iri/wpcontent/uploads/2011/08/CR-3-12-15.pdf). The listing rules for the Singapore Exchange, for example, require every listed company to prepare an annual sustainability report on its sustainability practices on a "comply or explain" basis with reference to five primary components: material ESG factors; policies, practices and performance; targets; sustainability reporting framework; and board statement. "SGX Sustainability Reporting Guide" in *Sustainability Guide for Boards: At a Glance* (Singapore Institute of Directors, KPMG and SGX, September 2017).

7 C. Williams, "Corporate Social Responsibility and Corporate Governance" in J. Gordon and G. Ringe (Eds.), *Oxford Handbook of Corporate Law and Governance* (Oxford: Oxford University Press, 2016), 16, Retrieved from http://digitalcommons.osgoode.yorku.ca/scholarly_works/1784 (citing Initiative for Responsible Investment, Corporate Social Responsibility Disclosure Efforts by National Governments and Stock Exchanges (March 12, 2015), Retrieved from http://hausercenter.org/iri/wpcontent/uploads/2011/08/CR-3-12-15.pdf).

8 Id. at 19 (citing KPMG, UNEP, Global Reporting Initiative and Unit for Corporate Governance in Africa, Carrots and Sticks: Sustainability Reporting Policies Worldwide 8 (2013), Retrieved from https://www.globalreporting.org/resourcelibrary/carrots-and-sticks.pdf.). A powerful and useful resource for monitoring actions regarding sustainability reporting among stock exchanges around the world is the United Nations' Sustainable Stock Exchanges (SSE) initiative (http://www.sseinitiative.org/), which is a peer-to-peer learning platform for exploring how exchanges, in collaboration with investors, regulators, and companies, can enhance corporate transparency–and ultimately performance–on ESG (environmental, social and corporate governance) issues and encourage sustainable investment. Among other things, the SSE has compiled a summary table of the sustainability reporting measures in place within G20 Members and by board members of the International Organization of Securities Commissions. Areas evaluated include the source of sustainability reporting initiatives, the scope of the reporting application, the scope of the subject matter, and the disclosure model.

9 Libit and Freier reported a dramatic increase in CSR-related reporting among S&P 500 companies from 2010, when approximately 20% of the companies provided such reporting, to 2012 when 53% of the companies reported on their CSR activities. B. Libit and T. Freier, *The Corporate Social Responsibility Report and Effective Stakeholder Engagement* (Chicago, IL: Chapman and Cutler LLP, 2013), Retrieved from https://corpgov.law.harvard.edu/2013/12/28/the-corporate-social-responsibility-report-and-effective-stakeholder-engagement/ (citing 2012 Corporate ESG/Sustainability/Responsibility Reporting: Does It Matter? Analysis of S&P 500 Companies' ESG Reporting Trends & Capital Markets Response, and Possible Association with Desired Rankings & Ratings, Governance & Accountability Institute, Inc. (2012)). The KPMG Survey of Corporate Responsibility Reporting 2013 surveyed an even bigger group consisting of over 4,100 companies and found that 71% of them were reporting on CSR. KMPG also reported that among the world's largest 250 companies, the reporting rate was 93%. Interestingly, however, only 5% of the companies were reporting on how environmental and social risks could impact their financial results and only 10% reported on linkages between CSR and executive compensation. As cited in H. Gregory, Corporate Social Responsibility, practicallaw.com (April 2014).

10 N. Cleveland, D. Lynn and S. Pike, "Sustainability Reporting: The Lawyer's Response", *Business Law Today* (January 21, 2015).

11 Id. See also C. Williams, "Corporate Social Responsibility and Corporate Governance" in J. Gordon and G. Ringe (Eds.), *Oxford Handbook of Corporate Law and Governance* (Oxford: Oxford University Press, 2016), 16–19, Retrieved from http://digitalcommons.osgoode.yorku.ca/scholarly_works/1784; and C. Williams, "The Securities and Exchange Commission and Corporate Social Transparency", *Harvard Law Review*, 112 (1999), 1197.

12 California Civil Code § 1714.43.

13 Ceres, The Ceres Roadmap for Sustainability (www.ceres.org/ceresroadmap).

14 For further discussion of sustainability reporting initiatives and frameworks, see A. Gutterman, *Sustainability and Corporate Governance* (New York: Routledge, 2020).

15 Finnish Textile & Fashion, *Corporate Responsibility Manual* (Helsinki: Finnish Textile & Fashion, 2016), 58.

16 ISO 26000, *Guidance on Social Responsibility* (Geneva: International Organization for Standardization, 2010), 77.

17 Id. at 77–78.

18 *UN Global Compact: Training of Trainers Course Guidance Manual* (New York: UN Global Compact), 53.

19 ISO 26000, *Guidance on Social Responsibility* (Geneva: International Organization for Standardization, 2010), 77–78.

20 Id. at 79.

21 *UN Global Compact: Training of Trainers Course Guidance Manual* (New York: UN Global Compact), 51.

22 Id. at 56.

15 Evaluating and Improving Sustainability Management

While organizational performance is a much discussed topic, the reality is that there is a good deal of confusion and argument regarding how it should be defined, conceptualized and measured. Traditionally, performance measurement systems relied almost exclusively on management and cost accounting principles, often resulting in an emphasis on short-term results and efficient management of tangible resources (i.e., fixed assets and inventory), which were easier to measure using financial metrics, and a lack of appropriate attention to non-financial intangible activities (e.g., nurturing of customer relationships, development of innovative products and services and implementation of high-quality and responsive operating processes), that contributed to the creation of long-term value for the organization.[1] These "old school" measurement systems were also useful tools in complying with regulatory and accounting reporting requirements.

As time went by, however, a consensus developed that traditional performance measures had become outdated and that managers needed a performance measurement system designed to present managers with financial and non-financial measures covering different perspectives which, in combination, provided a way of translating strategy into a coherent set of performance measures.[2] For example, one commentator described organizational performance as the extent to which the organization is able to meet the needs of its stakeholders and its own needs for survival.[3] This formulation broadened the concept of organizational performance beyond strictly market-focused measures such as profit margin, market share or product quality, all of which are important to certain stakeholders and overall organizational survival, to include a number of other non-financial indicators of organizational performance and success including job satisfaction, organizational commitment and employee turnover.[4]

At the same time, researchers interested in measuring corporate social responsibility (CSR) and corporate sustainability began to develop variables to measure environmental and social performance including ethics policy, philanthropic contributions, stakeholder interests and relationships (i.e., investors, shareholders, customers, suppliers, employees and the community), governmental relationships, urban development, minority support programs, health and safety initiatives, community involvement and development, conserving natural resources, employee eco-initiatives, voluntary environmental restoration, eco-design practices and systematically reducing waste and emissions from operations.[5]

The "Balanced Scorecard" Framework and Sustainability

The "balanced scorecard" (BSC) perspective, first advanced by Kaplan in the 1980s, is based on the premise that measurement of organizational performance should take into factors that are not purely financial in nature since many of the financial indicators that are generally used are based on operational performance.[6] The balanced scorecard framework is a multi-disciplinary view of organizational performance that includes measures such as market share, changes in intangible assets such as patents or human resources skills and abilities, customer satisfaction, product innovation, productivity, quality, and stakeholder performance.[7] The balanced scorecard takes into account the potential value of opportunities for the future that have been created but which have yet to be realized financially, an aspect that is outside of generally accepted accounting principles. The balanced scorecard includes, and attempts to "balance", financial and non-financial measures and seeks to include customer value and customer satisfaction and/or retention, internal business processes impacting product and service quality and efficiency and employee learning and growth (often called organizational capacity) perspectives along with financial perspective measures that are used to track how well improvements in the other three perspectives are working.[8] It cannot be stressed enough that the use of the term "balanced" does not imply equivalence among the various measures that are used in the framework but rather is intended to ensure that users of the framework understand that not all key performance metrics are financial and that non-financial measures should be considered when looking for ways to improve long-term organizational performance.

Proponents of the balanced scorecard approach point to the introduction of a broad array of non-financial indicators that can be used to improve decision-making and selection and implementation of strategies. According to the Balanced Scorecard Institute, business and industry, government, and nonprofit organizations worldwide have embraced the balanced scorecard, with studies by the Gartner Group and others suggesting that more than half of major companies in the US, Europe and Asia are using the scorecard and that use in growing in those areas as well as in the Middle East and Africa.[9] A global study conducted by Bain & Co placed the scorecard fifth on a list of the top ten most widely used management tools around the world—strategic planning was first—and the scorecard has also been recognized by the editors of the Harvard Business Review as being one of the most influential business ideas of the past 75 years.

Crawford and Scaletta argued that because the balanced scorecard had become a recognized and established management tool, it was well positioned to support a knowledge-building effort to help organizations make their values and vision a reality.[10] In addition, they believed that the balanced scorecard was an effective way to help executives, managers and employees make day-to-day decisions based upon values and metrics that could be designed to support an organization's sustainability initiatives. The balanced scorecard also allows organizational leadership to articulate its sustainability strategy, communicates the details of the strategy throughout the organization, motivates the members of the organization to execute the plans associated with the sustainability strategy and enables leaders to monitor results using both financing and non-financial metrics. Finally, the balanced scorecard is well suited to sustainability and CSR given that the scorecard framework explicitly incorporates and balances shareholder, customer and employee perspectives.

Crawford and Scaletta recommended that organizations should adapt or introduce a balanced scorecard that specifically included and integrated key market forces driving CSR and the indicators of sustainability performance and impact taken from the Global Reporting Initiative (GRI) Standards. The market forces would be "objectives" in the balanced scorecard framework and success or failure toward achieving the specified targets (i.e., the level of performance or rate of improvement required) would be tracked through measures taken from the GRI Standards. For example, an objective for the customer perspective might be addressing erosion of trust and push for transparency of among consumer and the company might decide to do so by implementing a policy and accompanying measurement target to eliminate all child labor in its own operations and its supply chain. For the internal business processes perspective the goal might be to combat climate change through initiative to meet specified goals for reducing total greenhouse gas emissions. Plans relating to organizational capacity might include implementation of policies, guidelines and procedures to address the needs of indigenous people in response to criticisms from civil society and non-government organizations.[11]

Crawford and Scaletta suggested that using the balanced scorecard framework to introduce and explain sustainability and CSR initiatives can overcome resistance to such initiatives among managers, employees and shareholders who may be skeptical of deviating too much from the traditional financial focus of organizational strategy and decision-making. For example, the balanced scorecard makes it easier to see the path that an organization might take to creating a competitive advantage based on cost leadership: investing in new technology and more effective and efficient processes that lead to improved ecological protection and better risk management that allows the organization to lower its cost of capital. Similarly, a differentiation-based strategy can be pursued through community-building activities that improve organizational reputation and brand equity such that customer satisfaction and demand for the organization's products and services is enhanced such that the organization is able to increase sales.

Evaluating and Improving Organizational Sustainability Performance

Performance measurement, coupled with verification and reporting, is important in its own right; however, the implementation and operation of the performance measurement system should also be seen as the catalyst for careful evaluation of the effectiveness and scope of the organization's sustainability and CSR initiatives and generation of ideas for modifying and improving those initiatives. Maon et al. recommended that in order to improve their sustainability and CSR programs, organizations should implement evaluation procedures based on measuring, verifying and reporting in order to determine what is working well, why and how to ensure that it will continue. In addition, organizations need to investigate what is not working well and why this is the case, explore barriers to success and what can be changed to overcome these barriers and, if necessary, revisit original goals and make new ones.[12] Maon et al. explained that regular reviews and evaluations of the organization's sustainability and CSR activities are a means for keeping stakeholders informed of the progress and activities, thus providing visibility and transparency. The legitimacy of the review and evaluation process can be enhanced by involving external auditors and rigorous reporting that includes a comparison of the organization's actual performance against previously established goals and targets. Maon et al. recommended that stakeholders be invited to verify the organization's sustainability performance and report publicly on their findings.[13]

Hohnen and Potts admonished organizations to use the results from their verification process, including information gathered from engaging stakeholders, to determine what is working well, why and how to ensure that it continues to do so; investigate what is not working well and why not, to explore the barriers to success and what can be changed to overcome the barriers; assess what competitors and others in the sector are doing and have achieved; and revisit original goals and make new ones as necessary.[14] While some might ask why this is necessary when a detailed report has been prepared at great expense, it is important to distinguish the data and other information in the report from the process of thinking deeply about what the data and information really mean in practice.

Questions that Hohnen and Potts suggested should be used in order to drive the evaluation process included the following:

- What worked well? In what areas did the organization meet or exceed targets? Has the organization celebrated its successes, an important way to continue motivating employees?
- Why did it work well? Were there factors within or outside the organization that helped it meet its targets?
- What did not work well? In what areas did the organization not meet its targets?
- Why were these areas problematic? Were there factors within or outside the organization that made the process more difficult or created obstacles?
- What did the organization learn from this experience? What should continue and what should be done differently?
- Is the organization using the right reporting indicators? Are they aligned with the company's overall mission and CSR commitments?
- Is the organization engaging with the right stakeholders?
- Have the right persons for advancing CSR initiatives inside the organization been identified and have they been given adequate support?
- Drawing on this knowledge, and information concerning new trends, what are the CSR priorities for the organization in the coming year?
- Are there new CSR objectives?

Another resource and framework for evaluating and improving social responsibility initiatives is provided by ISO 26000 ISO 26000 Guidance on Social Responsibility, developed and released by the International Organization for Standardization (ISO).[15] Section 7.7 of ISO 26000 addresses the reasons and procedures for continuously reviewing and improving the organization's actions and practices related to CSR, noting that effective performance with respect to social responsibility depends in part on commitment, careful oversight, evaluation and review of the activities undertaken, progress made, achievement of identified objectives, resources used and other aspects of the organization's efforts. While many of the monitoring and review activities are internal—tracking metrics on progress toward sustainability-related goals tied to operational matters (e.g., reduction of CO_2 emissions)—consideration must also be given to the opinions and insights available from external stakeholders. ISO 26000 also points out that organizations must continuously review changing conditions or expectations, legal or regulatory developments affecting social responsibility and new opportunities for enhancing its efforts on social responsibility.[16]

Evaluating the performance of sustainability-related programs and activities begins with establishing and maintaining monitoring procedures.

Section 7.7.2 of ISO 26000 counsels organizations to focus on those activities that are significant and seek to make the results of the monitoring easy to understand, reliable, timely and responsive to stakeholders' concerns. Organizations can choose to conduct reviews at appropriate intervals, engage in benchmarking that includes comparing performance to comparable organizations and obtain feedback from affected stakeholders. Performance evaluation can also be facilitated through the proper setting and use of targets and indicators, as described above in this chapter, in order to properly measure both qualitative and quantitative aspects of performance and progress and compare the current state of affairs to historical information.[17]

Section 7.7.4 of ISO 26000 addresses the important issue of verifying the reliability of the information collected during the review process and the manner in which such information is stored and managed, and calls on organizations to engage independent people or groups, either internal or external to the organization, to examine the ways in which data is collected, recorded or stored, handled and used by the organization. ISO 26000 also points out that reliability can be improved through good training of data collectors, clear accountability for data accuracy, direct feedback to individuals making errors and data quality processes that compare reported data with past data and that from comparable situations.[18]

Section 7.7.3 of ISO 26000 calls on organizations to carry out reviews at appropriate intervals to determine how it is performing against its targets and objectives for social responsibility and to identify needed changes in the programs and procedures. Reviews not only look at progress against targets and indicators established at the beginning of a particular reporting period, but also involve comparisons against results from earlier reviews to assess overall progress. The review process is also a good way to focus attention on important intangibles relating to the sustainability and CSR program—things that are admittedly difficult to measure—such as changes in attitudes relating to CSR throughout the organization and how well sustainability and CSR is being implemented and integrated. Among the review questions suggested by ISO 26000 were the following[19]:

- Were objectives and targets achieved as envisioned?
- Did the strategies and processes suit the objectives?
- What worked and why? What did not work and why?
- Were the objectives appropriate?
- What could have been done better?
- Are all relevant persons involved?

An effort should be made to gather information from a variety of perspectives regarding these review questions including external stakeholders.

The process should be documented and described in the organization's sustainability reporting and communications, and stakeholders should be informed about how the results of the review were used to make changes in sustainability-related strategies and programs to improve performance.[20]

Obviously the review process should be used to collect the information necessary for appropriate reporting and other communications regarding the organization's sustainability activities; however, the results of the review should also be used to identify and implement new ideas for improving the organization's performance on social responsibility and, as appropriate, making changes to the goals and targets of its sustainability programs. For example, an organization may decide that it is necessary to invest additional resources in a particular program and/or broaden the scope of a program to generate greater environmental or social impact. The review may also uncover new opportunities to deliver social value while expanding and improving the organization's line of products and services. The review process is a good way to ensure that there is regular dialogue with key stakeholders, since their views are essential to tracking sustainability performance. Finally, measurement of sustainability performance and progress toward sustainability-related goals should be integrated with periodic assessments of the performance of senior executives, thus illustrating the seriousness of organizational commitment to sustainability.[21]

Evaluations need to be done regularly, no less frequently than annually, and procedures should be established for tracking the results from evaluations year-over-year in order to gauge progress and identify any relevant patterns or trends. When conducting evaluations input should be obtained from people throughout the organization as line-level employees may have very different impressions of sustainability initiatives than managers higher up in the organizational structure. When small businesses conduct an evaluation it need not be time consuming. In fact, a good deal can be learned from having everyone in the company get-together for a working meeting and planning session to go through and discuss each of the questions laid out above.

Certifications and Ratings Systems

Another way that organizations can measure and demonstrate their commitment to social and environmental responsibility is through participation in ratings agencies and ratings systems that have been created in order to give external stakeholders a means by which they can assess the social and environmental impact of the organization's activities. In order to participate in these systems, some of which actually offer opportunities for certification, organizations must be prepared to adjust their internal structures in order to comply with the requirements of the system and ensure that the information necessary for measurement can be collected, analyzed and properly reported. While there are similarities among the most popular systems, there is still no universal standard and many of the systems operate without extensive efforts to verify or audit the information provided by organizations, although organizations should expect that they will be required to submit to site visits and renew their certifications on a regular basis.[22]

Perhaps the most well-known certification program is overseen by B Lab Company (B Lab), a Pennsylvania non-profit corporation that administers certification as a Certified B Corp., which offers access to the Certified B Corporation logo often seen as being a "Good Housekeeping Seal of Approval" for sustainable businesses. In order to become "certified" a company must achieve a minimum verified score on a "B Impact Assessment" that assesses the overall impact of the company on its stakeholders taking into account various factors such as number of employees, sector and location of the company's primary operations. The questions in the B Impact Assessment have by created and revised by the Standards Advisory Council, a group of independent experts in business and academia, and cover financial performance; suppliers; the impact of the business on all its stakeholders; best practices regarding mission, measurement and governance; and the company's "impact business model".

Companies that complete the B Impact Assessment will receive a B Impact Report that contains an overall score based on performance in three key impact areas (i.e., workers, community and the environment) and will move on an assessment review and submission of supporting documentation. At this point, the focus will be on the operations of the company and demonstration of practice relating to the company's social and environmental impact. Additional steps in the assessment process include completion of a disclosure questionnaire, which allows companies to confidentially disclose to B Lab any sensitive practices, fines and sanctions related to the company and its partners, and background checks by B Lab staff which include a review of public records, news sources and search engines for company names, brands, executives/founders and other relevant topics.

Around 10% of certified B corporations are randomly selected each year for an in-depth site review, which takes place either in person or virtually and typically takes six to ten hours depending on the size and scope of the business. Site reviews are considered to be a crucial step for verifying the requirements of the Certified B Corp. certification and confirming the accuracy of the responses of the specific company. Companies wishing to maintain their Certified B Corp. certification are required to update their assessment every two years by providing additional documentation and achieving a minimum score on the impact assessment. Recertification requirements provide assurances that companies are continuing to engage in a high level of impact with their stakeholders even as their businesses grow or change. The recertification process also provides companies with opportunities to set their own internal improvement goals against B Lab standards and benchmark their performance over time.[23]

Various product, safety and environmental certifications are available depending on the industry and activities of the organization. For example, UL (www.ul.com) helps companies demonstrate safety, confirm compliance, enhance sustainability, manage transparency, deliver quality and performance, strengthen security, protect brand reputation, build workplace excellence, and advance societal well-being through a range of services including inspection, advisory services, education and training, testing, auditing and analytics, certification software solutions, and marketing claim verification. UL's Sustainability Quotient (SQ®) Program provides organizations with the opportunity to achieve third party sustainability certification for their whole enterprise, demonstrating clear market leadership and a commitment to environmental stewardship at every level of business operations. The SQ® Program is a comprehensive system of assessing, rating and certifying the sustainability initiatives of corporations. With a focus on the environment, governance, workforce, customers/suppliers and community engagement/human rights, the SQ® Program promotes the adoption of a standardized language and rating platform for corporate sustainability. UL also tests and certifies products, processes and materials against current environmental standards and maintains a database of validated and certified products that can be accessed by industry professional and consumers.

Costs to organizations for attempting to comply with certification programs and standards will vary and consideration should be given to fees that must be paid to the agency and the investments that must be made in order to fulfill the agency's requirements. Organizations must also consider the potential impact of participating in a particular rating or certification program, or complying with a formal reporting regime, on the organization's governance or regulatory obligations depends on the program. However, the costs and disruptions to traditional operating procedures must be balanced against the benefits of being able to provide potential investors and stakeholders with reliable information to accurately assess the social impact such companies make, thus making it easier for organizations to raise capital from investors seeking to support socially responsible ventures and attract employees and customers want to do business with companies that are having a positive social and environmental impact.[24]

In addition to formal assessment, feedback on sustainability initiatives comes from other groups who watch and monitor industry activities and the behaviors of individual companies. Shareholders have become much more aggressive in questioning the activities of management and companies can also expect to be scrutinized by labor unions, consumer activists, environmentalists and other community groups. The possibility of government regulation has often motivated industries to "self-regulate" by adopting standards and codes of conduct to be followed by industry members. One place to look for ideas about measuring sustainability is in the financial community where various indexes and other measures of corporate performance on various sustainability-related criteria (e.g., governance, human resource management, health and safety, environmental protection and community development) have been developed to assist public and private investors, including mutual fund managers and venture capitalists, in making investment decisions. Interest in measurement has exploded as more investment capital is being set aside for "socially responsible investment".

It is important to understand how a particular index defines sustainability and CSR. Many earlier indexes focused on screening out companies that operated in undesirable or risky industries; however, as time went by the metrics became broader and more sophisticated and included positive factors such as leadership approaches, planning processes and management practices in areas such as governance, social impact and the environment. Notable examples of sustainability indexes include the Dow Jones Sustainability indices and the MSCI ESG indexes. An extensive library of reports and self-reported climate change, water and forest-risk data is available through the CDP (www.cdp.net), which works with companies, investors and governments on issues and projects relating to environmental risks.[25] Indices of sustainability and CSR have been supplemented by efforts to list and rank the most socially responsible companies. For example, Corporate Knights releases an annual list of the "Top 100 Most Sustainable Corporations in the World".

Notes

1 R. Kaplan and D. Norton, *The Strategy-Focused Organization: How Balanced Scorecard Companies Thrive in the New Business Environment* (Boston, MA: Harvard Business School Press, 2001).
2 I. Abu-Jarad, N. Yusof and D. Nikbin, "A Review Paper on Organizational Culture and Organizational Performance", *International Journal of Business and Social Science*, 1(3) (December 2010), 26, 31 (citing R. Chenhall, "Integrative Strategic Performance Measurement System, Strategic Alignment of Manufacturing, Learning and Strategic Outcomes: An Exploratory Study", *Accounting, Organizations and Society*, 30(5) (2005), 395).
3 R. Farooq, "A Clever Approach to Measure Organizational Performance: An Overview", *Prabandhan Indian Journal of Management*, 7(5) (February 2014), DOI: 10.17010//2014/v7i5/59321
4 R. Mayer and F. Schoorman, "Prediction Participation and Production Outcomes through a Two-Dimensional Model of Organizational Commitment", *Academy of Management Review*, 20 (1992), 709; and R. Mowday, L. Porter and R. Steers, *Employee-Organization Linkages: The Psychology of Commitment, Absenteeism and Turnover* (New York: Academic Press, 1982).

5 I. Montiel, "Corporate Social Responsibility and Corporate Sustainability: Separate Pasts, Common Futures", *Organization and Environment*, 21(3) (September 2008), 245, 260.

6 R. Kaplan, "Yesterday's Accounting Undermines Production", *Harvard Business Review*, 62(4) (July/August, 1984), 95. See also R. Kaplan and D. Norton, "The Balanced Scorecard—Measures That Drive Performance", *Harvard Business Review* 70(1) (January–February, 1992), 71.

7 R. Carton, *Measuring Organizational Performance: An Exploratory Study* (Athens, GA: University of Georgia Doctoral Dissertation, 2004), 48.

8 Id. at 34 (citing R. Kaplan and D. Norton, "The Balanced Scorecard: Measures That Drive Performance", *Harvard Business Review*, 70(1) (1992), 71; R. Kaplan and D. Norton, "Using the Balanced Scorecard as a Strategic Management System", *Harvard Business Review*, 74(1) (January–February 1996), 75; R. Kaplan and D. Norton, *Transforming Strategy into Actions: The Balanced Scorecard* (Boston, MA: Harvard Business School Press, 1996); R. Kaplan and D. Norton, "Linking the Balanced Scorecard to Strategy", *California Management Review*, 39(1) (1996), 53; and R. Kaplan, and D. Norton, *The Strategy-Focused Organization: How Balanced Scorecard Companies Thrive in the New Business Environment* (Boston, MA: Harvard Business School Press, 2001)). The discussion of the various perspectives of the balanced scorecard perspective is based on R. Kaplan and D. Norton, *The Balanced Scorecard: Translating Strategy into Action* (Boston, MA: Harvard Business School Press, 1996) and the summary of that work available at http://www.maaw. info/ArticleSummaries/ArtSumKaplanNorton1996Book.htm (accessed May 4, 2020), which also includes an extensive bibliography of books and articles covering various aspects of the balanced scorecard framework.

9 http://www.balancedscorecard.org/BSC-Basics/About-the-Balanced-Scorecard (accessed May 4, 2020).

10 D. Crawford and T. Scaletta, "The Balanced Scorecard and Corporate Social Responsibility: Aligning Values for Profit", *CMA Management,* 79(6) (October 2005), 20.

11 Id. at 25.

12 F. Maon, V. Swaen and A. Lindgreen, Mainstreaming the Corporate Responsibility Agenda: A Change Model Grounded in Theory and Practice (IAG- Louvain School of Management Working Paper, 2008), 35–36 (citing P. Hohnen (Author) and J. Potts (Editor), *Corporate Social Responsibility: An Implementation Guide for Business* (Winnipeg: International Institute for Sustainable Development, 2007)).

13 Id. at 36.

14 P. Hohnen (Author) and J. Potts (Editor), *Corporate Social Responsibility: An Implementation Guide for Business* (Winnipeg: International Institute for Sustainable Development, 2007), 73–74.

15 ISO 26000, *Guidance on Social Responsibility: Discovering ISO 26000* (Geneva: International Organization for Standardization, 2014) and *Handbook for Implementers of ISO 26000, Global Guidance Standard on Social Responsibility by Small and Medium Sized Businesses* (Middlebury, VT: ECO-LOGIA, 2011). ISO 26000 is available for purchase from ISO webstore at the ISO website (www.iso.org) and general information about ISO 26000 can be obtained at www.iso.org/sr.

16 ISO 26000, *Guidance on Social Responsibility* (Geneva: International Organization for Standardization, 2010), 81.

17 Id. at 81–82.

18 Id. at 82.

19 Id. at 82.
20 For further discussion, see Chapter 14 (Reporting and Communications) in this volume.
21 ISO 26000, *Guidance on Social Responsibility* (Geneva: International Organization for Standardization, 2010), 83.
22 *While Legal Structure is Right for My Social Enterprise?: A Guide to Establishing a Social Enterprise in the United States* (London: Thomson Reuters Foundation and San Francisco, CA: Morrison & Foerster, September 2016), 111–112.
23 For complete information about becoming a Certified B Corp., see the B Lab website at http://www.bcorporation.net/ (which is the primary source of the summary description in this section) and R. Honeyman, *The B Corp Handbook: How to Use Business as a Force for Good* (Oakland, CA: Berrett-Koehler Publishers, 2014).
24 *While Legal Structure is Right for My Social Enterprise?: A Guide to Establishing a Social Enterprise in the United States* (London: Thomson Reuters Foundation and San Francisco, CA: Morrison & Foerster, September 2016), 114–115.
25 P. Hohnen (Author) and J. Potts (Editor), *Corporate Social Responsibility: An Implementation Guide for Business* (Winnipeg: International Institute for Sustainable Development, 2007), 10.

Index

Note: Page numbers followed by "n" denote endnotes.